A Lancer for the Emperor

CHLAPOWSKI IN THE UNIFORM OF AN ORDERLY OFFICER OF
THE EMPEROR

A Lancer for the Emperor

The Recollections of a Polish Officer During the Napoleonic Wars

Désiré Chlapowski
Edited and Translated by John H. Lewis

LEONAUR

A Lancer for the Emperor
The Recollections of a Polish Officer During the Napoleonic Wars
by Désiré Chlapowski
Edited and Translated by John H. Lewis
The editor and author, John H Lewis, asserts his rights for copyright purposes.

ILLUSTRATED

FIRST EDITION IN THIS FORM

Principal text first published in French under the title
Mémoires sur les Guerres de Napoléon

Leonaur is an imprint of Oakpast Ltd

Copyright in this form © 2023 Oakpast Ltd

ISBN: 978-1-916535-26-8 (hardcover)
ISBN: 978-1-916535-27-5 (softcover)

http://www.leonaur.com

Publisher's Notes

Contents

Introduction to the Leonaur Edition

I declare that I have much sympathy for those who professionally translate books into English or into any language other than the one in which the book was originally written. So far as those whose task it is to translate 'literature' where style, nuance and whatever else is present to be interpreted—well—'in awe' would not be an exaggeration for how I regard those people. I am not, need it be emphasised, one of those people.

Fortunately, books of military memoirs tend to be fairly straightforward in their delivery, though they are not without issues which are required to be overcome. The first one that applies to this book was that it was originally written in Polish, though I imagine (based on my experience of other works of this kind of vintage) in an archaic form which was commonplace during the first decades of the 19th century, but which would mean it would possibly be difficult as a straightforward read for a contemporary Polish people. This Polish text was then translated into French (for this book is based upon a French language edition) which was also a form of that language not in use in every sense today. That text was then translated into English and so it will come as no surprise—given its pedigree—that the outcome was not a narrative that could simply reproduced and be readily understood by modern readers.

Problematic though all the foregoing undoubtedly is, those were not the only considerations in preparing a book of this kind for contemporary readers. One must give consideration to the likelihood that the authors of these books—who were primarily soldiers rather than writers—might not have possessed—for a number of reasons—very much talent or ability for the written word. As the original editor of Rees Howell Gronow's reminiscences, which included his time as a guards officer during the Peninsular War and Waterloo campaign, noted, 'Captain Gronow was deferentially apologetic as to possible defects of style, due to inexperience, merely claiming to have jotted down the anecdotes "in the best way he could." He wrote: "Soldiers are not generally famous for literary excellence, and when I was young, the military man was, perhaps, much less a scholar than he is at the present day." Furthermore, the subject material touches on matters—using words and phrases—that rarely, if ever, arise in our modern world.

I will not claim that producing such a book suitable for the modern reader is difficult, but it is an undertaking that requires time and consideration. I also cannot claim that my own methodology in the undertaking is faultless, since it is one of my own untutored contrivance. When I first embarked on these kinds of projects, I would spend much frustrating time grappling with complicated word structures in sentences, but then I received the inspiration (if that is the right word for it) that a 'word for word' translation of this kind of book was less essential than that I could understand what the writer was essentially trying to tell me. If I could understand what that was, then it would be a straightforward business—unshackled—to convey that information to others. So, when those occasions arose, I have simply written a fresh sentence.

That having been said, I knew that I could rewrite the book in a form that would give the impression that the author was born in a 20th century English county, but that treatment would inevitably take away much of the continental flavour of the work and, indeed, the impression of its place in time. Most readers know that is an easy trap to fall into which is why some contemporary historical fiction lacks authenticity by its use of modern parlance. So, I have deliberately left Chlapowski's narrative with a flavour of foreign language.

I have read a fair amount of Napoleonic period history and so it was apparent to me that I could litter the author's work with annotations and corrections, but I have not succumbed to that temptation to any great extent. This French edition, however, actually did include some interesting editorial asides and I have retained them. On a couple of occasions, I confess, I have added my own when I thought that was absolutely necessary. They are all readily identifiable in the text, because everything that was not penned by the author appears in italics.

Chlapowski's work was divided into six large sections. In this edition it has been divided by me into smaller chapters to hopefully make the chronology of the narrative somewhat easier to access.

The original work did not include illustrations so where they appear they are unique to this Leonaur edition. I am aware, incidentally, that this is not the first occasion Chlapowski's work has been translated into the English language, but at time of writing I have not seen a copy of that edition personally, so obviously made no reference to it in the course of my own project.

Need it be emphasised if I have compounded any issues with my own contributions I apologise unreservedly. I hope the reader enjoys spending some time in the company of this remarkable Polish soldier as he fought Napoleon's wars—often in the company of the emperor himself.

JHL, 2023

Foreword to the French Translation from the Original Polish

Désiré Chlapowski was born in Turwia (Grand Duchy of Posen) on May 23rd, 1788. His family belonged to the old nobility of Great Poland: his father, Joseph Chlapowski, was Starost of Kosciana; his mother, Ursule Moszczenska, was the daughter of the Senator Palatine of Inowrocklaw.

After a period of tutelage under the French *émigré*, Abbé Steinhoff, Désiré Chlapowski entered into the service of Prussia as a cadet in the Briesewitz Dragoon regiment on 24th June 1802, and studied at the Military Academy in Berlin. In 1806, when the war was declared between Prussia and France, his father, not wanting to see him exposed to fight the French, in whom Poland put all its hopes of recovery as an independent nation, had his name scratched from the role of the Briesewitz regiment, but succeeded, in consequence of his influential connections, to enable his son to continue his studies at the Academy.

Désiré, therefore remained at Berlin until the arrival of the French in the city and having seen them in person, he then rode alone to Posen to herald the inspiring and momentous news. Of course, he joined the army in French service at the earliest opportunity

Chlapowski was admitted (November 4th, 1806) into the Guard d'Honneur of Emperor Napoleon I formed at Posen by General Dombrowski, and was thereafter appointed on December 8th to the 9th Polish Infantry Regiment, commanded by General Sulkowski. It is in this period that his brilliant military career began.

The young officer was soon called to headquarters of Dantzig, and commanded during this campaign a company of *voltigeurs*. Following of the combat of Dirschau (Tczew), where his actions became noticed, he received the Knight's Cross of the Legion of Honour. Having been taken prisoner in front of Danzig during an enemy sortie, he was taken in captivity to Riga, and was not released until after the Peace of Tilsit in July 1807.

On September 24th, 1807, Prince Poniatowski named him captain *aide-de-camp* to General Dombrowski and soon afterwards the emperor, who remembered his enthusiasm and his valour, called him to his personal service as an orderly officer: this appointment was dated May 9th, 1808.

Chlapowski joined the emperor in Bayonne, thereafter serving in the Spanish campaign of 1808, and assisting at the battles of Burgos and Tudela. He then returned with the emperor to Germany, took part in the campaign of 1809, and assisted at the Battle of Wagram and the combat of Znaim.

On August 15th, 1809, he was awarded the Chevalier de Polognai military order; later the emperor conferred upon him the title of Baron of the Empire, by letters patent of January 4th, 1811.

On January 13th, 1811, he was appointed *chef de squadron* to the 1st Light Horse Regiment of (Polish) Lancers of the Imperial Guard and it was in this capacity that Chlapowski served in the campaign of 1812, where his regiment, constantly employed, continued to set an example of fearlessness and dedication.

After the retreat from Russia and the reorganisation of his regiment, Chlapowski served in the Saxon campaign of 1813: but, after the Battle of Bautzen, he learned following an inadvertent indiscretion on the part of Baron Fain, Napoleon's secretary, that the emperor was willing to sacrifice Poland and the Polish cause. In his indignation he then left the service of the emperor and offered his resignation from the army. He was removed from army lists on 1st July 1813, having obtained an absolute discharge by imperial decision on June 19th.

He then went to Paris where he fell seriously lying ill as a result of the fatigue of his recent campaigns; it is during this period of sickness that the fall of the First Empire of the French occurred.

The Restoration of the Bourbon monarchy offered him the rank of colonel in the Royal Guard, but he refused to accept it. He travelled to England, and finally returned to Turwia, to support his elderly father; devoting himself completely to the administration of his property.

Although once again, by fortunes of war, a Prussian subject, he nevertheless retained all his independence of character, and refused the military pension which was his due for his services, because he would have been compelled to apply to the Prussian Government to receive it. Possessed of the same conviction in 1817, when he was offered, through the mediation of Prince Radziwill, cousin of the King of Prussia, the rank of colonel in the Prussian Army: Chlapowski refused, replying "that on the chest of an officer of Napoleon there was no place for the Prussian cockade."

He returned once again to England, where he lived for eighteen months to thoroughly study agriculture and thereafter returned to Turwia, where he promptly reorganised the administration and development of its domains.

In 1821, Désiré Chlapowski married the Antoinette Grudzinska, and in so doing became the brother-in-law of the Grand Duke Constantin, brother of the Emperor of Russia, Governor of Poland, and chief of the army; the grand duke married Countess Jeanne Grudzinska.

In 1830, Chlapowski was vice-president of the Diet of Posen, when the uprising broke out in Poland. At the news of the insurrection of Warsaw (November 29th, 1830), he returned to Poland, was appointed colonel and formed a cavalry brigade. He was distinguished in combat at Rozan and the Battle of Grochow (February 1831). Promoted to brigadier-general on 21st May 1831, he went to Lithuania where he was welcomed as a liberator, and operated in conjunction with the General

Gielgud; but the two generals were pushed back by Russian forces before Wilna, forced to retreat and withdraw into Prussian territory, where their corps was disarmed on the 1st June 1831. Chlapowski was appointed General of Division and Commander-in-Chief of Lithuania: though this nomination did not reach him until he was already in Prussia.

He was interned in Memel (July 1831) and it was not until July 1832 that the Prussian Government allowed him to return to Turwia, where his assets had already been confiscated.

On May 9th, 1832, the trials, brought about by the Prussian Government against Poles who had taken part in the uprising, began: more than 2,000 of them were the object of convictions; Chlapowski was sentenced to two years in prison, with the confiscation of his property, and deprivation of political rights. However, the King of Prussia showed clemency and reduced the sentence to one year in prison and 22,000 *thalers* fine (82,500 *fr.*); he even offered to Chlapowski a complete amnesty, if he would give up his property in Turwia and take in exchange a domain of the crown in Brandenburg. This offer was refused. In May 1833, he went to Stettin to undergo his detention within the fortress. This detention was terminated after six months following the intercession of the Princess Radziwill, born Princess Royal of Prussia.

Returning to his lands, Chlapowski resumed his agricultural work: rallied to the Prussian Government, becoming a life member of the House of Lords and from that point forward, he remained a stranger to temptations of fruitless efforts for the emancipation of Poland. Désiré Chlapowski died in Turkey on March 27th, 1879, aged nearly ninety-one years.

While in detention in Memel, General Chlapowski had written, to explain the circumstance of his retreat before the Russian Army, a pamphlet which appeared in Paris in 1832 and was reproduced the same year in Berlin under the title: *Lettres sur événements militaires en Pologne et en Lithuanie.* He also published in Posen in 1852 a remarkable work on agriculture.

He left military memories which were published in Posen

in 1899 and curated by his sons. These memories are comprised of two parts: the first, devoted to Napoleon's wars from 1806 to 1813; the second, relative to the Polish uprising of 1830-1831.

It is the first part: *Wars of Napoleon* of which we offer in the French translation. Some fragments had already been published in French in the *Polish Bulletin* (1897-1898). These memoirs are of great interest, both by the importance of the events to which they relate, but also as a view of the personality of the author and his privileged close position with of the person of emperor.

We would like to especially thank Mr. Casimir Chlapowski, last survivor of the general's three sons, and a member of the House of Lords of Prussia, who has wanted to encourage us to publish this translation of his father's *Memoirs*, and has pointed out a few errors that had slipped into the Polish edition.

Our thanks also go to Mr. Waclaw Gaziorowski, the well-known Polish writer of the publication of the *Memoirs* of J. Grabowski which he pulled back from oblivion, and who was kind enough to collect and verify the information and biographical details that we have presented on the glorious and full military career of General Chlapowski.

★★★★★★★★★★★★★★★★★★

We give following a statement of services of General Chlapowski, according to the document items existing in the archives of the Ministry of the war.

CHLAPOWSKI (ADAM-DÉSIRÉ)

Born at Turwia, Grand Duchy of Posen, May 23th, 1788.

Entered as a cadet in the regiment of Briesewitz (dragoons of Prussia), June 24th, 1802.

Admitted to Honour Guard of S.M the emperor, formed at Posen, November 4th, 1806.

Lieutenant in the 9th regiment Polish Infantry (commanded during the campaign a company of *voltigeurs*), December 18th, 1806.

Prisoner of war, March 26th, 1807.

Returned from captivity and named by Prince Poniatovsrsky captain *aide-de-camp* to General Dombrowski, September 20th, 1807.

H.M. Orderly Officer of the emperor, May 9th, 1808.

Squadron leader in the 1st regiment of Light Horse Lancers (Polish) of the Imperial Guard June 13th, 1811.

Resigned, June 19th, 1813.

Served in the campaigns of 1806 and 1807 in Prussia and in Poland (under Marshal Lefèvre), from 1808 to Spain and from 1809 in Germany (under the orders of the emperor), from 1812 in Russia, from 1813 in Saxony.

Baron of the Empire (letters patent of January 4th 1811).

Member of the Legion of Honour, March 9th, 1807.

Chapter 1: The events of 1807

"If youth knew, if old age could!"

It is this apposite proverb that gave me the idea to write my *Memoirs*, which I thought may be useful to young people. So, I decided to rather describe the many events I personally witnessed during this glorious time, rather than reporting all of my personal adventures; of these I tell only what is necessary for the understanding of the facts.

So, I will not speak of my birth or of my education and I will only begin at the period which stands out for the importance and the general magnitude of its events that took place within it.

In November 1806 Napoleon's French troops arrived at Posen, (November 9th-10th-11th.)

★★★★★★★★★★

As soon as the French entered Berlin, the author of these Memoirs set out on horseback from that city to Posen, to carry the news of these recent momentous events. The Prussian Army commandant at Posen ordered Chlapowski to come before him, and then began to reprimand him for spreading false news. But when the latter assured him that he himself had seen the French forces marching through Berlin, the commandant exclaimed in astonishment, "Was wirkliche Franzosen?" (What! REAL French!). The next day the Prussian troops promptly evacuated Posen.

★★★★★★★★★★

The French cavalry, the 1st regiment of Chasseurs à Cheval, commanded by Colonel Exelmans (who later became a well-known general), were the first to enter in to the city at nightfall. The first squadron, sabres drawn, trotted straight through the town and went into position beyond the Warta, on the Warsaw and Thorn roads. The other squadrons halted in the marketplace, where some of the inhabitants ran up to them and welcomed them with a warm cries of "*Vivat!*" I correctly emphasise 'some' of the inhabitants, because the remainder of them were at that time largely composed of foreigners.

During the religious persecutions in Germany, our ancestors had welcomed, with their habitual tolerance, the German exiles; then after the partition of Poland, our country had received even more of these strangers. When the Duchy of Warsaw was created, a portion of these new elements then left Poland, especially those employed as civil servants; but in 1806, these foreigners, including Jewish people, represented (at time of original publication) nearly half of Posen's population.

The newly arrived *chasseurs* in the city dismounted and soon understood, based on their conversations with the numerous inhabitants who thronged around them, that they had found themselves in the midst of new friends and so they quietly took to their quarters.

Two days later General Dombrowski arrived in the city. He found already in Posen a number of martially minded Poles who had been drawn to the city since recent developments were answers to their prayers and it was from among them that a guard of honour was recruited to receive the emperor upon his arrival. This honour guard consisted of 100 cavalrymen. General Dombrowski gave the command of this unit to Uminski, who later became a renowned general officer. Uminski had been well known to Dombrowski since the days of the campaign led by Kosciuszko; he was then a young man of just fifteen years old, who performed the duties *aide-de-camp* to General Madalinsky.

This guard of honour was exercised each day at troop and squadron school, until the arrival of the emperor, on the fields on the side of the Buk, behind the windmills. Uminski appointed me to the rank of squadron adjutant and at the same time to the duties of an instructor, because he knew that I had previously served four years in the Prussian dragoons, and so had been trained in both infantry and cavalry service. This had been the dual role of the dragoons since their origin, though in later years, in Prussia, they became light cavalry. I had served actually within this Prussian regiment for only six weeks, during the time of the Autumn manoeuvres; the rest of the year I took courses at the Berlin Académie Militaire (artillery-academy), whose instructors were artillery officers of some talent. A few of them became famous, like General Scharnhorst, at that time a captain and later the organiser of the *Landwehr*. My tutor was Lieutenant Perlitz.

I continued in this service from 1801 to 1805. When in 1805 my regiment was ordered to march on the Rhine, my father, not wanting me to interrupt my studies, obtained from General Brûsewitz, commander of the regiment, permission to leave me at Berlin, and I stayed in that city until the arrival of the French in 1806.

It was this background of mine which led Uminski to designate me, though the youngest officer, to be an instructor of the honour guard. The drill instruction on foot went well enough and progressed quickly assisted by our young soldiers who were inspired to learn, but the instruction on horseback of those same guards of honour was very painful. Almost all of them owned and rode horses which were too lively to be able manoeuvre together and, in consequence, their ranks were nearly always in total disorder. It is absolutely necessary to avoid taking mounts for the cavalry which are too lively as they will always get as excited as though they were back in the days when they were running in herds of their siblings.

It is with the greatest pleasure that I am able to mention here the names of those who served with me in this honour guard: Among them were Suchorzewski, Morawski, Tomicki, Ziemecki, all to become generals later. Our *legionnaires* from Italy had also just arrived one after another; they were General Sokolnicki, Downarowicz, Sierawski, Muchawski, Hauke, Cedrowski, etc. We, of course, welcomed them warmly.

The foremost French infantry division, belonging to Marshal Davout's corps, arrived and made a great impression on me. Several of us went to meet them. About an hour from the city, we saw the countryside was covered with infantry, dressed in greatcoats of different colours; they were carrying their rifles with their butts in the air, and seeking out the driest places to cross over the fields, because the roads were so wet and well-travelled that anyone walking upon them soon had mud up to their knees!

In front of the town, near the aforementioned windmills, drums were beaten and the soldiers, coming in from all sides, gathered together and resumed their ranks. In the blink of an eye, they rolled up their greatcoats, adjusted their hats (because at that time all the infantry still wore tricorn hats), and suddenly this was the most perfect troop that ever presented itself, a regimental band at the head of the column, ready to enter at a quick march into the city.

They stopped in the marketplace, piled their arms, out of their bags came brushes to remove the mud from their shoes and they began chatting with vivacity and amusement between themselves as if they had only travelled only one league instead of one hundred and fifty leagues to arrive.

I gazed in amazement at these infantrymen, composed of fellows who were so animated and, until that moment undefeated on the battlefield. All of them were as fresh as for the start a dance. The Prussian infantry who had just left Posen were quite a different proposition; they were in the main at least the head of more taller than the French, and seemed overall individually physically stronger, but they were stiff, heavy, and seemingly already tired when their column halted after only a league of marching.

I had learned in reading the history of warfare that it is the infantry that wins the battles and it is the foot soldier that decides victory, for although the cavalry also sometimes had a decisive role to play, this was almost always most effective after an assured victory when its role is to gather in the harvest. Studying closely and admiring these brave agile French infantrymen, I clearly understood the vital importance of this weapon, and accordingly I became resolved to begin my real military career in the infantry.

Chapter 2: Encounter with Napoleon

We finally received the news that the emperor was on his way and would soon arrive at Posen. Our guard of honour left Posen, with the intention to stop at Miendzyrzec to receive the emperor when he crossed the Polish frontier: but arriving towards evening at Byton, we found him already there. We went forward and escorted his carriage, walking both in front and behind it: the *Chasseurs* of the Imperial Guard, *i.e.* a troop of twenty five men commanded by an officer, who had escorted the emperor until that time, passed behind us, so we were able to demonstrate that we had confidence in ourselves.

The night was very dark, and so we could hardly see in the gloom the white turban of the Mameluke, Roustan, sitting on the seat of the imperial carriage. During the journey and the relays, the emperor chatted with General Dombrowski, who stood beside his horse near the carriage door. The mud was so thick, the carriage could only progress at a walk.

When they reached Posen, the emperor made his quarters in the former Jesuit convent; Twenty-five of our guards were ordered to remain in the same building to serve him there and we received a good room for our quarters on the ground floor.

The next morning, around 10 a.m., the emperor mounted his horse. Our honour guard was assembled in full in the yard; four of ours received the order to march mounted before the emperor, the rest of the unit following behind his retinue. The emperor set off at a gallop, crossed the bridge and followed the road to Warsaw through appalling mud and upon arriving at the small town of Swarzendz, he took a right turn across the fields, looking for the highest points, stopping here and there to examine the ground as if he had a enemy army in front of him.

Having been most often one of four honour guards who was at the head of the column, I was able to see and examine the emperor at my ease when he stopped, and it seemed to me that I had already known him from a long time, having seen his portraits which were strikingly similar, especially those who represented him on horseback. I noticed it was almost impossible to distinguish the colour of his eyes, because they were always moving; at that moment they seemed to me dark, probably because of the depth of his gaze. Later, when I found myself near enough to the emperor to speak with him, I saw perfectly that his eyes were very clear. When Napoleon spoke to someone, he did not look him in the face, but he looked at the floor or next to them. It was very rarely that he fixed his gaze directly on the eyes of his interlocutor.

We returned to Posen around 5 o'clock in the evening. The next day the emperor rode at around noon, and was shown a Polish palace. After crossing the city, he set off at a gallop towards Stenzew and only stopped at Konarzew. On the third day, December 13th, he rode beyond the other side of the town, first to Winiary, where he stopped and surveyed the country, then riding across fields, inadvertently straying into an area which appeared to be sound but which was, in fact, merely a grassy covering of deep mud into which he almost sank together with his mount. His escort could not follow him, because the cavalrymen accompanying the emperor and some of his generals had themselves passed with difficulty and accordingly the ground was now in such a poor state that it was impossible for any others to move forward to his assistance.

★★★★★★★★★★★★★★★★★★

We will report here an incident which had a profound significance to the author's career. At this time when the French officers could not cross the mud pit in a meadow, the author came forward saying: "Here is a Polish solution!" and indicating a safe way, the emperor crossed over the muddy area behind him. After the Peace of Tilsitt, Napoleon demanded that we send him this young Pole who "was able to go everywhere", and so appointed him as his orderly. (Editor's note to the Polish edition).

This anecdote is told a little differently in Épisodes politiques et militaires, by Baron Paul de Bourgoin former ambassador to Spain, Paris, 1864:

"I was told since in Warsaw that one day the Emperor Napoleon advanced on horseback, followed by his staff, having at his side a young Polish gentleman, Count Chlapowski, belonging to the first families of Posnania. He came to the edge of what seemed like a green meadow, and wanted to enter it to cross over. He was suddenly stopped by his young guide, who pointed out this meadow though covered with grasses was a deep muddy swamp, hidden under a thin layer of topsoil. The emperor, impatient to advance, did not want to heed this warning, but the intrepid Pole preceded him by rushing to demonstrate the danger which he had refused to believe. The dedication of the young man had the potential to be fatal to him. Scarcely had he taken ten steps the layer of turf opened, the horse and the rider sagged into a liquid mire. The rider alone was saved by extraordinary efforts.

To reward him for his courage, so worthy of noble nation which was then fighting alongside us, the emperor the soon after named Chlapowski his orderly officer."

★★★★★★★★★★★★★★★★★★

Then the emperor, accompanied only by us and by some of his own *chasseurs*, arrived at Radojew, from where he was rafted to the other side of the Warta; he went as far as Owinsk where he visited an abandoned convent. He demanded to know how this area came to belong to Trescow. I was able to satisfy his curiosity, for I knew this family by chance. My aunt, Madame la Contesse Engoestroem, *née* Chlapowski, lived in Berlin in a house that belonged to the Trescow family.

During my own stay in that city, I dined at her home every Sunday. My aunt had given a warm welcome to Marshal Duroc, when he visited in 1804 on an extraordinary mission to Berlin to announce the emperor's coronation. The marshal was received everywhere quite coldly, except at my aunt's home at that time. We did not know the French in Berlin, but the population were not afraid of them yet. Marshal Duroc remembered my aunt and the warm welcome she had given him; maybe he said a word to the emperor, and that was probably the reason why, back in Posen, the emperor once called me and gave me a seat at his table for dinner.

★★★★★★★★★★

The Gazette de Posen of January 7, 1807 reports that, on December 13, 1806, the Emperor Napoleon invited to his table the son of the former Koscian vedette Chlapowski.

★★★★★★★★★★

There were only three people at the table; the Emperor Napoleon, Prince Berthier, who took his place opposite him, and me. The table was so small that we could hardly have placed another person in front of me. A single servant brought and served food and other necessities. The dinner did not last more than half an hour, as far as I could judge; though during this time, if short, the emperor however asked me many strident questions, each delivered very quickly, as if it had been an examination. He knew I had previously served in the Prussian Army: he asked me about my studies, about the teachers of artillery, about the schools and made enquiries in general about the Prussian Army. He asked me how many Poles there were in the General Lestocq's corps on the other side of the Vistula.

I could not precisely answer this question, but I remarked that there must be many Lithuanians, because this corps was recruited in Prussian Lithuania, that is to say in the province of Augustow, assigned to Prussia during the last partition of Poland. At the same time, I allowed myself to make the observation that in Lithuania, landowners alone were Polish, but that the peasants themselves were Lithuanians. Napoleon knew nothing of Lithuania and had no idea how this province had been reunited with Poland; I had to explain that to him.

In general, he barely knew anything of our history and knew that of Prussia only from the times of Frederick the Great; so, he was astonished when I told him that in the corps of Lestocq there were principally Lithuanians and Samogitians, rather than Poles; I added that although these two peoples speak little of the Polish language, they were devoted to Poland; the same sympathy exists in the Lithuanian provinces that belong to the Russian Government.

The emperor also questioned me about the state of the peasants. I knew from my father that at that time in the kingdom of Poland, peasants were less severely treated than under the Prussian yoke. Agriculture became simpler than it had been formerly and required less hard labour, except as always during the harvest time. But when the Prussian Government took possession of the territories which had belonged to Poland, all the property of the church, the crown and the "*starostwa*" was redistributed to Germans who then increased the heavy hand of servitude and imposed harder labour and more work days. Polish born landowners, burdened with debts since the last wars, of necessity took their cue from the newcomers and imitated them.

The emperor listened to me attentively then suddenly he asked me about the Jewish people; saying he thought the Jews had come to Poland from Asia. I replied that on the contrary they had arrived from the West, at the time when they were oppressed almost all over Europe; indeed, our ancestors had always been acknowledged by their excessive tolerance for all religions. Napoleon also bade me tell him why the province of Kœnigsberg belonged to the electors of Brandenburg.

I didn't know France yet, so I didn't know how little the French care about what is happening outside their homes. They know in depth all the anecdotes of the court of France, and know very little of the history foreign nations. The emperor also questioned me about my family, and when I told him that my mother was a native of the vicinity of Cracovie, he asked for details of this country and of the University of Cracovie. I could not inform him about the state of this university, but I explained to him its origins and its influence, as well as its hostility towards the Jesuits.

Napoleon rose from the meal after having taken his coffee and complimented me on not having taken wine. He showed me the bottle, saying that he only took half a bottle of Chambertin himself, but emphasised that it was a bad habit.

Then, while walking around the room, he returned once again to the organisation of the Prussian Army; he knew it well enough himself, but he spoke to me again about the military schools, asking how far the study of mathematics was pursued. He was surprised when I told him it ceased at at conical sections. He asked me if they also learned geometry there, but I didn't know myself about that subject at the time, but only learned more later whilst in Paris.

That same evening, several Polish ladies from around the region had gathered in a living room near to our dining room waiting to be presented to the emperor. He joined them and thereafter often asked them the oddest questions, in as few words as possible and you could easily see that his thoughts were far away from his immediate engagements. He approached the men present however, who were dressed in coats, stockings and shoes, to tell them they should have worn boots and spurs.

The city of Posen gave a grand ball in honour of the emperor at the theatre. The room was so full of people that there was barely enough room for the dancers to move. The emperor walked here and there chatting with the Polish audience. As for me, I was more often in the street than in the hall, because I had to make sure that the honour guards did not enter all at the same time leaving their horses to the grooms, but on the contrary were always ready to escort the emperor when he decided leave the ball. A few days later an *aide-de-camp* from Prince Murat brought the news of the occupation of Warsaw by the French.

Chapter 3: Light Infantryman

The next day the emperor left Posen, and was escorted by honour guards for three hours. Thereafter he dismissed us and ordered General Dombrowski to grant each man, who had been a member, the patents of second lieutenants. Uminski was appointed lieutenant-colonel; Suchorszewski, major; Gorzensky (a former lieutenant of Prussian *cuirassiers*) and I were made lieutenants.

However, General Dombrowski began to organise four infantry regiments of the line and two of cavalry and beside these regular troops, to train irregular troops. The emperor himself appointed to colonel, the Prince Sulkowski; an officer of the same name had been his *aide-de-camp* in Egypt and had been killed at the Battle of the Pyramids.

The following noble Poles, who had on their own fortunes and so clothed and equipped the troops under their own commands, were named colonels: Mielzinski, Eacki, Poninski and Garczynski. General Dombrowski appointed in each regiment a lieutenant-colonel or major ("Gross major"), chosen from among the former *legionnaires*, and the latter were in reality the practical commanders of these regiments. The commanders of battalions, commanders of companies and squadrons were all former serving experienced officers; only some lieutenants and sub-lieutenants were new to the service. Following my father's wishes, I entered our army as lieutenant in the regiment of Prince Sulkowski, who was my uncle.

★★★★★★★★★

Prince Sulkowski was son of Elisabeth Przebedowski, daughter of the Woïnode of Malborg, and sister of Mme Mosczenski, Woïnodine of

Inowroclaw, grandmother of General Chlapowski; therefore Sulkowski was his uncle.

★★★★★★★★★★

I was placed in Captain Puchalski's company of *voltigeurs*. This officer had formerly been an officer in Kosciuszko's time. The sub-lieutenant of this company was Gorzensky, an excellent officer and well regarded by the soldiers. Gnesen was assigned to us as a garrison; I found there 2,000 recruits, almost all volunteers, and all the officers. I was immediately sent down to my company and put into service. The organisation, clothing distribution and military education were pushed along with great speed.

General Dombrowski sent us rules of service which were a Polish translation of the French rules. Already knowing the Prussian equivalents, I quickly learned the new ones, which were more straightforward and so easier to understand and learn. We did not have to wait long to be issued with our guns, almost all of which, incidentally, came to us brand new from the arsenal in Berlin, because the Prussians did not have enough time to carry them away before the French entered the city. However, the Prussian bayonets were too long, so they were quickly replaced by French bayonets.

The young soldiers began their instruction drill unarmed; but as soon as their guns arrived, the recruits soon learned to march and maintain their formation better. In my opinion, it is perfectly useless to turn out recruits to drills for very long without their arms, in the so-called soldier's school; as soon as they have the weapon in their arms, they are soldiers in their own minds, their pace improves, the alignments happen on their own.

We led a pleasant life in Gnesen, with exercise in the morning and after lunch; the evening after "the *génerale*" (roll call), the Lieutenant-Colonel, Majaczewski gave instruction on tactics to officers. Major Rogalinski gave appropriate tactical instruction to the non-commissioned officers.

Almost every day some detachment of the French Army was passing through the city. Prince Sulkowski always received the arriving officers with kindness. We were well entertained ourselves and often had balls at the Casino which were attended by the lieutenant-colonel, who had a young lady on his arm. We also often had dinners and evenings with the artillery soldiers.

Finally came the order to depart. That winter was mild but occasionally damp. We wore French Army shoes instead of boots. Shoes with tight gaiters on the legs prevent the blood from going down to swell the feet. It is true that if you walk in the snow or in the mud, the shoes get wet very quickly, but in the evening, in quarters, at the camp or at the bivouac, they dried much faster than boots, which incidentally get wet like shoes in any event. While we were drying our shoes, gaiters and stockings, we put on dry ones from our packs, because, of course, it is easier to carry two pairs of shoes than two pairs of boots. It has been pointed out that one can easily, in thick mud, lose one's shoes; but that only happens if the gaiters are done up wrongly; if they are properly adjusted, shoes hold up better than boots.

It is, of course, essential for infantry to have their legs in good condition, and to keep them that way. It is a good idea to rub them with *eau-de-vie* in the evening, when you change your shoes; this prevents the foot from swelling and at the same time preserves the skin from developing abrasions. Our soldiers prefer to rub their legs and the feet with grease, and envelop them with strips of linen, instead of socks. This practise should be forbidden to soldiers, because if these bandages are not fitted very well on the feet, they hurt them and, in any case, make them very smelly.

Every man should have three pairs of socks and wash them regularly. I give all those details about the legs and feet of infantrymen, because it is upon them that the speed of the march depends. Has not a distinguished general said that victory is found in a soldier's legs?

During our march we regularly received rations of bread, meat, porridge or beans, and brandy. From Gnesen to Gniew, we always lodged with the peasants. A selected *voltigeur* cooked for us and this was designated as his job upon his entering the regiment. Our captain, who was quite old, fell ill and had to stay behind; we saw him no more. I therefore commanded the company and fortunately my second lieutenant was a very good officer.

The four sergeants, and the few soldiers designated for the watch ate with us, especially if they weren't stationed too far apart. This was a habit we borrowed from the French.

I had in my service a servant whom my father had given me; he rode my horse which was also loaded with my wardrobe. As for me, I never rode a horse, but walked with my company. Second Lieutenant Gorzenski did the same, although he also insisted on having a horse at his disposal.

Our marching stages were long, we were covering about 4 leagues (post leagues of 7 *versts* = 7½ kilometres) per day following the road to Gasaw, Bromberg, Swiecie and Gniew. General Dombrowski found us in this last city, and brought together several battalions of the division to manoeuvre with them.

The movements in columns went well, but when the battalions deployed in lines, with fixed bayonets, they held their alignment very badly at the quick march. The young soldiers were not yet sufficiently trained to maintain direction without turning their heads to discern where they were going. When soldiers turn their heads, their bodies do not can keep the same direction, the pitch becomes irregular, the whole line floats, the troops huddle against each other or become confused.

That same day I received the order to leave with my company for Cieplo, where our vanguard was posted, about half a league from Gniew, by the side of the Vistula. The snow fell heavily all through the night, and soon the road and paths were covered over and marching became difficult. Arriving in Cieplo, I presented myself to Major Suchorzewski, who commanded a detachment of 150 lancers forming the great guard.

The major assigned my company to one of the three houses in this small village; the two other dwellings were occupied by him and his lancers. The inhabitants, all Poles, welcomed us, but we were too tightly packed in for comfort: I allocated the largest bedroom to the soldiers and I reserved a small room for the two officers and the three sergeants.

I went out with the major, who had inspected the position the day before, to place the vedettes. It was the first time we found ourselves so close to the enemy.

The major told me that we had seen hussars and enemy *chasseurs* on the bank of the Vistula. The night was dark and the snow was falling continually. We stayed in this position throughout the next day. In the evening I received the order to leave for Mlynow, 2 leagues to the left: Taken by a guide, I only got there about dawn, because we could only walk very slowly impeded by deep snow. Eventually, however, I saw on the left side of the village the bivouac fires of our division. An officer brought me an order to report to General Dombrowski and I found him in a cottage, stretched out, fully clothed upon a bed of straw.

He sent me with Lieutenant-Colonel Hurtig to collect my company. Instead of going into camp as we expected we were led to the right of the village to man a ditch whereupon we placed sentries everywhere. It was permitted to light a fire at the bottom of the ditch so we could begin cooking for the men.

I had read various regulations on manoeuvres produced by different nations and I thought (and still think today) that it is the Austrian cavalry which has the best instructions. So, I placed the sentinels on the highest points, and I came back to my company, which had already lit fires in the silos where potatoes are normally kept, though these had been long since emptied. I placed myself in a hole to shelter myself from the wind, and, wrapped in the folds of my coat, I fell asleep. In reality, it was not a coat because they are very difficult to walk in, but a cloak fitted with a collar. I slept for a few hours; my sub-lieutenant, who had rested before me, relieved the sentinels.

The next day, a staff officer brought the order to rejoin the regiment. It is from him that I learned that the whole division had moved on the left of Mlynow, for the Prussian corps had entered Danzig, and wanted to cut us off. A unit of ours, commanded by Prince Michel Radziwill, and which was called the "Legion du Nord" single-handedly defeated the enemy and occupied Starogrod. This legion was 3,000 strong, almost entirely comprised of former Prussian Army soldiers made prisoners after the Battle of Jena. Their officers, who were Poles, came from the Italian Legion.

We returned once again to the great road to Danzig, not to Gniew, but in a neighbouring village whose name I forgot, because I was immediately sent to the vanguard. The commander of the troops was Jan Dombrowski, the general's son; he took up residence at Sulkow, about a league from Dirschau (Tczw, in Polish; pronounce Tcheff). I received the order to place myself behind the village. The local peasants, all Polish, very generously brought us food in abundance.

Chapter 4: Action at Dirschau

The next day, very early in the morning, it was still dark when General Dombrowski arrived, and the officer who accompanied him gave me the order to cross the village and to stop before arriving in Dirschau. There I found the general surrounded by senior officers giving his orders for the forthcoming attacks. As commander of a company of *voltigeurs*, I was called into the circle of officers to take orders.

The general ordered me to walk behind the first cavalry squadron, which was to stop next to the suburban gardens; my second lieutenant, with half a company, was to take his men as *tirailleurs* into the gardens, and then I, with the remainder, was to swiftly advance into the houses of the *faubourg*, moving forward as far as the gate known as the "Porte de la Vistule". This gate had to be taken by our battalion, including the grenadier company. The second battalion was intended for the assault from the second entrance, at the "Porte du Moulin". The cavalry, during the attack, was to pass behind the town, on the left, and get into position beyond the "Porte de Danzig", ready to attack the enemy during his retreat. All these provisions were clearly explained by General Dombrowski so that we all understood them perfectly.

The advance immediately began, and continued for about two hours. When we saw the city and before it skirmishing Prussians hussars as we accelerated our march. Our cavalry and that of the enemy traded rifle and pistol shots, but as usual these discharges didn't really hurt anyone. When our supporting cavalry squadron arrived near to the *faubourg,* they moved to the trot and passed towards to the left as planned. I left my second

Conflict at Dirschau

section, as instructed, in the gardens, and with the first ran towards the *faubourg*, whilst the *tirailleurs* crossed over and through the hedges.

The Prussians allowed us to approach near to the houses, from where they welcomed my half-company with heavy fire from the windows, doors and loop-holes made in the walls. The sergeant running beside me was instantly mortally wounded. Some of our *voltigeurs* also fell, several wounded went back for aid. This first fusillade made a great impression on us: the people who were killed, knocked down or seriously injured naturally remained lying in the places where they fell; the rest scattered out of control. I confess that I lost my composure in this moment: my sergeant, named Morok, fell so suddenly that I almost became unmanned. When I saw his face as pale as the snow and his inanimate body, I lost my mind. In short, we all fled about 150 paces, running back the way we had come until the company of grenadiers who marched at the head of the battalion came into view. Our courage then returned, I rallied my *voltigeurs* and we ran ahead of the grenadiers and threw ourselves into the houses. The Prussians, however, had not waited for the attack of the whole battalion and as we continued our race through the houses of the suburbs, we could see the Prussian troops fleeing before us.

A few enemy horsemen also took to flight and we followed them closely, but when they threw themselves into the city, the gate was closed after them. When we were about 100 paces from the gate, a hail of bullets fell upon us anew. Once again, several *voltigeurs* fell under this fire: Lieutenant-Colonel Sierawski gave the order to take shelter behind the nearest houses, saying: "Wait here, the cannon has just arrived and is going break down the doors". He himself remained in the street, smiling in the midst of a hail of bullets which pierced his blue coat. I watched him whilst sheltering behind a house, admiring his composure.

After being exposed to a few more minutes of Prussian fire, Sierawski turned and calmly returned to his battalion, which was hidden like us behind rear the houses. Thus, the street became free again, but the enemy bullets nevertheless found several of our solders including Lieutenant-Colonel Muchawski and Adjutant Major Josef Bojanowski. Despite the continuous hail of projectiles, the wounded were taken back to the safety of the houses by their comrades; there were eleven stricken men in my company.

Well over half an hour had passed before there was any sight of cannons or the gunners who were to fire them. A moment before they arrived an old officer, with the *aide-de-camp* of the General Dombrowski, Bergenzoni came up, but this latter was mortally wounded and fell from his horse near the house where we were. The Frenchman, his companion, did not move, lying, as if unaware that the other had fallen next to him. The first cannon shot passed so close to him that his gold embroidered hat turned on his head. The shot third found its mark, the doors fell to pieces; this officer then addressed these words to me: "Forward, young man, earn 'the cross' for yourself and enter the town!" No sooner had he said the last word than we were running down the street following the fleeing Prussians who did not stop to defend themselves. We followed hard on their heels to the market place, where the battalion arrived with us.

I received the order to cross the city whilst the 2nd company was pursuing the Prussians down a street to the right. I later learned that these troops had taken refuge in the church, but they surrendered, except for a small group which fled by attempting to traverse the ice on the Vistula, where most of them were drowned. The Prussian General, Roth was taken prisoner with the 800 of his men who had taken refuge in the church. These soldiers were almost all elite *chasseurs* who had fought so well from the windows and battlements that day, that they killed 150 men of our battalion.

I stopped briefly outside the city, then I received the order to move forward half a league, until we reached Stamberg, a small village made up of six poor peasant houses, to place my sentries.

That first fight of mine at Dirschau made me reflect that young soldiers who haven't seen fire yet should not be expected to act independently as experienced *tirailleurs* do. It is more prudent to keep them in ranks, or to create a command of small detachments each led by an officer. Small detachments thus constituted, and placed at a certain distance from each other, will occupy the same front as an equal number of soldiers placed as *tirailleurs* in pairs.

General Dombrowski was wounded near our second battalion; General Kosinsky replaced him in command, though he was replaced himself a few days later by the General Gielgud, who was a hunchback.

The battalion, with Colonel Prince Sulkowski, had entered the city almost in same time as us and we could see it as it entered the streets. During our march towards Stamberg, we heard a distant fusillade and a fairly strong cannonade which we estimated to be at nearly a league ahead of us. We learned, some hours later, that an enemy column had was sent from Danzig to the aid of the garrison of Dirschau, but that General Ménard marching towards Stagarod with the Northern Legion, stopped it and forced it to retreat after a fight of barely an hour.

★★★★★★★★★★

The officers and soldiers named below received the decoration of the Legion of Honour for the Dirschau affair, following the agenda of General Dombrowski of the March 14, 1807, published on March 21 in the Gazette de Posen:

1. Hauke, Colonel, Chief of Staff.
2. Pakocz lieutenant-colonel adjutant, coming from the 1st infantry regiment.
3. Prince Sulkowski, Colonel.
4. Majaczewski, Lt. Col.
5. Muchawski, Lt. Col.
6. Bojanowski, Adjutant Major.
7. Puchalski, captain.
8. Chlapowski Lt.
9. Chojnacki, Sergeant Major.
10. Bojanowski, Sergeant Major.
11. Malinowski, sergeant.
12. Szalin, Corporal.
13. Czuprynkiewicz, soldier.
14. Charlet, French artillery officer.

Chapter 5: Stamberg and Zblewo

As soon as I arrived in Stamberg I realised what the necessary positions must be and so placed vedettes on the two breakwaters; one of these dykes led to a village that you could see about half a league away and was in mid-flood; the other ran parallel to the Vistula; the roads placed on these dykes started from the village at right angles, to later become roughly parallel. In this season, you could only move on these dykes, between which the flood covered grasslands everywhere.

When I left Dirschau, I was also given command of a second company of *voltigeurs*; so, I had under my hand 200 *voltigeurs* and 50 sharp-shooters; the latter having previously been commanded by Captain Golaszewsky, who had been recently killed in action.

On each of the dykes I positioned a guard of 40 men, which I considered to be strong enough for defence if attacked; each main guard detached two sentries who were instructed to walk 200 steps during the day and 100 steps during the hours of darkness. The next day, having learned that we would remain several days in the same place, I built in front of each guard a high barricade made of carts and planks taken in the village. We also erected huts to protect our men from poor weather and from a sudden attack. So although the outposts were a few hundred paces from the village, the main command was able to rest quietly in the houses. The main guards were all changed at twelve o'clock, both noon and at midnight, so that everyone could take turns doing kitchen duties and eating in the houses. One hour before day light, we were always under arms. Order was thus well established.

During the daytime we had nothing to fear from the enemy, because looking over the flooded plain the least object or movement could be distinguished from afar. General Kosinski came to inspect us on several occasions during the day and the night, and always found us in satisfactory order. We stayed four days quietly in this position and so we were able to rest after our most recent exertions. The enemy still did not appear, though on the fifth day one of our outposts saw some enemy horsemen near a village which faced our position. This village, named Zblewo, was about half a league from Stamberg. All the countryside being inundated, this cavalry unit could not move freely other than on the dry ground upon the dykes.

I decided to undertake a reconnaissance in the direction of this village so I moved forward about 1,000 paces from one of the outposts, with a small patrol of just 6 soldiers who I had ordered to divest themselves of their packs and swords so as to be more nimble and as quiet as possible. From cover I discovered that there were in fact enemy infantry in Zblewo. Upon returning to Stamberg, I sent a report of this development to Dirschau carried by a sergeant mounted upon a horse borrowed from a local peasant. The next day, early in the morning, I received 30 French sappers under the command of a sergeant, who told me he carried the order for me to dislodge the enemy from Zblewo with my two companies supported by his sappers.

Ideally, I did not want divide my forces, because it behoves any commander to have them together as much as possible in any military operation large or small. I left, nevertheless, on the dyke, near our barricade, 30 men under Second-Lieutenant Gorzenski, in whom I had full confidence following his bravery during the Battle of Dirschau. I was unconcerned overall, because I knew that the enemy cavalry would have the difficulty of negotiating this dyke to have any chance of cutting off our retreat. As for the enemy infantry, they could never run fast enough to overtake us.

So, I kept almost all my resources under my hand. However,

when I organised the vanguard, the French soldiers immediately demanded to be a part of it, saying that it was up to them, old experienced soldiers, to set an example for young people. I would have preferred to keep them as a reserve, which would have been more prudent, but I yielded to their entreaties. I made the French sergeant advance 100 paces in advance of the main force with 5 sappers and 5 *voltigeurs* and they set off at such a rapid pace that our men could barely keep up with them.

We took almost an hour to reach our objective and the sappers and men from my own company were fired upon several times. At the same time, several Prussian hussars put themselves *en route* behind the village and took the dyke from the left; they soon found themselves behind us on the left; but I was sure that Gorzensky would stop them at his barricade so I rushed on the village with my first detachment, crossed through it and didn't stop until I had passed it by. A few shots were fired at us. I soon lost sight the sergeant of the French sappers and his little detachment as they pursued the Prussians. I also saw some fleeing hussars on the road to the left and learned later that they had some wounded with them that they were carrying back to their own lines.

My French sergeant had not returned with his 10 men so I took two horses from the peasants and with one of my men we rode them bare-back so as to speedily catch up with him, since he was by this point near another village. Zblewo itself was quite large with very nice houses; the owners were German, but spoke Polish, because all the servants, men and women, were Polish. The latter were very happy to see us; their masters, probably out of fear, gave us something to eat and drink to refresh ourselves.

We returned to Zblewo with the sergeant of sappers. I had to stand close to him to hold him in check during our return journey on the road, for he was bent on killing or taking a Prussian and was most reluctant to return, as he said, "empty-handed". I was really concerned that he would disobey me and refuse to turn back.

I stopped at Zblewo and began to write my report to General Kosinski. My men were eating, when a sentry came to warn me that a few hundred more of our infantry were coming towards us from Stamberg. They were two companies of the 12th regiment (Colonel Poninski), who had orders to support me in case of need. The captain who commanded them handed over his instructions which stated that if the enemy withdrew from Zblewo, we should we go immediately to Skarszew (Schoeneck), where our regiment had moved; the sappers should be sent back to Dirschau.

Chapter 6: Zulawek

My regiment had set out on the morning for Skarszew; I only got there in the evening with my two companies, and upon arrival we found our quarters had already been prepared. Prince Sulkowski appointed command of this place to Captain Stanilawski, who had lived in France for a long time, and spoke German though with a strong French accent. He was very kind to me and gave us good quarters. He told me that the inhabitants, part of whom were Germans, were afraid of him, because they took him for a Frenchman based upon his accent.

This country had been in the power of the Prussians for several years, that is to say since 1772, the date of the first partition of Poland. There were many Germans, but less than I thought there would be. The Germans attach themselves easily to the earth that nourishes them. Each nation has its own character. In almost all nations, men who are forced by the need to leave their homeland suffer of from nostalgia, and do not settle abroad without bitterness. The Germans on the contrary go abroad without regret in the hope they will find an improvement in their existence. They stay, settle and keep their national identity alive whilst respecting the laws of the country in which they then reside, trusting to its justice to protect them.

I had in my company some Germans who came from around Leszno; I promoted one of them to the rank of sergeant and on the whole was very pleased with them. Though they were weaker than us when it came to bearing fatigue, the Germans are much more cautious and especially careful about maintaining their good health. When they entered the regiment, my

GENERAL OFFICER

Ulanenoffizier der 1. Legion.   Chevaulegeroffizier.
1807.

POLISH CAVALRY OFFICERS

Tambourmajor Grenadier-Trommler   Grenadier   Stabsoffizier
2. Inf.-Regiment.   5. Inf.-Regiment.
1808.

Voltigeur   Grenadier
vom 4. Inf.-Regt.   vom 17. Inf.-Regt.
1809.

POLISH INFANTRY

Germans did not speak Polish; they learned it, however, soon afterwards, and stood well under fire everywhere they fought alongside our own men. I made sure that the Poles did not make fun of them, and that on the contrary always treated them as comrades as they should. I often noticed that our soldiers carried the rifles of their exhausted German comrades which was a good sign.

There were everywhere, in the countryside, Polish peasants and in the beautiful villages Polish speaking, and well-behaved Germans were ready to employ Poles, men or women who were more vigorous than they and always ready to work hard.

After two days of rest, we once more marched and arrived at Zulawek, a village closer than 2 leagues from Danzig, and where we found our vanguard. On arriving, we saw Dziewanowski's lancers. This regiment of lancers had been formed at Bromberg with the Prussian regiment named "Towarzysz" (In Polish, 'Companion'), most of whose riders had joined us at Fordon, as soon as they glimpsed us across the Vistula; they were all excellent soldiers. A few elder officers and quartermasters of this regiment had belonged to the Polish Army of Kosciuszko. These officers, with almost the whole regiment, 600 men, had entered the service of Prussia immediately after the partition of Poland. They were all from the province of Augustow, which was assigned to Prussia.

These 600 horsemen still received from around Bromberg 300 recruits, bringing the strength of this excellent regiment to 900 men. It had been the only Prussian lancer regiment dressed in the Polish style, dark blue *kurtka* with crimson lapels and facings, pennants of red and white on their lance tips

The village of Zulawek, was both beautiful and clean and was reasonably well located. It belonged to an owner whose name I have quite forgotten, quite wrongly on my part as it happens, because we were welcomed very cordially by him. He was an old man, who had been appointed chamberlain by Frederick II, but had never wanted to live in Berlin. After the first partition of Poland, many Polish aristocrats had sold their estates for

45

a meagre price, or had given away their less valuable properties to their employees, whilst they themselves went to settle in the part of Poland that remained independent. Frederick II did his best to get rid of the Polish nobility and to have them replaced by Brandenburgers.

Chapter 7: Assault on Danzig

We left Zulawek to retire 3 leagues from Danzig. At the end of two hours' march, we saw on the roads, both right and left of us, our divisions as they marched on this city. We were in the centre of the host. In front of us were the lancers of Dziewanowski, and behind us the French batteries of artillery. On our right marched the French 2nd regiment of Light Infantry, followed by the Saxon Division. To our left the 10th *Chasseurs à cheval* regiment of French cavalry, followed by a battery and a brigade from Baden. Further on, always on the left, advanced the Legion of the North under Prince Radziwill, and before them rode General Sokolnicki's cavalry, composed of insurgents from the provinces of Posen and Kalisz. The show was superb, it was just like a review.

The advanced riders of the cavalry of both sides had on several occasions exchanged pistol shots with each other. The enemy also fired several cannon shots at us, but from our side, I did not see any battery respond, or even take a position to do so. Our division stopped at Bomfeld, but our regiment soon received the order to turn left on the village of Schoenfeld, where we subsequently arrived and where we spent the night encamped. At the beginning of that night, we saw a great fire: the enemy had clearly set fire to the suburbs, which burned throughout the whole night. It was so bright that within our camp that we could see to read our letters easily.

We stayed two days at Schoenfeld; the third day we were replaced by the 12th regiment and went to occupy the village of Kowal. We thereafter replaced each other after two days, I don't know why, because we were all camping, the general staff alone was housed in the cottages. We had enough straw to lay down upon and materials enough with which to build shelters. Furthermore, supplies came up to us regularly. There was no sickness in the ranks and men quickly become used to life in the fresh air without being inconvenienced by it. So, life passed pleasantly among happy and good comrades.

We had outposts and sentries in front of our camp, and my turn came to command them several times. I wrote in my notebook that the night of March 12th, passed on full guard, was particularly stressful, because hardly had we come to settle down, when Lieutenant-Colonel Cedrowski, gave me the order to advance towards the burnt-out suburb of Schotland. He forbade us to light a fire for ourselves, for fear of being seen by the enemy. Without straw and without fire, we spent a cold and damp night there, stamping the soles of our feet to warm ourselves in the mud and snow. I placed my vedettes very close to the guard, because the night was very dark. However, in reality the whole company was on guard, because no one could go to bed. I don't remember a more uncomfortable night.

When day broke, our soldiers brought a few planks from the burnt suburb on which Gorzensky and I slept a little, in turn, because it was impossible to lay down on the ground where, if one stood erect, there was mud up to the knees. No, I will never forget this night which seemed so long to me! In fact, I want to recount the memory of it so that young soldiers know what awaits them in war; it's not the cannonballs they have most to fear, but the lack of everything they have come to expect as perfectly normal and so be ready for any deprivation. But good comradeship, once again, diminished our miseries. My *voltigeurs* didn't complain, I heard some humming this old Polish military song from the time of Kosciuszko:

> *Czy to w boju czy to w czancu*
> *Zolniez zawsre jakby w tancu*
> (Either in battle or in garrison,
> The soldier always likes dancing!)

But there were quite a few who murmured an additional lyric: "cold, hungry and far from home."

Around 9 a.m., when we began to wonder why we were not relieved, the regiment arrived in its entirety, and we set off towards the burned suburb. We stopped in a hollow as the 12th Regiment passed in front of us, then we received the order to stand at ease and wait.

We soon heard a veritable storm of shooting. After a one-hour fight, the 12th captured Stolzenberg. The enemy retreated to Fort Bischoffsberg, and began to shell us with artillery from within the stronghold. The 12th regiment lost many fine soldiers on that day, because the enemy, hidden in the ruins of the burnt suburb, fired upon them with deadly precision.

The wounded were brought to us; the cannon thundered, but their shots fell beyond our line. It was a good test for our young soldiers, because they were able to convince themselves that although we were very close, the cannonballs would always pass over our heads. We stayed quiet, noticing that the sound and whistle of cannonballs can only be heard when they pass, because the cannonball that kills you cannot be heard.

Four companies of the 12th regiment remained in the burned-out suburb of Stolzenberg, the rest of the regiment retreated to Kowal. Our regiment went to Wonnenberg, where we installed our camp and our bivouac, and where we could, after twenty-four hours of movements, light a fire and begin cooking our meals. I am sure that almost no one from our company had eaten a piece of bread during these last twenty-four hours. We were inexperienced in those days and had nothing edible with us. I note here for beginners that a soldier should always have a piece of bread somewhere about him.

On March 17th, the trenches were opened in front of the fortress. In the evening, I was sent with my company as support for a French officer and 40 sappers. When night fell, they went to work. During the night, the Prussians who occupied the forts of Bischoffsberg and Hagelsberg sent patrols on the side of the lines.

(In Polish: Biskupiagora and Goragradowa, literally Bishop's Mountain and Hail Mountain. We have adopted the German names of these two forts.)

These patrols soon heard the sound of pickaxes of our sappers and began to fire on us. Soon they were throwing fire bombs to illuminate the place and it was not long before the enemy also began to cannonade the working party. This trench was begun in the ruins of burned houses. Before the sappers had time to dig down deep enough to be sheltered from enemy fire, one of them was wounded and another was killed. But the work was so advanced before daybreak, that in the morning, although the enemy had doubled his fire upon us, we were able to stand upright in the trench. Cannonballs struck the parapet, however, and so it was necessary to continuously repair it. During the day we placed gabions, filled with earth, to increase protection. We should have employed these gabions from the outset, but they were only brought forward in the morning by detachments of sappers.

About a thousand paces behind us the rest of our division was waiting, weapons at the ready, outside range of the fort's cannon, in order to prevent sorties of the enemy which might upset our works. I learned later that we had opened trenches in two other places. The next day a company arrived to replace us, but as it was almost daylight when it approached the trench, it was greeted with volleys from the enemy, which also accompanied us during our return to Wonnenberg; however, no one was hurt. In the following days the companies were sent out to the trenches in the evening when darkness had fallen, and likewise before dawn had broken, so that the fort could not fire upon us.

At Wonnenberg camp we heard roar the cannon all day and night: we could hear it on the right side of the Saxons, to the left on the side of the Badois. Those troops were also involved in trench work, but we could not see them from our position at Wonnenberg. Nor could we, from the camp, see our sappers working in the trench, accompanied by own our guard companies. Four companies always stood ready half way between the camp and the trench. These were relieved every twenty-four hours; we changed the companies actually in the trenches every twelve hours, because they helped the sappers in their work, and no one could sleep in the trenches. Every day the whole regiment stood to arms before dawn and remained under arms thereafter.

However, despite all these precautions, the enemy made a sortie from Hagelsberg upon the Badois, who they chased from their trenches, and went on to the Ziganenberg (Mountain of the Bohemians), opposite the fort of Hagelsberg. A few hundred Cossacks fell on the Badois who fled and took a few prisoners. The *Chasseurs à Cheval* rode forward to their assistance, but disengaged, either because they saw the Cossacks for the first time or because there were too few of them.

From Wonnenberg where we were, we could see only part of Ziganenberg; we saw two squadrons of Saxon dragoons advance fearlessly against the Cossacks, who retreated into the fort. The *chasseurs* had advanced as foragers against the Cossacks, who did not move, but when they saw the dragoons advancing in close formation, they forthwith fled.

On March 22, Marshal Lefebvre arrived to review us and have us execute some movements. He passed through our ranks with his staff and inspected us in detail. Then he ordered the companies in the centre of each battalion to form into columns; the four companies that were ahead of us united with their battalions; the marshal deployed once more, and put them to the quick march as though for a bayonet attack against a battery of cannon.

Then we formed squares in three rows, then whole squares, detaching troops to cover the gaps. In a word we executed all the movements which are most used and most useful in war. All these movements were fairly well executed, despite mud and snow. That same day Marshal Lefebvre transferred his Prusztch headquarters at Pickendorf, a better choice for a position at the centre of the works of attack. Dantzig, a large stronghold surrounded detached forts, was easier to besiege that one might have believed at first glance: although quite large, it was for most part covered by flooding. We were on the side of the Vistula, and so could not approach in this season.

We could only lay siege on the side of the south, where the city was covered by the two forts from Bischoffsberg and Hagelsberg; if you had managed to take the city from another side, these two forts could always have held out, be readily defended and were in a position to destroy the city.

It was therefore not necessary to completely invest the city, it was enough to wrap around the southern half of it and to build the trenches and the parallels only on that side. If the above-mentioned forts could be taken, the city could no longer defend himself. On the other side of the Vistula, to the east, one must establish a bridge of communication between Prusztch and the spit of sand that runs along the edge from the sea, and then place an observation corps on this spit of sand, near Pillau. If this body of men was strong enough, it could occupy the island of Holm, which lay between the Vistula and the canal; communication was thus cut off from Dantzig with the sea, and with the two forts positioned at the mouth of the Vistula, Weichselmünde and Fahrwasser. This mission was reserved for General Oudinot's division, which arrived later.

Our division was in the centre of the line of investment; to our right, the Saxon division; on our left the Baden brigade; on the far left, the Northern Legion. General Sokolnicki's cavalry brigade were established at Langfur and guarded the land to the west until it reached the sea. This cavalry brigade were often called upon to fight against the enemy and especially to oppose his sorties at the beginning of the siege, before the investment of Danzig was complete.

The two strong approach works before us were carried very quickly, and thereafter began the construction of the batteries for our large calibre guns. The sappers were working especially at night, but the enemy sent fire bombs to illuminate the works. The enemy's elite sharp-shooters were also advancing against our guards and firing at close range. When the flames revealed our men valiantly filling the gabions, they fired upon them, but fortunately without much effect.

On March 26th, it was my turn again go into the trenches with my company. At 4 o'clock in the morning, I had replaced a company of the 12th regiment and we had barely taken their place in the trench and deposited our haver-sacks when a hail of bullets fell on us from the left flank. It was still very dark; however, thanks to the reflections created by the snow, I could see enemy *tirailleurs* running forward to cut off any retreat on this side. I was almost certain that the Baden troops had surrendered or had fled without firing a shot, for these *tirailleurs* passed by only a few hundred paces the trenches occupied by the Badois.

At that moment I believed it was all up for us, because behind the *tirailleurs* was a column of enemy infantry which had almost overtaken us. The *tirailleurs* themselves were heading straight for our position, so we left the trench and retired towards Stolzenberg. It was impossible to fall back on our companies which had been placed in reserve, despite the fact that they had been positioned precisely in the event of a sudden attack, because the Prussian infantry was already behind us.

The burnt-out suburb of Stolzenberg was on our right, and the trenches were occupied there by 10th and 11th companies of the line so that is where we headed through the gardens, running under a under the hail of bullets delivered by the Prussian *tirailleurs*. But to our dismay when we were just halfway to our destination, we saw that Stolzenberg was already occupied by the enemy, who greeted us with a well-directed fire.

Thanks to the darkness, we only had a few of our men injured. Nevertheless, we had to get out of these gardens because we were now caught between two fires. Our best option was to escape to the right. This we did firing at the enemy as we went and taking some wounded with us, we retired across the fields onto our four reserve companies, which advanced to assist us.

Major Malczewski, commander of this reserve, came to us on his horse, followed by our own *tirailleurs* who ran to our aid, and in so doing halted the advance of the enemy *tirailleurs* who had almost cut off our retreat. We finally joined the reserve. The day, however, was just beginning. The major, on high from his horse, saw several enemy skirmishers emerging from the city. He gave the order everyone to turn around to the right and retrograde on Wonnenberg. As for us, who were still 100 or 150 paces from the reserve, the major ordered us to follow the others, remaining deployed as skirmishers.

We ran for a few hundred of steps following this command, the four companies of reserve in columns, my own men as *tirailleurs* about 150 paces behind. We fired upon some Cossacks, who had formed a curtain in front of their infantry. Behind them, I saw regular cavalry organising themselves into line. I ordered my bugler to give the signal to rally my *tirailleurs*, and keeping 10 men with me, I ordered the sub-lieutenant to continue the retreat; I followed him with my 10 men at 50 paces. Alas! My decision came much too late!

ENTRENCHMENTS OF THE BATTLE OF DANZIG–

ASSAULT ON DANZIG BY THE FRENCH 1807

Chapter 8: Taken Prisoner

Two enemy cavalry squadrons charged us in line at the gallop; One of them passed right over the top us and I fell, knocked down between two horses after receiving a blow in the back.

I lost consciousness, though I don't know for how long. However, when I came back to my senses, I found that I was lying on the ground and stripped of my uniform. I was surrounded by Cossacks on horseback, and next to me was one of my *voltigeurs*, from whom only his greatcoat had been taken. A Cossack officer told me to get up, but that was impossible. I could not move my arms, and my body and legs were stiff. He held out his hand to me, raised me, and then dismounting one of his Cossacks, he told me to mount his horse.

The Cossack led his horse himself, without allowing me take the reins. We crossed the suburb between the Bischoffsberg and the Hagelsberg, then Stiglitz, into the city.

After passing through the city gate, the Cossack helped me down and there I sat down on a bench to rest, shivering with chattering teeth, for I was almost completely undressed. The colonel of the Cossacks eventually arrived, dismounted and offered me some brandy together with four of my *voltigeurs* (of the 10 who were previously with me). He then asked me what uniform I wore, and after a quarter of an hour, it was returned to me, with the ribbon of the Legion of Honour still in place upon its breast, though without the cross. It was this cross that I had received following the combat of Dirschau: the chief of staff of the Marshal Lefebvre tied it to my chest himself. This officer was next to the Dirschau gate when we blew it up.

My cap was lost, but the colonel of the Cossacks presented me with a warm Cossack hat and I liked this cap better than everything. We found Lieutentant Sokolowski among the prisoners. He was an officer of one of the four companies which were overturned by the cavalry charge together with my own company. Also taken prisoner were a French soldier, four of my own *voltigeurs*, two French artillery officers and engineers and finally a Baden officer and several of his soldiers. Prussian officers of different arms surrounded the French soldier, who was from 2nd Light Infantry Regiment; those who spoke French themselves chatted with him, for he was inclined to be talkative. The two French officer captives, however, did not say anything.

This French soldier gave the following answer which then found its way around the army. One of the officers Prussian officers said to him: "You Frenchmen, you only fight for the money!"

The other responded quickly: "And you? Why do you fight?"

"For us, it is for glory!" said the Prussian.

"You are right: you are fighting for what you have lacked!" resumed the Frenchman.

We were taken to a building, then after two days of incarceration marched during the night, in Fahrwasser, where we were embarked upon a Swedish ship, which transported us first to Pillau, then to Klejpeda, and finally to Riga. We stayed six weeks on this boat, very malnourished so that we were all became affected by scurvy.

With us were Uminski, Malet (A French engineer officer who later entered in the service of the Duchy of Warsaw bearing the name of Malecki), and around 200 soldiers. We formulated a plan to seize of the boat, whose crew was small: but upon hearing that the war was soon to come to a conclusion, we gave up our project in the hope that we would ere long be repatriated. We were lodged in Riga and received half of our balance. Almost all officers and soldiers, one after another, fell ill of a nervous fever derived from the poor food we had been given on the transport vessel. I was one of the last to succumb, and remained several days without knowing anything; a haemorrhage through the nose and mouth saved me.

Chapter 9: Liberated

Finally, the Peace of Tilsitt was signed and we were set free. I took advantage of my liberty immediately and left for Wilna, where I knew I would find M. Oginski, a gentleman I had known in Berlin. He received me with open arms, and gave me all the money necessary to travel onwards to Warsaw. I spent a few very pleasant days with him visiting the surrounding countryside. As soon as I arrived in Wilna, I introduced myself with General Governor Korsakow, the same officer that Masséna had beaten in Zurich. It was a very polite old man. He invited me to dinner and spoke of the Swiss campaign in which he had taken part and seeing that I knew its background, he spoke to me about it in great detail.

I noticed that the Lithuanians were happy with his company. I met several Lithuanian families in consequence, in particular, Mr. and Mrs. Tyzenhauz.

I left Wilna by post chaise, for I now had the money for the fare, and did not stop on the way, except for one day in Grodno, to visit the city and its monuments, which remind the Poles of so much of our past. In Bialystok, one could readily notice the effects of the well-established Prussian administration. Several houses were newly built slightly "*à la Prussian*". The country is not as pretty as the surroundings of Wilna and Grodno, though quite pleasant. From Tykocin to Ostrolenka, we witnessed the sad results of the war: devastation everywhere. From there onwards, I encountered detachments of our troops.

I stayed a week in Warsaw, to visit the city and to re-equip myself. After presenting myself to Prince Joseph Poniatowski and our generals, I went to my parents where I found my father in good health. Whilst living in my father's house, I received a letter announcing my appointment as orderly to the emperor.

★★★★★★★★★★

A copy of this appointment is in the Archives of the war, we give below:

Extract from the Minutes of the Secretary of State.

Bayonne, May 9, 1808.

Napoleon, Emperor of the French, King of Italy, and Protector of the Confederation of the Rhine, We have decreed and do decree the following:

Art. 1.—Sir Désiré Clapowski (*sic*), Polish *État-Major* officer, is appointed one of our ordinance officers.

Art. 2.—Our Minister of War is responsible for the execution of this decree.

Signed: Napoleon.

By the Emperor,

The Minister of State.   *Signed*: Hugues B. Maret..

The Minister of War.   *Signed*: Clarke.

For extension

The magazine inspector, general secretary,

Fririon.

Collated

The head of the law office,

Arcambal, the eldest.

★★★★★★★★★★

I immediately left for Paris. Although our title given was that of ordinance officers, we were actually the assistants of the emperor's camp, that is 'orderly officers', because the general *aides* of camp never did the service as such: they often commanded army corps, like Junot, Marmont, Rapp, Savary, Bertrand, Mouton, Lauriston, Drouot, Lebrun, Lemarais, Durosnel and Caffarelli. When Marmont was named marshal, he was replaced by Narbonne, then in 1813 by Flahaut. There was usually two of these *aides-de-camp* to the person of the emperor, some sometimes only one, sometimes also none. When I took my service as an orderly officer, we were at peace, so I got permission to take courses at the École Polytechnique.

I rented accommodation from this school. Above all, I became particularly attached, among the different courses, to that of descriptive geometry, on which I could not answer the questions asked by the emperor at Posen. Alongside mathematics, I studied various courses including geology, chemistry, botany and mechanics. The polytechnic of Paris was, at that time, the best military school and preparatory military sciences were promoted there to the highest degree.

The commitment of the pupils of 1st and 2nd years was excellent, so much so that we never talked about subjects other than science. Besides, we didn't have much time to talk, because the tutors came from 6 o'clock in the morning in our lodgings, two hours before beginning of the first lesson. We had so all be ready before 6 o'clock.

Classes lasted from 8 a.m. to 11:00; then came a very short lunch. From noon to 5 o'clock the courses followed each other; at 5 p.m., dinner, then, from 7 to 10 p.m., teachers came to us to review the courses that had been made for us. They often stayed until 11 p.m. and midnight with the students who were less intelligent. They were extremely conscientious in their duties. During meals we usually chatted, applying to wars both ancient and current the theoretical knowledge we had acquired. Each of us was convinced that experience is necessary, but that experience without theoretical studies cannot make a good general.

After class I went back to my lodgement, at Doctor Markowski's house, who, at the time when our country still had a political existence, had been sent by the University of Cracovie to Paris, as one of his most distinguished students, to improve medical sciences. Our country had been divided for twenty-six years, the French Revolution had passed, and Doctor Markowski remained in Paris, always studying and the best of tutors. I advised him to return to Poland, invoking the duty of every good citizen to be useful to his country. But it was not until 1809 that he decided to return. Another one of our tutors, of the name of Livet, also decided, according to my advice, to go to Poland, where he later became a teacher at the applied school of Warsaw.

It is to him that several of our artillery officers owe their extensive knowledge in mathematics; certainly, many of them enjoy remembering this professor of distinction.

I want to mention here the names of some professors of the polytechnic school of that time, who became famous; they were Monge, Fourcroy, Faujas, de Saint-Fond, Thénard, Jussieu, etc. It is easy to understand that young people as busy as we were, hardly thought of the pleasures of the world; also, as I said above, there was hardly any talk other than of military subjects, the development of our progress and of our intelligence. It was only on Sunday that one of us went to the theatre and then always to hear some tragedy, our thoughts being always serious. It is therefore not surprising that the students of l'école Polytechnique later played important roles in life.

During the holidays, I went to Berville, near Fontainebleau, to pay a visit to General Kosciuszko. He lived with his close friend Mr. Zeltner, a Swiss, who owned a house and a small farm, where our distinguished chief involved himself in agriculture. I found him in a French farmer's costume, with a straw hat, a grey coat, short pants and shoes. He had already lost his upper teeth, which interfered with his pronunciation. He was very kind to me, telling me of various incidents of the campaigns he had commanded. I can still see him in my mind, as he recounted the attack on the Russian battery at Raclawice. He leaned over as if being pushed, and sprang forward, shouting, "*Naprzod, wiara!*" ("Forward! my friends!"), pressing down upon his head his straw hat so violently that he demolished it. Certainly, during this story, his imagination had transported him in the past to the extent that he made on his straw hat the same gesture as he had on the Krakow cap he was wearing at the time of the attack.

He also told me that he rode a roan horse at the Battle of Maciejowice, at the end of which he sank into a swamp, where he was wounded and taken by the Cossacks.

He said to me the following words, which remained forever etched in my memory, and which undoubtedly related to my position as an orderly officer of the emperor:

"You do well to serve and study. Work hard, and when the war comes, be a careful asset. Placed near the emperor, you can gain a lot of knowledge and experience everything. Increase your knowledge as much as possible to be useful later to our unfortunate country. You are in a good school. But don't believe that he (Napoleon) is going to reconstitute Poland! He thinks only of himself, not of our great nation, he does not care to give it back its independence. He is a despot; it is only his satisfaction, his personal ambition that matters to him. It will never create anything lasting, of that, I am sure. But don't let all this discourage you! You can learn a lot from him; experience and especially strategy. He is an excellent master. But, although he does not want to reconstitute our fatherland, he can prepare for us a good many officers, without whom we can't do anything worthwhile, if God allows us to find ourselves in better circumstances. I repeat to you once again: Study, work, but he will do nothing for us!"

In the month of May, 1808, I received the order to go to the Emperor at Bayonne. I did not pass my polytechnic examination until my return from Niort. That was before General Bertrand, who was then the senior commander. He was kind to me during the exam, not asking me as many details as he would have done to the real students of the school, who had entirely completed their studies.

Chapter 10: Bayonne

I arrived in Bayonne on the same day that the old King of Spain, Charles IV, with the Queen and the Prince of Peace (Godoï), were leaving for Valençay where the emperor had them 'installed'. The king left his country after the revolution at Aranjuez, which caused him to lose the crown and give it to his son Ferdinand. The emperor also summoned Prince Ferdinand to Bayonne; he did not recognise him as a legitimate heir to the throne, and so sent him to join his parents in Valençay. Later on, the King, Queen, and Queen of Etrurie had to leave Valençay for Italy and thus, thereafter, Prince Ferdinand remained alone at Valençay.

★★★★★★★★★★

The Château de Valençay belonged to the Prince of Talleyrand. The latter complained to the emperor that the enforced residence of the Spanish royal family cost him much more than the indemnity he was paid to keep them, because the court of the Spanish king was so numerous. As the emperor was inclined to offer a deaf ear to these complaints, Talleyrand went on: "But then, what do I say?" "Tell him mass!" answered Napoleon caustically. Talleyrand had been a priest and a bishop before the revolution.

★★★★★★★★★★

At Bayonne, the emperor and the empress lived in the castle of Marac, a quarter of a mile from the city, on the road towards Pamplona. This *château* was not large; in the middle there was a rather large living room, into which one entered directly from the garden, without an antechamber or corridor. This was used by the duty officers. On one side there were two rooms, the emperor's bedroom and the one where he took his meals with the empress; on the other side two rooms also, entirely occupied by the empress. On the upper floor lived the ladies-in-waiting (one Italian, the other Irish), and *vis-à-vis* with them the chamber ladies.

In neighbouring houses, belonging to the merchants of Bayonne, lived the Marshal Berthier, Chief of Staff of the Grand Army, *i.e.* Grand-Marshal Duroc, the Archbishop of Malines Pradt, chaplain to the Emperor, the minister Secretary Maret, the Minister of Foreign Affairs, Champagny, the *aides-de-camp*; the generals Mouton and Durosnel, and later General Bertrand, then M. de Senfft-Pilsach, ambassador minister of Saxony, much loved by the emperor, accompanied by his wife, a very kind person and very intelligent, but a little deaf.

★★★★★★★★★★

Fragment of the Memoirs of Count de Senfft- Pilsach, former minister of Saxony.

"The emperor lived in the castle of Marac, a half-quarter of a mile from the Porte d'Espagne, and M. de Champagny occupied a neighbouring house. M. de Senfft had arranged an adjoining house for his home. A squadron of the Polish guard, established at the bivouac in a nearby wood, did the service of the palace. The Vistula Legion and the fine regiment of lancers commanded by Colonel Konospska (sic, instead of Konopka), and the lancers several times executed their brilliant manoeuvres in front of the terrace of Marac. As soon as they arrived in Bayonne, Mr. and Mrs. de Senfft received their special invitation to the palace to spend the evening with the empress. From half-past nine to midnight the court, who were on the trip, gathered including the ladies of the palace: Madame de Montmorency and Madame Maret, the beautiful Mme Gazani, reader of the empress, the Grand Marshal of the palace (Duroc), General Ordener, first equerry of the empress, Generals Bertrand and Lebrun, sons of the archbishop treasurer, a young Polish ordinance officer, named Chlapowski, whom the emperor had taken a liking to and who was then enjoying a favour from Chérubin at court. Of the Polish MPs (these were the Woïvodes Stanislas Potocki, Bilinski and Dzialinski), were admitted to the same privilege during their vacation."

★★★★★★★★★★

In front of the castle, and so close that there was only room for passage of a carriage, was installed, under canvas, a battalion of the Grenadiers of the Imperial Guard. Near them were two hundred Basques of the Pyrenees, organised as a guard of honour for the emperor; they had red dolmans, black pants, stockings and shoes and were wearing blue berets. These people were fine featured, full of life and, I was told, excellent marksmen. Five hundred paces further down the road to Pamplona, there was stationed a squadron of Polish Light Horse, commanded by Captain Dziewanowski. Whenever the emperor rode out or was driven by carriage, an officer and twenty-five of our cavalrymen served him as an escort.

The palace quartermaster fixed my quarters with M. Taubin, an old ship's captain who was very amiable and whose house was very close to the Spanish Gate. When I realised that we would be at war with Spain, I met with a Spanish language teacher, who came every day to my billet at 6 o'clock in the morning, because I had to be at 8 o'clock in the service lounge. It was at this the hour when the *aides-de-camp* and the orderly officers were to be in the first chamber of the emperor, where we were given (in five or six minutes) the orders for the day. We then went to the living room of service, where each man occupied himself as he saw fit until he was called upon by the emperor. We talked or read; I often played chess with Chamberlain Bondy.

At 11 o'clock we went to have lunch at quarters of Marshal Duroc, who lived in a house next to the castle. After lunch we went back to the service room, where there came a crowd of visitors throughout the day, because this was where the ministers arrived and waited for the moment to be received in turn by the emperor. Archbishop Pradt always passed a part of the day at the service lounge and was never short of interesting anecdotes to tell us. Besides all of this, many generals and incoming couriers continually arrived from all over Europe. These latter were announced to the emperor by one of the senior *aides-de-camp*, or failing that, by one of us.

Three or four hours before dinner, which was regularly

served at 6 o'clock, the emperor rode out almost every day on horseback or was taken by carriage to the seaside at a place which offered a very nice stroll near to Biarritz. A squire accompanied the imperial carriage which was followed by an escort of twenty-five Polish Light Horse commanded by a lieutenant. Dinner was served, as I have said, at 6 o'clock. The emperor always dined with the empress and often also with the Prince of Neuchâtel (Berthier). In the evening we met in the *salon* of the empress; the emperor came there sometimes; he would then walk about in the drawing-room, chatting with various people. Everyone except the ladies remained standing. Sometimes he sat with us. One day he came into the living room, a little book in his hand, saying, "It's not interesting, it bores me, I have nothing to read", and he threw the book on to a chair. We can truly be amazed that such a man actually found the time to read novels. It is the best proof that his whole political and military machine was well constructed.

We sometimes played cards in the evening, 'Krebs'.
(*Editor's note: possibly the game now known as 'Mus' which originated in the Basque region and was well established by the early 19th century*).

In general, no one lost, nor won, although the table was covered with gold. Indeed, we were not trying to win, and we didn't pay much attention to the game. One evening, however, Lady Luck was with me and I won many gold *napoleons*; I was not embarrassed by my good fortune, because I had not given the game any more attention than others had done.

The empress always won at games; it is probable given there were only a few players present and seeing the fun she had by winning that most purposely lost out of politeness. However, she never took away the money she won, because she always withdrew before midnight. I don't know what happened to that money, because as soon as the emperor and empress were leaving the *salon*, everyone else was also leaving.

Shortly afterwards, I received the order of the emperor to carry despatches to Spain.

★★★★★★★★★★

This order was as follows:

"The Orderly Officer Chlapowski will leave immediately. He will arrange to arrive in Vittoria before 4 o'clock in the morning; he will deliver the attached letter to General Verdier in person; he will continue on his way to Burgos without stopping, and give Marshal Bessières his letter; he will stay in Burgos until the Marshal dispatches it.

N.

At Bayonne, June 3, 1808."

★★★★★★★★★★

Chapter 11: Abroad in Spain

I left immediately, and before dark I stopped to change my post horse by the Bidassoa River. From this place everything changes, the country as well as the people. It is said that there may not be in Europe a border that separates such different countries as France and Spain. Everywhere else on the continent we might notice a gradual change from one place to another, but here it is sudden; on one side of the Bidassoa, a small, cheerful and lively population, on the other bank live a tall, serious and pensive people. On our side there are maisonettes with pretty gardens on almost level ground; on the other side stands the city of Irun with its stone houses and immediately beyond the rising mountains, so that on leaving the city one enters 'parades'. These 'parades', which lead from one mountain to another to Vittoria, have a length of 33 Spanish "*leguas*", it is that is, nearly 24 of our leagues.

A Spanish postilion preceded me, dressed in his great coat. Bells were attached on his horse's head, so that travelling by night, I heard him in front of me even though I couldn't see him. The Spanish horses are very good riding horses and can gallop easily uphill or downhill, so that we could very well traverse 2 leagues in half an hour.

I arrived in Vittoria in the morning, in Burgos at noon, and the following day in Madrid. But when I arrived to this last city, I could no longer feel my legs or my arms. I had to be taken to the marshal, because I could not stand up. After giving him my despatch, I was recognised. He took me to my accommodation, where I found a good bed, and where they gave me a servant to tend to my needs.

The *aides-de-camp* helped me to undress, but my legs were so swollen they couldn't take off my boots, they had to cut them off, though I had chosen them with extremely wide legs when purchased them in Bayonne. I couldn't sleep that first night. I had a fever all over my body and I still could not feel my limbs. However, although it seemed to me that my head was no longer attached to my body, my thoughts remained clear and free.

During my journey, always on horseback, it was impossible to eat; on the second day I was only thirsty and drank sweet water from each stop. Also, on the second day I had to be helped to ride a horse, because I couldn't do it any more unassisted. It was only after the second night, during which I slept well, that they allowed me to take a bath: then, after a good lunch, I was ready to resume my journey. But I was held back a few more weeks in Madrid.

I recount this trip here for the benefit of young people. If they have to travel on post horses, day and night without stopping they must choose to wear very wide boots, have stirrups with the soles lined with wood and use a saddle with a longitudinal recess. They must eat shortly before departure; they will not be hungry on the way in spite of that. If they travel during the hot season, they will have dry mouths and so they must then have a small bottle of cognac, with which to rinse the mouth, without swallowing it. Every time one takes a strong drink, one increases one's fever, which is inevitable after forty-eight hours of this kind of travel.

On May 2nd, the Madrid revolution broke out. This revolution was not intended to break out until the 3rd of the month, during the bullfighting, the favourite amusement of Spaniards. All French officers were invited; the intention was to massacre them and this was believed to be an easy task because the soldiers of the French garrison in Madrid only comprised 4,000 infantry (Fusiliers of the Imperial Guard), gunners with twelve guns and 200 Mamelukes, stationed nearby the Royal Palace. Most of the cavalry was confined to small villages a league and a half from the city, for there were no villages in the immediate vicinity.

The surroundings of Madrid form a plain, but one cut by numerous ravines. The plot had been well organised. The conspirators had brought together a few thousand inhabitants of the two Castilians, who approached the city during the night, passing through ravines and parades well away from the busy main road utilised by our troops. They stopped near to the city on the night of May 2nd.

However, on 1st May, the plot had been discovered, and the order was immediately given that all officers who had their homes in the city were to live in the barracks of Buen-Retiro. The conspirators had probably known of this order and decided to act immediately without waiting for May 3rd. They hastened in consequence the arrival of the peasants. At dawn on May 2nd, a few thousand insurgents of all ages rushed into the city, and after overwhelming the few soldiers who were on duty in front of the main door, seized the Arsenal. The people of Madrid gathered on the main squares, armed with swords and especially with long knives, though some had guns. Most of crowd gathered in the square in centre of Madrid, named Puerta del Sol. The streets leading to this square were also full of insurgents so quickly descended into the greatest disorder.

They shot at the officers on horseback that we had sent to carry orders. Murat's *aide-de-camp*, Gobart, crossing at a gallop the Puerta del Sol square, received several stab wounds to the legs; luckily, he rode a large horse. He succeeded nevertheless to cross the whole city and to carry orders to the Fusiliers of the Imperial Guard. Upon the receipt of this order the fusiliers marched immediately and recovered the Arsenal without firing a shot. During their march, they routed a crowd of insurgents, who were in possession of some old guns which they were unable to fire.

The order was given to shoot 'on the spot' all Spaniards who had taken up arms and the city was restored to calm in less than two hours. (The cavalry had entered town at the end of the riot, and played no active part in it, Mamelukes excepted.) The 2,000 prisoners (*bourgeois* and peasants of the surrounding countryside) that had taken were driven out of town and received the order to kneel down. A battalion placed themselves in close ranks opposite them and the order to fire was given. All the Spaniards fell face down. . . .but not a single one was killed or wounded.

The soldiers had fired in the air: was it by order, or were those old grumblers unwilling to shoot at unarmed people? I do not know. Surely the generals were convinced of the feelings of their soldiers and did not want disobey the superior orders they had received, they gave the order published in the proclamation; the officers and the soldiers executed it according to their own ideas. After the salvo, the battalion returned to its barracks, and the Spaniards, finding themselves quite alive, fled to their homes.

It is truly amazing that so many thousands of men, almost all well-armed, could do nothing in the presence of a few thousand disciplined and experienced soldiers. Only one explanation can be found and that is Spain had not had a war for a long time and lacked, as a result, good officers.

I made the acquaintance of several nice Spanish men, and I noticed that many the peasants were brave and ready to sacrifice, as much as the "great" that is to say the aristocracy who they believed were made effeminate and corrupted by American gold. The length of the previous peace had caused the most fatal results for the nation. Only one, among all the Spanish officers, Palafox, Captain in the Regiment of Horse Guards, showed himself full of energy, and deeply felt the humiliation of his country which was subjected to the foreign yoke.

(It might be fair to comment that the above view of the Spanish uprising in Madrid is an unusual one. Chlapowski's version of the events of Dos de Mayo certainly does not align with those of contemporary historians. The French casualties are offered as in the region of 30 killed and in excess of 100 wounded, whereas the Spanish are said to have lost in the region of 200 killed and 300 executed. Editor)

Chapter 12: The Oath to King Joseph

On my return to Bayonne, I related to the emperor all that I had observed in Spain. I did not hide from him my conviction that if the Spaniards learned the fate of the family royal, and realised that the emperor, instead of keeping Ferdinand on the throne of Spain, was preparing to present it to his brother Joseph, a general insurrection would break out. The Madrid insurrection had been the work only a few men: the Spaniards did not yet know that Ferdinand had been sent to Valençay and would not return, so the insurrection ended with the riot in Madrid. The emperor used to ask clear and brief questions; answers should follow immediately. When I expressed my opinion on a general insurrection, it again was questioned sharply, doubting the veracity of what I had told him. However, I confirmed my conviction.

During my interview with the emperor, the empress was seated nearby on a sofa. That evening, when I found myself at the reception of the empress, she sent for me, and with great goodness, urged me to be more careful in the expression of my thoughts when I was speaking to the emperor, because, she advised, he did not like to hear anything that did not support his own opinions. The empress added that I must have noticed the discontentment displayed by the emperor when I spoke of the uprising in Spain. I thanked the empress for her advice, but I did not change anything in the manner in which I made my reports to the emperor, and I never noticed that he was displeased; he always showed, until the end of my services, the greatest benevolence. This warning from the empress proved her good heart, but perhaps did not reveal a great finesse of mind.

Soon after my return to Bayonne, the members of the Cortès, to the number of about a hundred arrived there; their president was Duke of l'Infantado. Dinners were given everywhere in their honour, at Maret, Duke of Bassano, Champagny, Duke of Cadore, Duroc, Duke of Friuli, and at the Saxon minister of Senfft-Pilsach, whose wife ran a very pleasant *salon*, where we often met in the country house of a merchant of Bayonne. All the Spaniards were lodged at Bayonne.

At last Joseph, the emperor's brother, arrived. He had abandoned the throne of Naples to take possession of that of Spain. The Cortès, on arriving in Bayonne, thought to find Prince Ferdinand there. Upon his leaving Spain, they had been informed that the emperor was taking him under his protection, though in reality he had sent him to Valençay, that is to say to a comfortable prison. Therefore, instead of finding Ferdinand they found Joseph, whom, by order of the emperor and motivated by fear, they were to recognise him as king and swear their loyalty to him.

To accommodate this ceremony, we arranged in one of the halls within the town hall a room to place the throne, where the Cortès met. The emperor arrived when everyone was already there. The king, Joseph had preceded him and had already taken his place on the throne. Napoleon stopped in the antechamber, or to put it more accurately in a hallway that led to the great hall, the door of which he had left half-open, so he could listen to the speech which was addressed to King Joseph by the Duke of l'Infantado.

The latter spoke in French, very distinctly and without a foreign accent. When his discourse drew to a close, the emperor heard nothing which alluded to any manner of oath, there were only compliments on the character and qualities of the King Joseph. The conclusion of his oratory was this:

So, when the Spanish nation will be undefeated by the qualities of Your Majesty, these qualities will attract on you the unanimous sentiment of the people, and we will decide. Sire, to take your oath.

The irritated emperor abruptly opened the door, entered

quickly into the room between the Cortès and the throne, pronouncing a French word impossible to repeat, and addressed to the Duke of l'Infantado the following words:

Why did you come here? First you must think or not come at all. But since you are gathered here to accept my brother as king, it is your duty to swear to him!

When the emperor entered and pronounced his first word, his brother left the throne as quickly as if he had been deposed, and the "greats" took off their hats, though they had enjoyed the privilege of wearing them as they stood before their king. The form of the oath was then read by the Duke of l'Infantado, and all the members of the Cortès by the repeated raising their hands.

The next day I was invited to dinner at the table of M. Champagny; I found myself seated near a member of the Cortès who, apparently warned too late of the summons to arrive with everyone else, had only just arrived in Bayonne and had come directly from his hotel to the minister's for this dinner. He knew nothing of what had happened the day before, because his other table neighbour, the imperial equerry, Cavalotti, hardly answered him out of excess of prudence, so he addressed himself to me.

I had no reason to hide what had happened; he would have learned it from all his colleagues in any event. So, I answered him that Ferdinand had been sent to Valençay, that the emperor did not recognise him as king, and had abdicated the king, his father, for the second time. Listening to me, the blood rose to his face, he couldn't say anything or eat anything. He was barely able to stand up as he left the table, and as I learned later, left Bayonne immediately. This gentleman was called Alava. I was happy to find a noble Spaniard who was aware of his dignity. King Joseph left Bayonne for Madrid with all the Cortès, under the leadership of a good Old Guard escort.

(Alava was, in fact, one of the most notable oath givers at Bayonne. He had fought on the French and Spanish side at the Battle of Trafalgar, subsequently served with the Duke of Wellington, was present at several notable battles of the Peninsular War and was finally among the duke's staff and by his side throughout the Battle of Waterloo, so

notably saw the final downfall of Napoleon at first hand. Editor)

The emperor's sister, Caroline, also came to Bayonne to find her husband, *(Murat)* who had received, as the French soldiers said, his "advancement" to become King of Naples. She stayed several weeks in Bayonne, animating the evenings of the empress: she had two ladies with her. After the unforgettable scenes at the town hall, the emperor began to foresee that the Spaniards would not accept his imposed change of the royal dynasty as easily as he had imagined and so he ordered several corps of his army to put themselves upon the march to enter Spain.

French regiments began to pass through Bayonne. One of the first was the regiment of Polish lancers commanded by Colonel Konopka. It was a former legion regiment commanded by Dombrowski, organised in Italy by Rozniecki from the Polish prisoners and deserted Gallicians from the Austrian Army. This superb regiment was comprised of only old officers and old soldiers. Klicki was major. (This regiment later became the 7th Regiment of Lancers of the Vistula).

In the morning before breakfast, the emperor passed in review and manoeuvred this regiment on a wide esplanade which was behind the garden. All manoeuvres were carried out with such speed and precision that the French officers present agreed that there was not, in their army, including the Guard, a better regiment. The emperor invited the officers to a dinner which took place in the camp of the Polish Light Horse of the Guard, and was very brilliant.

Captain Dziewanowski and the officers, such as Krzyzanowski and André Niegolewski did the honours. The Light Horse received the lancers of Konopka beneath the trees under which they were encamped. The imperial service paid for everything. We had fun until late into the night. The next day the regiment of lancers left for Spain. A few days afterwards three Polish infantry regiments also arrived in Bayonne. These regiments came from the old Legion of Italy, and formed the Legion of the Vistula. They were three fine regiments, commanded by General Grabinski (then later by General Chlopicki). They were also passed in review by the emperor, who ordered his own infantry regiments to receive them and offer them a dinner. The French officers received their Polish comrades, the soldiers received their fellow soldiers.

A few days later, the two squadrons of Berg's (German) lancers arrived at Bayonne. They had been equipped and dressed in the Polish style by Murat. But we noticed, although their uniform was much richer, a great difference in their attitude and in their movements compared to their Polish counterparts. About the same time there passed by twelve Portuguese regiments, sent to France by Junot, *aide-de-camp* to the emperor, who, frankly, had not much confidence in them. These regiments were very weak and incomplete, because there had been many desertions during the crossing from Spain. What was left was in good enough condition; the Portuguese were small and thin, but very skilful.

One after another, these regiments were reviewed by the emperor, and were sent into garrisons in the south of France. They walked very fast, much faster than the French. Their uniform was white, with collars and facings of different shades. Two squadrons of Portuguese *chasseurs* also arrived. They had brown uniforms, one with green collars, the other with red collars. It was said that he left two more regiments of these *chasseurs*, in Portugal. Then passed several regiments of French infantry and dragoons. Each of them, before their departure, was reviewed by the emperor.

Chapter 13: A Return to Central Europe

On August 6th, the emperor and empress left for Paris travelling *via* Pau, Agen and Bordeaux. I had orders to follow the emperor so I left two days after him, bringing with me the reports of two generals who still had to work about Bayonne with their brigades. I caught up with the imperial court at Agen, because the emperor had spent one night in Pau and one in Toulouse, and I rode without stopping until I reached Agen, where I arrived half an hour before emperor and empress entered the town.

An old colonel was waiting, seated in the living room. The emperor, alighting from his carriage, noticed him sitting there but realised, when he entered the living room, that this colonel didn't recognise him personally, and so said to him as he approached him:

"How is it, Colonel, you do not recognise me, I do not know! Yes, especially since you once had me jumping through hoops?" This colonel had been a captain in the regiment where Napoleon had served as a lieutenant. The emperor then told the old officer that he was the same Second-Lieutenant Bonaparte that he had previously known, had given a hard time including arrests and so the conversation concluded with the poor man wondering whether he would receive his retirement pension.

The next day we set off by Bordeaux, Rochefort, La Rochelle and Nantes for Paris, or more accurately for Saint-Cloud directly. It so happened that I was the only orderly officer present, and so consequently always of royal service for several weeks. In Saint-Cloud I was allocated to a good room. Visitors were numerous every day and during the evenings above all. Queen Hortense, daughter of the empress, also lived in the palace: she was not pretty, but a very attractive lady.

Soon three of my old comrades arrived, Tascher, from Italy, Talhouët, from Saint-Pétersbourg, and Eugène Montesquiou, from Spain. At their arrival, we did the weekly service between us. The Queen of Holland, Hortense, invited me to come to her castle of Saint-Leu, a few hours from Paris, to attend a party that she was giving on the occasion of the marriage of General Bertrand, *aide-de-camp* to the emperor. I accompanied Tascher, who was the uncle of the bride.

A few days later, on September 18th, the emperor sent me to meet General Caulaincourt at Erfurt, having accompanied the Emperor Alexander from St. Petersburg. I bade him announce the day and time when the emperor was going to receive the emperor from Russia.

Emperor Alexander stopped for a while at his sister's home in Weimar, and arrived in Erfurt with his brother Constantin together with a large suite of retainers, after the arrival of Napoleon.

★★★★★★★★★★

The Grand Duke Constantin, noticing that we were wearing Nanking breeches because of the heat, instead of leather overalls, was surprised him and he approached us to feel the cloth and asked us if they were allowed.

★★★★★★★★★★

The King of Saxony and several German princes also arrived there. Everyone stayed in Erfurt for twelve days. The princes lived in different houses within the city, but they always found each other to dine with the emperor at the Archdiocese; their officer aides dined with us. Only English uniforms were missing, because almost all Europe nations were represented; those wearing Austrian uniforms were represented by some generals. All of the princes had at their disposal the emperor's horses and carriages and servants of the emperor were, furthermore, at their service.

Napoleon brought to Erfurt the actors of the Théâtre-Français, and a show was performed every evening. Among other pieces was played Britannicus, wherein the actor Talma pronounced the following apposite verse:

The friendship of a great man is a blessing from the gods,

Alexander, who sat between the emperor and the King of Saxony opposite the stage, rose with considerable noise to be well noticed and then bowed deeply before Napoleon.

(Chlapowski is making a small mistake here. The quoted verse is found in L'Oedipe by Voltaire which was, admittedly, also played in Erfurt on this occasion. The incident is also recounted in the l'Histoire du Consulat et de l'Empire by M. Thiers).

After a rest of twelve days in Erfurt, we all returned to Paris. We received the order to send our horses on to Bayonne. But the emperor then left Paris abruptly, and we who were following him, then had to buy two saddle horses each so we might reach Bayonne and thence all haste move towards Spain. The first stop in that country was in Irun.

Chapter 14: War in Spain

We did not rejoin the emperor until near to the city of Burgos, where he had stopped, because the main Spanish Army had massed there in the plain. During that engagement he had part of the French Army at hand, that is to say a body composed of three infantry divisions, a dragoon division and half of the Guard. He had them deployed, not in line, but in columns of battalions, preceded by *tirailleurs*.

The *tirailleurs* were the only ones directly engaged, though nearly 500 cannon shots were fired. We saw some evident disorder in the Spanish Army. The enemy only tried to charge us once. A certain regiment of black uniformed hussars, which I had never seen before, launched a fierce attack, but did not succeed, because they set off at a gallop at 1,000 paces from us and after 500 paces, they had already become disunited. A regiment of dragoons was sent to meet them at the walk; seeing that the hussars were no longer advancing, the flankers alone moved forward, easily taking prisoner the worst mounted hussars who were unable to escape on their blown horses. However, all these hussars whether dismounted or wounded, defended themselves bravely. They were missing, unfortunately, experienced officers.

The emperor entered Burgos on the same day with part of his Guard. Some of us were sent on different missions. I was sent to Marshal Lannes, who was to be found in Tudela in Catalonia; I arrived on November 22nd. Marshal Lannes had in front of him a numerous Spanish corps, 40,000 men, it was said; the Marshal had only 18,000 men. The Spaniards, commanded by General Blake (an officer of English family, but born in Spain), were placed in an advantageous position, on perhaps too dominant heights, because their artillery could do no great harm to our troops below.

The marshal was a little surprised at the order I brought him to attack the enemy, but he answered without hesitation: "Orders will be executed.", and he took his measures to begin the attack the next day at 4 o'clock in the morning. Two infantry divisions headed towards the heights, in four columns, preceded by *tirailleurs*. The Spanish vedettes who were at mid-height fired upon us and fell back towards the summit and from there the artillery began a sustained fire all along the line; all the balls fell beyond the French lines. The French columns advanced for two hours without stopping and soon our *tirailleurs* showed themselves on the peaks.

An officer immediately ran to tell the marshal that the whole Spanish corps was in retreat and were seen to be retiring in disorder. The marshal had left in the ravines a brigade of cavalry, having been unable to suppose that the infantry alone would so easily dislodge the enemy. He sent for them now, but it was already too late. With the exception of two Spaniards taken by the *tirailleurs*, no prisoners were taken.

The battles of Burgos and Tudela, if we can call 'battles' movements of troops which last no more than two hours, justified the manner in which the emperor expressed himself in his proclamation:

"Soldiers! the defeated Spaniards could not bear your gaze!"

When I returned from my mission to the Marshal Lannes, I met at Tolosa, Tascher, who had just left Marshal Soult. Escorted by twenty hussars, we set out in haste for Mondragon. The Spaniards were shooting our isolated officers on the roads and they often massacred small parties brutally. A short distance from Mondragon where we had to change post horses, Tascher and I quickly took to the front, telling the officer of the hussars to go more slowly, for the horses were tired. After crossing a small bridge over a torrent coming down from the mountain, we nevertheless left at full gallop, me riding beside the postilion, and Tascher behind us.

Suddenly we heard shouting from behind brushwood: "*Para!*

Para!" (Stop! stop!) These words were probably addressed to the postilion. At the same time some shots were fired, and bullets hissed passed our ears. The postilion, who happened to be nearer to their side, stopped. Not a bullet hit me; it is probable that they didn't want to open fire so close to the Spanish postilion, but Tascher's horse was wounded, and he even received a few grains of black powder in the face, demonstrating how closely he had come to the assailant's fire.

A few seconds later, following the sound of the shots fired, the hussars came back to us full of contrition, while our aggressors fled away into the mountains through the brush.

★★★★★★★★★★

Tascher recounted this assault in a slightly different way. When his horse was wounded, the Spaniards threw themselves on him and wanted to take him with them, but Chlapowski turned his horse around, and threw himself on the Spaniard who was already holding Tascher, firing his horse-pistol into his body; Tascher was thus freed and escaped.

★★★★★★★★★★

We changed horses at Mondragon, then continued our route through Vittoria, Miranda, Burgos, Lerma, Aranda, and arrived at Somo-Sierra two days after the famous battle that had been fought there, of which we heard the news on the way. We saw some corpses of Polish Light Horse troopers still lying in the snow which already covered the mountain of Somo-Sierra.

We stopped for half an hour at the village, (Bocequillas), where I found some of our men seriously injured and that we had not yet been able to carry away. They told me of the charge of the squadron led by Dziewanowski and affirmed to me that all the officers and the greater part of the squadron had been killed; the rest of the squadron had nevertheless succeeded in seizing the Spanish position and the sixteen guns which had defended it. It was believed that the lieutenant must have already been dead before he finally fell, he had been so riddled with wounds. Ambulances arrived to transport the rest of the wounded to Madrid.

The ambulance surgeon told me that following the attack on

RECONNAISSANCE IN SPAIN

POLES AT SOMO-SIERRA

Somo-Sierra, the emperor had handed over to the Old Guard the entire regiment of Polish Light Horse. He had taken away the usual progression; because, in general, a regiment passed from the Young Guard to the Middle, and it was only after a brilliant action such as this one that he allowed direct progression to the Old Guard. This advancement gave each man two grades higher, so that a soldier of the Old Guard could, if required, command as a brigadier in a line regiment.

The Old Guard included the following troops: *Chasseurs à Cheval*, Grenadiers *à Cheval, élite Gendarmerie*, Foot Grenadiers, and Foot *chasseurs*.

The Middle Guard consisted at this time Dragoons and Fusiliers (Fusiliers grenadiers and fusiliers *chasseurs*).

The Young Guard, up to the Battle of Somo-Sierra, included only Light Horse and the *tirailleurs* (grenadier and *chasseur tirailleurs*).

The emperor had watched the charge of the Poles at Somo-Sierra, and had found it so brilliant, that he elevated them from the Young Guard to the Old Guard, ordering the existing troops to the Old Guard to present arms to the valiant squadron of Light Horse.

★★★★★★★★★★

This fact is confirmed by the letters addressed in 1851 by Colonel Niegolewski, a former lieutenant to the Polish Light Horses, to M. Thiers: These letters are published in the book: Poland and the Poles by a former Polish Light Horse officer of the Guard of the Emperor Napoleon I against errors and injustices of French writers MM, Thiers Ségur Lamartine Paris, Dumineray library, 1854.

★★★★★★★★★★

After a half-hour stop at Somo-Sierra, we left, but there was no post office. In every post office, two *élite gendarmes* had been placed, who replaced the original postmasters in whom there was no trust. These *élite gendarmes* were very experienced and knew how to get out of trouble. There we found horses and also something to eat. Naturally, they knew each of us and knew that we always carried the orders of the emperor and even the most important dispatches. Anyway, in a city or a small village abandoned by its inhabitants which was at first sight deprived of everything, the *élite gendarmes* knew how to find everything one might need and almost always whatever food that could be found there. These *élite gendarmes* of the Guard formed four squadrons, that is to say 600 men. They had for their chief General Savary, the emperor's *aide de camp*, then later the minister responsible for Fouché's police.

We crossed Buytrago and San-Augustin, and arrived in Madrid, from where we left immediately for San-Martin, a quarter of a league from the city, where the imperial headquarters were situated. The castle of San-Martin, with its buildings and annexes, belonged to the Duke of l'Infantado: it was in a deserted place, like all the surrounding areas of Madrid.

We returned to Madrid, where I received the order to stop for three days: I had to visit General Belliard, governor of Madrid every day then depart to rejoin the emperor, who was on his way to Salamanca, and bring him the news from Madrid. Though I roamed about the city in all directions, during these three days I was still able to rest completely from my fatigues; I spent the evenings and nights with the governor.

I met with Niegolewski, covered in bandages: he had already received his award of the Legion of Honour. I left on the evening of the third day on a post horse. I passed l'Escurial and crossed the Guadarrama during the night; the mountain was covered with snow which sometimes was as deep as the chest of my horse, but my postilion knew his way. At dawn I arrived at Villacostin, then I passed by Arrevalo, Medina del Campo, Tordesillas, and finally, on the evening of December 11th, I joined the headquarters in Medina del Rio Secco.

The emperor was not yet asleep, I found him dressed in a white *piqué* dressing gown, wearing green slippers, and upon his head, a white nightcap tied with a green ribbon. The Mameluke, Roustan was in the room and departed when I entered. The emperor asked me the most minute details about affairs in Madrid. When the emperor kept one of us several days in the same place, our instructions were to learn everything, to know in particular which troops were arriving or had passed by, to visit hospitals and take doctors' reports.

Chapter 15: In pursuit of Moore

I found my servants at headquarters and grooms for my horses. The next day we set out to Valderas, leaving the road to Salamanca. The English Army commanded by General Moore had left Salamanca and was retreating on Corunna where a flotilla of transports awaited to evacuate it.

The emperor wanted to cut off the route the English were taking through Valderas and Astorga, but the rain which lasted several days saved them, for they were on a good gravel road. Snow and cold rain soaked the terrain and the paths so thoroughly that it took three days instead of one to reach Valderas; men and horses entered knee-deep in mud. The old grenadiers, by means of contrast, remembered the muds of Pultusk. I was told that a few of them, unable to follow the column, committed suicide in despair so as not to fall into the hands of the Spanish guerillas whose detachments were fighting throughout the country.

General Lefebvre-Desnouettes, who left with the *Chasseurs à cheval* of the Guard long before the emperor, had taken the same route, though before the rain had done its worst, but he was moving too fast and ranging too far ahead of the main army. He forded the River Esla near Benavente.

The whole English cavalry division fell upon him and his *chasseurs à cheval* in the plain near Benavente, undoubtedly informed by their spies that the French Army was still far away.

Lefebvre-Desnouettes was forced to retire immediately, but he was taken prisoner with nearly sixty of his *chasseurs*, on the edge of the river, where he had wanted to hold to the last.

We arrived on the edges of the Esla which was very swollen

by the rains. We found there the regiment of *chasseurs* in much disarray, because never had such misfortune befallen them in the past. The fault for the affair fell solely on General Lefebvre-Desnouettes, because any other regiment present would have suffered the same fate. The *chasseurs*, numbering 500, had to fight against 2,400 English cavalry.

Among those who were able to save themselves by recrossing the river, there were many wounded by the rifle and pistol bullets. Several *chasseurs* showed us bruises on their backs and arms, and black marks on their faces; they told us that the English were hitting them with the flat of the sabre instead of the cutting edge, their sabres having wide blades which ensured their strokes were not as effective as ours were.

★★★★★★★★★★

(Modern historians do not subscribe to Chlapowski's version of events in this cavalry engagement. The retreating British Army was hard pressed, continually harassed by French pursuing cavalry and the British cavalry was almost constantly at work fending them off. There were 550 French horsemen engaged in this affair, but as it transpired opposed by no more than 600 British cavalrymen of the 10th and 18th Hussars. Both sides lost a similar number in killed and wounded, between 50 and 60, but the French suffered most in those captured which amounted to 3 officers and 70 other ranks including, of course, their general. British cavalry swords were inferior and given to blunting in their metal scabbards. French troopers suffering severe bruising from sword blows could count their blessings. The British blades were not sharp enough to deliver the intended cuts, so were in effect, despite the intentions of those that wielded them, less lethal metal clubs. Editor)

★★★★★★★★★★

The emperor sent some of us with detachments of the Guard, right and left, along the river to look for boats or trees to make rafts. A thousand paces away, near an abandoned village, I found in the bushes some small boats, I placed in each boat three *voltigeurs* and we came back rowing upon the oars towards the emperor's position.

★★★★★★★★★★

The author does not say that these boats were found the other side of the river, and that after crossing the Esla by swimming, he captured them under enemy fire. For this an action of daring, he was appointed officer of the Legion of Honour.
(Account by Count Tascher.)

★★★★★★★★★★

Each of these boats passed over the river propelled by some *voltigeurs*, accompanied by Ordinance Officer, Fodoas. A few cavalry squadrons followed the *voltigeurs*, fording when the water was shallow enough or swimming in the places where it was deep.

The whole cavalry division, as well as the artillery by now also arrived. The emperor ordered the cavalry to cross the river by a ford that we found a little higher upstream. By making the squadrons close up as much as possible and positioning the officers within the ranks, this tight column formed a living dam, downstream of which the water level fell. The emperor sent forward the artillery, which thus succeeded in crossing the river without wetting its ammunition. When they were on the opposite bank, the emperor crossed over with all of us. We arrived in the evening in Benavente, frozen and wet. It was at the end of December (1808).

The emperor sent me to Marshal Bessières, who had left a few hours previously towards Astorga with his division. The night was very dark and the road ran through badly maintained fields, without trees on their edges. I left the reins loose on the neck of my horse, which followed the tracks upon the ground left by the cavalry. I caught up with the marshal at 2 o'clock in the morning, at Banoza, 2 leagues distant. In half an hour, the division remounted. We departed through Astorga, and on the same day we joined Marshal Soult's vanguard, upon its arrival in Leon. This vanguard was under the command of General Colbert.

Bessières' division halted near Astorga, and General Colbert left for Manzonales.

Colbert met a little further on, beyond the village of Carcavellos, Scottish *chasseurs* placed in a position behind the village. One of them had found an advantageous position to wait for the ideal opportunity. Several shots rang out, and General Colbert, struck by a bullet in the forehead, dropped dead. As I retreated, an English soldier from the Scottish regiment barred my road which was narrow; he seized my horse by the bridle and pointed his bayonet at me: I was forced to kill him with my sword. It was the only time in my life when I found myself in the need to kill an enemy, I always tried to simply defend myself.

★★★★★★★★★★

(This is an interesting anecdote from the author and one which will be curious for most students of the Peninsular War from the British perspective. Of course, no regiment that might be reasonably described as Scottish 'chasseurs' existed. A Scottish infantry regiment was present in the second line within the British rearguard on the field beyond the village of Cacabelos, which was divided by the River Cúa. The British were on one bank—the French upon the opposite one. The shot that killed Colbert has become legendary in the annals of the famous dark green uniformed riflemen of the 95th, because it was fired by Rifleman Thomas Plunkett with his Baker Rifle at maximum range—approx. 250 yards—across the dividing river. In fact, a second shot from him killed Colbert's aide-de-camp. How Chlapowski found himself in very close proximity to an enemy soldier he identified as Scottish—given the respective positions of the protagonists—is a mystery that is now possibly impossible to resolve. Editor)

★★★★★★★★★★

When I arrived near the emperor, who was in in Baneza, I informed him of the death of Colbert, for which he expressed deep regret. The emperor eventually reached Astorga, but after receiving reports from Marshal Soult, who was following in pursuit of the English, he came to the conclusion that he was no longer able to catch up to them before their arrival in Corunna. The English succeeded in embarking their troops onto their waiting ships, but they could not save their horses, and so as not to leave them to us, they cut off the legs of these poor animals.

Chapter 16: Mission to the German Princes

We went from Astorga to Valladolid. From this city, the emperor sent me on a mission to German princes, so that they put their contingents on a war footing, because Austria was preparing to invade Bavaria.

★★★★★★★★★★

Order.

Mr. Chlapowsky will travel to Mainz. He will deliver the letter attached to the Prince Primat From there he will go to Cassel and will deliver the enclosed letter to the King of Westphalia. From there he will go to Warsaw, where he will deliver the letter to the King of Saxony; if the King is in Dresden, he will pass by Dresden to give it to him and will then travel to Warsaw. He will stay there eight days, see everything that is done there, the spirit that animates the Duchy, what they say and made in Gallicia, and will come to find me in the place where I will be.

Signed: *Napoleon.*

Valladolid, January 15, 1809.

P.S, If the Prince Primat is not in Frankfurt, you present the letter to the governor of Frankfurt so that he can pass it forward.

★★★★★★★★★★

Concerning Marbeuf—his father was once Governor of Corsica, and had sent the young Bonaparte to the school of Brienne; that is why the emperor had taken a liking to the son: the son, like his father, was an excellent man and an excellent officer. We travelled together through the south of France up to Strasbourg and Carlsruhe: Marbeuf left from there to Stuttgart and Munich, whilst I went to Darmstadt, Frankfurt and Kassel, to the King of Westphalia. I did not find the King of Saxony at Dresden, but in Warsaw, where I had the order of wait for a period of time in any case.

I arrived in Warsaw in the morning, after a trip of nineteen days and as many nights, during which time I did not stop anywhere, except for a few hours with the German princes. Everywhere, after delivering my despatches, I was obliged to give news of events in Spain.

From Valladolid to Bayonne, I travelled on post horses, but from Bayonne to Warsaw I used my own resources. On the advice from an experienced old traveller, I only drank hot milk with toast, three times a day, in post offices, when I was hungry. The season was cold, and from Leipsig, the cold became so sharp that I was forced to buy myself a fur coat.

When I arrived in Warsaw, I only stopped at the Hôtel de Vienne, where lived the French minister, M. de Bourgoin. He hitched up his carriage at 8 o'clock, and when I had changed, led me to the King of Saxony, Duke of Warsaw. The king received me kindly, went over the despatches I brought him, questioned me about the events in Spain, and ended up inviting me to dinner. That same evening there was a royal ball in the castle. The king ended the ball at 10 o'clock in dancing a *polonaise*; Prince Joseph Poniatowski stayed a little longer, but was not long in leaving; I also withdrew to rest from my fatigue.

I felt very happy in Warsaw: I got to know almost all of our *alumni* officers. Although the organisation of our army was not over, the spirit of our soldiers was excellent. We suffered, however, in almost every regiment the lack of experienced officers, and the contrast was great between these new regiments and those I had seen and frequented in Spain, especially the Light Horse of the Guard and the Vistula Legion. The Light Horse of the Guard, commanded by Vincent Krasinski, had all their *état-major* composed of former officers, and had taken as models the regiments of the Imperial Guard which they had soon equalled.

The Vistula Legion had only veterans officers from the Italian Legion of Dombrowski and Kniazewicz's Legion of the Rhine. Almost all the sergeants were also old soldiers; so, service was undertaken calmly, with precision and accuracy. In the Polish Army of the Duchy of Warsaw it was not the same. If the infantry was good, the cavalry, on the other hand, needed more exercise. The movements prescribed by the old regulations were too slow, and the new rules had not yet been published. The artillery lacked experienced officers, but the gunners were beginning to know their craft. The whole army had a good spirit, cheerful and confident, which gave me hope for the future.

Finally, there were only a few troops in the duchy, because they provided the garrisons of Danzig, Stettin and Cüstrin. The money that was sent to these garrisons never returned to Poland. In fact, Poland's financial situation was disastrous; minted money had left the country, which possessed neither industry or manufacturing The only product of the country was wheat, which it was unable to sell. Taxes were above the country's resources to pay. Skilful officials were lacking, for the Prussians had never employed Poles, and it was necessary to employ many unskilled staff who absorbed income.

I stayed a week in Warsaw and I did not did not leave before receiving information on the state of the Austrian Army in Gallicia. This information was given to me by Roman Soltyk, officer of our horse artillery, whom I had known a year before at polytechnic school. His father lived in Sydlowiez, a small town still belonging to Austria and he had inquired about the number and the locations of Austrian troops in Gallicia; the search for this information being part of the instructions I had received from the emperor on my departure. Mr. Niemcewicz, whose wife was my cousin, also provided me with useful details about the Austrian Army, as well as advice that was later of positive use to the emperor.

Marshal Davoust suddenly left the Duchy of Warsaw with its army corps, to go to Silesia, then on to Bavaria. He received from the emperor the order to hand over the command of the Army of the Duchy of Warsaw to one of his three generals of division at his discretion. He preferred Prince Joseph Poniatowski and thus handed over command of the army to him.

★★★★★★★★★★

At that time, the Polish Army consisted of 3 divisions:

1st division: General Prince Poniatowski,
2nd   " "   : General Zajonczek,
3rd   " "   : General Dombrowski,

★★★★★★★★★★

The Saxon Army was soon put on war footing, received the order to march, and entered Bavaria at the end of April. When I returned to Paris, I found the emperor at the Elysée-Bourbon, ready to depart for Germany. We all too soon followed him, only stopping at Strasbourg.

Our servants and our horses received the order to leave Spain and join us in Strasbourg with the Guard. But they were still far away and so each of us received 10,000 *francs* to re-equip ourselves. I purchased one of my horses at the post office in Stuttgart, and another at Ingolstadt. I had a servant with me, and I hired a groom to look after my horses who was a Wurtemberger postilion. It is only near Vienna that our valets came up to us from Spain. Just at this moment the emperor made use of cavalry of the King of Württemberg.

Chapter 17: Pfaffenhofen

On April 13th the emperor left Paris at 4 a.m.; on the 15th he arrived at Donauwerth. (We only left ourselves on the 16th). The next day our headquarters was in Ingolstadt. During our trip, I noticed that the lines of the Lech had just been fortified. The emperor, while hoping to move forward quickly, had taken the precaution of fortifying his position in the event of an enforced retirement. On his arrival in Ingolstadt, he had examined the old city fortifications and had immediately begun the necessary work to restore them. Not having yet having forces superior to those of the Austrians, he first, as a precaution, prepared for the defensive.

While walking on the ramparts, we heard a lively cannonade from the direction of Ratisbonne. Towards evening, an officer sent by the Marshal Davoust arrived with the news that the marshal was in retreat before the entire army of the Archduke Charles, and that he had left a delaying garrison of 3,000 men at Ratisbonne. These were forced to surrender, after having held out against the enemy all day, but the marshal had won himself one day in time; finally, a dispatch announced that the Bavarian Army had been beaten and had hastily withdrawn.

At one o'clock in the morning, the emperor called me, made me sit at his work table and bade me trace on his special map the route from Ingolstadt to Pfaffenhofen. When this was complete, he ordered me to take a squadron of Württemberg *Chasseurs à Cheval* (who were engaged in escort duties at Imperial Headquarters, because the Guard, which had been recalled from Spain, was still a long way off), and make a reconnaissance in the

BAVARIAN CUIRASSIERS

Jäger-Regt. z. Pf. Nr. 4 König.
Chevauleger-Rgt. Nr. 1, Prinz Adam.
Leib-Chevauleger-Regt. Nr. 2.   Jäger-Rgt. z. Pf. Nr. 3, Herzog Louis.

WURTTEMBERG CAVALRY

direction of Pfaffenhofen. He advised me to approach this city with caution, because the Austrians probably sent patrols towards Ingolstadt themselves. He added that Marshal Masséna was on the march from Augsburg to Pfaffenhofen, and had received the order to attack that same day, at 8 a.m. The Austrian left wing was commanded by Archduke Louis. The distance from Ingolstadt to Pfaffenhofen is four German leagues, (Approximately thirty kilometres.)

At 4 a.m. it was, of course, still dark and I was on horseback in front of the Württemberg cavalry squadron when General Mouton, *aide* of emperor's camp, introduced me to an officer of Bavarian *cuirassiers* accompanied by six of his men, telling me that this officer could to be useful to me on account his perfect knowledge of the country we were entering. Although very young, he transpired to of invaluable service, because he was indeed from this same countryside.

We marched for a good two hours before the day dawned. At the first inn we saw, I purchased brandy for the whole squadron, and I noticed that it came at very little cost, two *Napoleons d'or*, so I made myself popular with all the soldiers. We continued on our way and arrived, so the Bavarian officer told me, at a point which was half way down the Pfaffenhofen road.

Our *avant-garde*, was composed of twelve Württemberg *chasseurs*, the officer from the Bavarian Army and two of his *cuirassiers*. When we came into a little fir wood, we heard gunshots though we in the main body were 500 steps away. I immediately deployed my squadron, sent to the rear a troop guard who trotted 500 paces back with orders to stop there, and then rushed at the gallop towards the vanguard. When I came up to it, I came upon some French *chasseurs à cheval* who were hard at work slashing at my Württembergers.

Our men were shouting, but the French clearly didn't understand them and had already dismounted two of my men and injured two others, taking them for Austrians. These French *chasseurs* had noted the helmets of the Württembergers which were unknown to them and the white uniforms of Bavarian *cui-*

rassiers had also deceived them; because they only imagined that Austrian troops wore that colour uniform which was why they called them "soldiers of cream". So far as they were concerned they were legitimately attacking the enemy.

The French troopers then recognised my uniform, and fortunately their officer at that moment arrived on the scene: a nice meeting! He was, in fact, my intimate friend, young Lauriston, son of general *aide-de-camp* of the emperor. He had been sent on reconnaissance himself by Masséna with 80 mounted *chasseurs* of the 20th regiment towards Pfaffenhofen, before the marshal attacked the city.

I immediately made the following arrangements: I sent back, to a convenient place, three troops, asking the squadron commander to place vedettes and to allow the men and horses to eat. I then begged him to have a good troop horse kept in reserve for me, which could bring me back to the emperor very quickly when the need arose. I left an officer with a troop where we had met the French *chasseurs*, and I gave permission to fetch food for men and horses from some peasant houses that I had seen not that far distant. I gave four gold *napoleons* to the officer so that the Württembergers and Bavarians did not take anything from the countryfolk without paying for it.

It is indeed disastrous, especially for officers who are making reconnaissances, to allow the soldiers take provisions and fodder without the permission of the inhabitants; because they henceforth run away from their villages, disorder reigns in the country, and the army can no longer find supplies. The paymaster of the imperial district reimbursed the orderly officers all their disbursements on the notes that we presented to him.

I also advised the same officer to place two vedettes to observe the surrounding countryside for as far distant as possible. Lauriston gave me a fresh horse and the assistance of a *chasseur* who knew the route to Pfaffenhofen. I galloped there and arrived when Marshal Masséna was approaching the town with his infantry. His cavalry was already positioned on the other side.

The Austrians made no attempt to defend the place, for the

situation of the city did not lend itself to it. They withdrew to Landshut, where the headquarters of Archduke Louis was located. I knew that the information of Marshal Masséna's entry into Pfaffenhofen was of great importance for the emperor, so I asked the marshal to lend me a good horse. He gave me one of his own which was naturally a fine creature and thus I did not take even an hour to return to my troop, where a good Württemberg horse was, as prearranged, waiting for me.

From there I made all haste to cover the distance that separated me from my other soldiers; the squadron leader was kind enough to give me the best of his two horses. So, while it took me four hours to go from Ingolstadt to Pfaffenhofen, I barely took two hours to do the same route back again, and when I presented myself before the emperor, his first words were:

"What happened to you on the way that prevented you from fulfilling your mission?"

The emperor was very pleased with the news which I brought back to him about the entrance of the Marshal Masséna at Pfaffenofen. It was by that time 10 o'clock in the morning; the emperor told me to go and rest; but after two hours I was called upon once again and had to leave, because the emperor had news of Masséna, who had set out to join the Bavarian Army. Command had been transferred to Marshal Lefebvre, because the Bavarians had been consistently beaten by the Austrians when they were under the orders of Prince Ludwig of Bavaria, the heir to the Bavarian throne.

When the emperor arrived at the camp of the Bavarians king, he called together their officers and entered alone with the crown prince and some Bavarian generals like de Wrède and Roy. Napoleon asked Prince Louis to precisely translate into German what he said to them in French. We couldn't hear any of his words, because we were too far from their circle and besides Prince Louis stuttered a great deal. But then we learned that the emperor had told the Bavarian officers that he had just rid their country of the Austrian invasion, that he was going to lead the Bavarians to Vienna and that they absolutely had to fight better in future.

After this speech, the emperor took control of the Bavarian Army, had it formed in columns and set it marching towards the conflict, because we heard half a league or a league from Ratisbonne a sustained shooting and from time to time the noise of cannon shots. The emperor, with the rest of us in pursuit, then galloped off to find the Bavarian cavalry, which we caught up to after half an hour. This cavalry corps was comprised of six regiments, with supporting horse artillery. Unfortunately, these troops presented clear signs of demoralisation.

Their artillery was firing at too great a distance towards the Austrian cavalry which, formed in two columns preceded many scouts (mostly *Uhlans*), was advancing bravely against the Bavarians. This was between Tann and Abensberg. But soon, to the left of the *chaussée,* Ingolstadt to Ratisbonne, there appeared a division of our infantry together with a brigade of French *cuirassiers* that soon changed the situation. When the Austrian cavalry command saw the *cuirassiers*, it had its scouts fall back, and thereafter it began to retreat behind its infantry. The *cuirassiers* forthwith deployed at a walk, though the brush-covered land was not in their favour so as they advanced against the Austrians it seemed like they weren't charging in line, but dispersed as foragers.

The *cuirassiers*, notwithstanding these impediments, fell on the enemy infantry with so much vigour that it did not linger to dispute the ground with them. Instead of forming, although it had its cavalry in support, it fell back in such a way that the Bavarian cavalry, inspired by the audacious charge of the French heavy cavalry, then took courage and hotly pursued the Austrians. The *cuirassiers* and the Bavarians captured a great many prisoners, especially from the enemy infantry and triumphantly brought them back to their emperor.

Napoleon dismounted, and ordered the lighting of a fire, for the day was beginning to fade. Davoust's second division had arrived and passed before the emperor. The soldiers, who still believed in the potential for victory in Spain, recognised him and acclaimed him with loud cries of " *Vivat!*" such as I don't believe I had ever heard. Almost at the same time a dozen *cuirassiers* brought in a column of about 500 prisoners, including several officers who fallen into our hands that evening.

An Austrian staff colonel was brought before the emperor, who invited him to sit near to him and then began to question him about the position and state of the various Austrian corps. The colonel began to answer, then corrected himself by saying that "you must not ask an *état-major* to supply information to his enemy".

"Don't be concerned", said the emperor, "I know everything already," and he then began to quickly enumerate in great detail the positions of the different corps and the names of the regiments which composed them and which opposed him.

The Austrian colonel, struck to see a well-informed *avant-guard* officer, exclaimed: "With whom do I have the honour of. . .?" The emperor got up a little, and lifting his hat, replied: "Monsieur Bonaparte!"

The French infantry continued to cheer their emperor. It was a great show: on one side, this confident infantry, full of enthusiasm, looking at their leader, singing with gusto as they marched; on the other side, a column of prisoners, some of whom (at least it seemed to us) also acclaimed the emperor with their "*Vivats!*"

It was at 11 o'clock in a very dark night, when the emperor remounted his horse and reached Rohr, the first small neighbouring village, where his quarters had been prepared next to a poor house which had been reserved for imperial quarters, there was another, composed of a single chamber. After a very short meal, we lay on the straw which had been prepared for us by the quartermaster from the palace. During dinner we were warned that we would only have two hours rest.

Chapter 18: Landshut and Eckmühl

At 3 a.m. we were riding once more behind the emperor marching on Landshut. The Archduke Charles was Commander-in-Chief of the Austrian Army; but, as we know, the council of the Empire sent him all the arrangements and all orders. The army was laid out according to orders from Vienna, as if the enemy had not yet begun to attack them.

The right wing, commanded by Field Marshal Bellegarde, was to the north and on the left bank of the Danube, from Ratisbonne to Amberg; the centre, under the orders of the Archduke Charles, in the south of the Danube and Regensburg; finally, the left wing, with Archduke Louis, was in Landshut. These three corps numbered about a hundred sixty thousand men; in addition, Austria had 60,000 men in Italy and 45,000 in Gallicia, plus another separate body stationed on the borders of Saxony.

The emperor could only put in the line 100,000 men; but, since his reunion with Masséna's force, he had them all under his own hand, and as we will see later, it possessed a numerical superiority at every point where he could be attacked. From 3 a.m. to 8 a.m., we left riding four leagues between the columns of infantry and cavalry who had marched the whole night on both sides of the carriageway; the artillery having walked in the middle.

The emperor came out of a wood and emerged onto the plain above Landshut just where Marshal Masséna attacked the camp of Archduke Louis: the emperor's column was therefore in front of the left wing of the Austrians. The emperor deployed by regiments the division of *cuirassiers*, and gave the order for the

103

first of these regiments to throw themselves on the enemy infantry which was deployed against us; at the same time, he opened fire with the artillery. Soon our infantry, which had marched all the night like the cavalry, emerged from the forest, formed into columns at the quick march, and to the sound of drums beating the charge, followed the *cuirassiers*. All Archduke Louis' troops retreated towards Landshut. We followed their movements very closely: the cavalry was the first to cross the bridge of the Isar at the trot, followed immediately by the infantry. Beyond the bridge, the central street of the city rose on a long hill which we could view from afar was crowded with soldiers of all the branches of the army.

Marshal Masséna's *cuirassiers* and the light cavalry captured a few thousand prisoners before arriving at the bridge, but when they approached it, they were stopped by a hail of grapeshot delivered by the enemy artillery from the top of the street, which was enhanced by the fusillade of infantry fire directed from the houses which commanded the bridge. Despite the ensuing carnage, our infantry column crossed the bridge at a run and rushed into the city where they once again captured many prisoners. By this point the emperor had many more resources in men and materiel at his disposal than had the Archduke Louis.

The archduke had been able to see from the top of the city all the French columns that were advancing against him. All the Austrian soldiers could also see the movements of the French Army which in half an hour or three quarters of an hour, had enveloped their positions. This demonstration produced such a considerable effect on their morale that we could easily understand, even before we began to fight, why the battle lasted so little time. The Battle of Landshut began at 8 a.m. in the morning, at 11 o'clock we were within the city and at half past twelve we were eating our lunches.

At one o'clock the emperor summoned me to ride to Marshal Davoust, whom he had left with only two infantry divisions facing the army of Archduke Charles, in command of an army of more than 60,000 men. I copied the path to follow from the emperor's special map and thereafter I departed on my mission. Instead of taking the main road I took a path on the right leading directly to Eckmûhl, where the emperor had told me I would find Marshal Davoust. I was ordered to inform the marshal that the emperor would arrive before midnight with his troops on the road to Ratisbonne near Eckmûhl.

The emperor, before sending me away, had said:"At 8 o'clock in the morning, I sent from the battlefield to Marshal Davoust an *aide-de-camp*, your compatriot, but I have seen from his appearance that it was probable that he would not arrive quickly enough; if he happens to arrive in time, however, it will be all to the good. Anyway, to be certain I want you announce to the marshal the capture of Landshut and the flight of the Austrian troops under Archduke Louis."

Three-quarters of a league from Landshut, I stopped in a small village in front of the house of the mayor, to ask him for a guide who would lead me to Eckmühl by the shortest route. The mayor, to whom I spoke without dismounting, answered me from his window and showed me into a bedroom occupied by an officer who was sleeping on a bed of straw, telling me that this officer also had asked for a guide, but only required him after 4 hours had elapsed.

I entered the room, I woke the sleeper, and recognised him F.P.; it was him that the emperor had sent in the morning to Marshal Davoust. I asked him to continue on the road with me, but he was undressed, and answered me that he had to eat first, because he had spent the whole night on horseback. When my guide presented himself on horseback in front of the house, I left with him without delay, leaving my compatriot at the mayor's house.

The emperor had judged him accurately. I believe Monsieur F.P had no vocation for the military profession. He hadn't intended to serve his country wherever that might be; he was elderly, married and the father of a family, and had been attached to Marshal Davoust's staff at Warsaw. I only mention this incident to show the emperor's judgment, and his appreciation at a glance of military skills in others. This quality is one of the most important that a commander in chief can possess.

My guide had a good horse, so I came to the marshal's side at 5 o'clock in the evening. On the way, I made haste because an hour before I arrived, I heard the cannon thundering without interruption, though when I arrived the cannonade had finished.

I found the marshal in front of his batteries, on a height, overlooking Eckmühl and the Austrians, who had been attacking him since morning, and had thus far been unable to drive out his two infantry divisions from the advantageous positions he had chosen for them.

The marshal told me that whenever the enemy columns were approaching the heights where he had placed his forces, he sent the horses of the artillery to the rear to show his soldiers that he was not thinking to retire. Three times the Austrian columns renewed their attack; each time, the marshal let them approach within half cannon range, and stopped them with a hail of cannonballs. The third time, after a salvo with all his guns, he himself led his first line of infantry and with fixed bayonets hurled back the enemy. The Austrians could not press their assault and so abandoned their offensive. A mass of Austrian corpses was strewn upon the ground from the foot of the heights upwards to only 100 paces from the artillery batteries. This superb defence earned Marshal Davoust the title of Prince of Eckmühl.

At Landshut, when the emperor saw his infantry enter the city, he gave the order to the light cavalry and the *cuirassier* division of set out for Ratisbonne. Most of the artillery and infantry subsequently also went in the same direction. Also, an hour after my arrival with the Marshal Davoust, that is to say around 6 o'clock in the evening, we saw the Austrian Army retreat to Regensburg: furthermore, from time to time, we could hear the cannon in the direction of Landshut.

It was likely that the Archduke Charles had placed detachments between Eckmühl and Landshut and that they had come into collision with the French cavalry arriving from Landshut.

It was also certain that he had already learned of the defeat of his brother Louis, and realised that it was the centre army, under direct orders of the emperor, which had come out on his left flank. So, he had his army manoeuvre towards Regensburg to join the corps of the Field Marshal Bellegarde.

When the sound of cannon shots grew, so much so that around 8 o'clock I could see their fire, I returned to Eckmühl (the servants of the marshal had taken care of my horse), and I found the *cuirassiers* were already arriving. After leaving Landshut they had walked for twenty-four hours, like all the troops commanded by the emperor, arriving eventually beyond Eckmühl, two leagues from Ratisbonne. Certainly, they had left a lot of horses behind them, nevertheless those who had arrived made such an impression on the Austrians that their generals lost their nerves.

The emperor arrived at Ergolzbach before midnight; we slept the rest of the night, and at 6 o'clock in the morning we were on our way to Regensburg. The emperor marched immediately after the 1st regiment of *chasseurs à cheval*. At 8 o'clock, we could see the towers of Ratisbon. The Austrians left a few infantrymen in all the villages. As we only had cavalry, we couldn't go through the villages, but we passed them by turning across fields. We saw in front of us the scouts of the hussars and of the *uhlans* of Archduke Charles, wearing their red *czapskas*. Austrian infantry detachments, seeing that we were turning around villages, hastened to fall back behind their horsemen.

Half a league from Ratisbon, the country was more open and higher than the valley where the city is situated. We could see, behind a village that extends in front of Regensburg, a mass of horsemen, in the front line of which were the *uhlans*. The emperor advanced onto a hill fairly close to a village, when shots from several rifles in the gardens were fired at us. We had for our escort a squadron of line *chasseurs à cheval*. (because the Guard was still held in the rear). The emperor ordered me to take this squadron and enter the village with it. The *chasseurs* rushed forward at a gallop under enemy fire, dismounted and attacked the

Austrians, a few hundred of whom soon surrendered. They belonged to the regiment named for Archduke Charles.

Among the prisoners was an officer named Ignace Ledochowski. When the *chasseurs* brought them back from the village, the emperor noticed this Ledochowski, who was walking at their head, and was distinguished by his fine bearing; he was young, wore a nice white uniform with light blue, collar and a golden helmet larger than that of his soldiers. The emperor had him brought before him and asked him his name. Guessing by hearing it that he was a Pole from Gallicia, he said, "Why do you serve the kidnappers of your homeland?"

After saying these words, he gave the whip to his horse and galloped off. Ledochowski was so close that the tip of the whip touched his helmet, and thinking that the emperor had done it on purpose, he felt the insult so strongly that he was on the point of crying. He would not have had this idea, if he had known as we did, that the emperor never used the spur nor the pressure of the calf to put his horse at a gallop. I could only explain to him that the emperor hadn't actually hit him and furthermore never had any thought to do so.

The French cavalry division approached, led by the Carabinier brigade. The emperor immediately deployed this brigade, because he had noticed that the Austrian cavalry, massed in columns in front of the city, was moving in our direction. In an instant, a regiment of *uhlans,* six squadrons strong, advanced 200 paces from the *carabiniers* charged them at a gallop and managed to pierce their first line, but without destroying them, because behind were the 2nd regiment and the whole division of *cuirassiers.* I noticed a few *carabiniers* wounded by lancers, but on the other hand I also saw a lot of *uhlans* upon the ground.

Prisoners were brought back, including a non-commissioned officer of *uhlans*, a very handsome man, who had received a terrible blow from a *carabinier* sabre, which split his face between the eye and the ear to the bone; the blood flowed to the ground from his green coat, his *czapska* had not fallen off his head nonetheless, and on the contrary it was very well adjusted behind his right ear. When the emperor learned that the Austrian *uhlans* were in fact Poles, he made me ask this non-commissioned officer if he did not know that the intention of the emperor was to reconquer Poland and give it back to us? This lancer answered bravely: "I know it, and I am sure that if a Polish officer arrived in front of our regiment, all our *uhlans* would follow him. But for now, when we are commanded to charge, we must charge, so that it cannot be said that the Poles were badly beaten."

After this charge, the Austrians withdrew towards the city, the purpose of the charge of the *uhlans* was to cover the retirement of the other cavalry. The emperor approached the city, took his place on a height from which one could see everything comprehensively and began to examine the Austrian positions with his spyglass. Enemy *chasseurs* were still holding the gardens of the suburbs and fired upon us. A spent ball struck the emperor in the foot. He dismounted, the *aides* removed his boot, and Ivan, the surgeon applied a bandage to his toes, which had turned black with the bruise, and cut off a piece of the boot so that it would not tighten it too much around the royal foot.

The emperor soon remounted his horse and rode at full gallop towards our troops. He formed all the regiments and in each one asked the officers to appoint one soldier who was the bravest among them. I saw the officers bring to the fronts of their regiments the one they had chosen. The emperor immediately named that individual, 'Baron of the Empire' and granted him an endowment. A few orderly officers were also named Barons of the Empire on the battlefield, with an endowment of 4,000 *francs* of income.

Chapter 19: Vienna

Ratisbonne (Regensburg), which has old ramparts, was occupied by the Austrian infantry. But hardly had our artillery arrived and had fired a dozen rounds at them, our infantry rushed into the town where they took several thousand prisoners. The entire enemy army had already taken refuge on the other side of the Danube departing in such a rush that they hadn't destroyed the bridge. The same day the corps of Marshal Davoust crossed the bridge and followed the Austrian Army. The emperor entered Ratisbonne and we stayed there all day, because the army was in need of rest after three days and three nights of forced marches; it had left a lot stragglers behind due to fatigue. After this day of rest, we returned to Landshut.

The corps of Marshal Lannes in pursuit of the remnants of the army of the Archduke Louis, had captured an enemy unit in charge of pontoons destined, so we were told by these prisoners, for the crossing of the Rhine. We crossed the Isar, then the Inn at Braunau, and on May 3rd we arrived at Wels. The Austrians had burned the Wels bridge. I was present when General Bertrand had a new bridge built and I was amazed at how quickly it was constructed, without pontoons, because the French Army had not brought any with it, and those we had taken from the Archduke Louis not followed on quickly enough.It is very easy to build new bridges in a country where the buildings are constructed of wood.

We first crossed to the other side by means of a small boat rowed by some sappers, who stretched a rope from one side of the river to the other. Then we tied this rope to different boats and rafts. If some boats sat higher on the water than others, we weighed them down with stones or bricks to bring them level, then we placed the beams and planks, etc. over the top. If we had an insufficient number of boats reach the opposite bank, we built rafts with pieces of wood taken from the houses. It is in this way that we made a bridge over which the artillery and infantry began to pass in six hours.

The emperor soon crossed between the troops and travelled by a small road to Ebersberg, where we arrived at night. This town had been stormed by the division of Claparède, from the corps of Masséna. The Austrians had bravely defended themselves there. We saw corpses of French soldiers before the bridge and on the bridge itself which almost touches a city gate. The enemy, however, had failed to destroy this bridge. After a fierce fight, the French had entered the city, killing and slaughtering many Austrians and the streets were full of their corpses. The Claparède division was composed of Corsican regiments, which had lost many of their people to attack on the city and so took their revenge with ferocity.

The emperor did not enter the city until the next day. It seemed to me that the sight of this carnage made a painful impression on him. We spent the night outside the town pitching our little tents made with our *schabraques* and laying down upon the ground. As I began to fall asleep near a ditch, I heard close by the rattle of dying, and these words pronounced distinctly: "*Jésus! Marie! Joseph!*" I got up abruptly and I saw an Austrian soldier on the ground, but he could not answer me and though he was still breathing he had already lost consciousness.

War is always accompanied by atrocities, and this war in particular gave us the most painful sensations, because everywhere we were pitting Poles against Poles. The emperor, immediately after crossing Ebersberg, retraced his steps and installed his headquarters two leagues away, at Enns. From Regensburg to Landshut, the Austrian reargaurd was almost always comprised of *uhlans*. The emperor offered them imperial service, by making them a Polish Light Horse squadron. This squadron, commanded by Lt. Col. Lubienski, had just arrived in Enns. It was sent to the vanguard, to that we could always place a few Light Horse as vedettes. Every time the *uhlans* in Austrian service saw them, they came over to join us, either singly or several at a time. After a few days, however, the Austrians replaced the *uhlans* in their rearguard with their own hussars.

Marshal Masséna went from Ratisbonne to Scharding on the Danube. Unaware that the emperor would cross the Danube near Enns, and would arrive by the opposite bank, he immediately gave the order to seize Ebersberg. He had certainly failed to keep in communication with the emperor, otherwise he would not have carried out this attack on May 4th, knowing that the emperor was to arrive the same evening on the other shore. The Austrians in this case would have had to withdraw or be taken prisoner.

The bridge near Enns had been destroyed by the enemy, but on May 5th we built a new one.

It is ridiculous to destroy a bridge in its own country, because it does not take much time to restore it for the army that is marching through and especially so for the French Army wherein the sappers are so skilful and so industrious that they are in good condition for this kind work. The time taken can be spent at rest for the main body, which is always necessary for the troops at some point, but a broken bridge results in greater loss for the inhabitants, because it is always necessary to demolish a few houses to replace it.

The emperor was *en route* from Wels to Ebersberg, when the news of the occupation of that city reached him. He immediately sent a warning to Marshal Lannes in the rear to no longer follow him, but to take the road from Wels to Steyer.

This corps joined us at Amstetten, where our cavalry had to execute several charges against enemy cavalry. I was then near Colonel Aldobrandini, whom I knew quite well and who understood how to command a regiment of *cuirassiers*. After his regiment had charged and had a *mêlée* with the Hungarian hussars, I noticed that after the enemy retreated the number of their dead that remained upon the field exceeded ours. The Hungarian hussar must make his stroke with the curved blade of his sabre, while the French *cuirassier* strikes with his straight sword blade at the point. I did not see one mortally wounded *cuirassier* cut down by the sword, though more than a dozen had been killed by cannonballs. We took about 100 Hungarian prisoners on that occasion.

On the 8th, headquarters was moved to Mölk, siting itself within a large Benedictine convent, situated in a beautiful location. On the 9th we found ourselves at Saint-Pölten, whence the emperor sent me at night with a squadron of *chasseurs a cheval*, with the order to approach people sleeping by the high road to Vienna, and to find among them someone who had been in Vienna that same day, or who possessed exact information on what was happening in Vienna.

I crossed through six very well-kept little villages, where everyone was already asleep, but finally in one of these villages, I saw some houses showing lights and within Austrian soldiers dressed in white; but as soon as my first *chasseurs* arrived, the lights went out and tranquillity set in. These were probably marauders who forthwith hid. I followed my path quietly; my captain of *chasseurs* would have liked to capture these marauders, but I had to deny him that pleasure. I would have been forced to stop and that would jeopardise my mission. I told him that we would take our revenge on our return journey.

However, I then ordered the commanding officer to lead the vanguard, made up of twelve horsemen, and to wake up the inhabitants of the main houses. Marching 200 paces back with the squadron, I wasted no time whilst this happened and I could talk with these inhabitants during the passage of my troop; once the rearguard past, I caught up to the squadron with my orders and my trumpeter.

It was not until the sixth village that I had the luck to find a priest who was in Vienna the day before and had just returned that same night. This priest told me that Archduke Maximilian commanded the garrison, consisting of twelve infantry battal-

113

ions. He was not aware that Archduke Louis had made his retirement. But the emperor knew he had crossed the Danube to Krems to join the Archduke Charles.

I was back in Saint-Pölten in around nine hours and the *chasseur* squadron came in two hours after me. I changed horses at Saint-Pölten and left following the emperor who, in four hours of galloping, arrived at Schoenbrünn and, without stopping there, pushed his horse in front of the outer parts of the Vienna in suburb called "Wieden". I there found before me an incomprehensible sight, which I would not have believed had I not seen with my own eyes and heard with my own ears!

The ramparts were covered not with a crowd, but with a large number of very well dressed Viennese. The emperor, still on horseback, advanced to the glacis; a ditch of only 10 fathoms separated him from the Viennese residents. These people recognised the emperor, having already seen him in Vienna in 1805. They took off their hats, which I thought was natural enough, but began to cheer him with loud "*Vivats!*", which seemed peculiar to me and, given the circumstances, quite out of place. I can't explain this action except to acknowledge the charm that a man like the emperor exerted on everyone. When I expressed my astonishment to the French officers present, they told me that they had seen a similar spectacle in Berlin in 1806, near the Brandenburg Gate.

The emperor turned left, following the ramparts of the *faubourg* for more than half an hour, to the barrier; sometimes he raised his hat to thank the cheering crowd as if he was making a processional tour of Paris. His escort squadron, which had accompanied the emperor from Saint-Pölten, had been ordered to halt, and then the escort was reduced to a picket of just twenty-five horsemen which followed him at 200 paces. It was only after coming close to the barrier that the emperor turned his horse away and, still at a walk, resumed the road to Schoenbrünn. Along the way he saw me and told me to hurry back to the palace and go to bed, ending his instruction as follows:

You will find a good bed prepared for you; After passing

so many nights on horseback you should now make your-self comfortable in a good bed courtesy of the Emperor Francis; however, you start running again tomorrow.

I went straight to the castle. I met *en route* the head of the column of General Oudinot's grenadiers and *voltigeurs*, who had already attired themselves in full dress with their plumes attached to their head-dresses in preparation to enter Vienna in triumph. I found, on arriving at the castle, the Imperial Quartermasters and as promised one of them showed me to the rooms which were allocated for us; in each one of which there were two beds.

A servant of the emperor brought me a superb pineapple, of which there was, he told me, a large quantity in the gardens, together with a bottle of wine, bread and some ham. After such a wonderful meal, I undressed and dutifully fell asleep.

My comrade Talhouët shared my room; he awakened me at seven o'clock in the evening for dinner, but he did not return to bed himself, for the emperor had sent him to General Oudinot, who had just informed him that after crossing the village, he had advanced in front of the town, where he had been received with cannon shots fired from the ramparts and that the Austrians seemed to want to split Vienna.

The emperor opened a trench under the barracks of the Hungarian guard, and there placed in position a battery composed of howitzers, by means of which they set fire to the city in several places. Not wanting to burn it down completely, the emperor ordered the division of General Molitor on the following day to take a detour around Vienna and stop at Ebersdorf, where he arrived with us on the morning of the 14th. Having discovered on the left of this village some boats, the emperor ordered Talhouët to cross the Danube with 200 *voltigeurs* and occupy the Prater triangle.

Pourtalès, Berthier's *aide-de-camp*, with a few *voltigeurs* had already crossed the channel of the Danube which separates Vienna from the Prater; it was around evening time. Archduke Maximilian, believing that the entire French Army had carried out the passage, promptly vacated Vienna before dawn with all of the garrison.

Our army entered the town on the 15th, though the emperor had already returned to Schoenbrûnn. The same day the emperor learned that enemy General, Chasteller, with the reserve division and Landwehr, was approaching Styria and Hungary. He immediately sent to Newstadt, Lieutenant-Colonel Lubienski with his squadron of Polish Light Horse of the Guard, with the order to choose a position near this city whence his emissaries and his patrols could monitor all the movements of General Chasteller. Lubienski was every day to relay a report to the emperor. I had to read all these reports, inform the emperor if Chasteller was approaching us and return to him an account of everything serious that was happening.

On the 18th, I received a report informing me that Chasteller had retreated south to meet Archduke John, who was retiring from Lombardy, followed in pursuit by the Viceroy of Italy, Prince Eugène de Beauharnais, coming from Udine. It may seem odd that the emperor had only sent one squadron to an area where, according to the news received, there manoeuvred an Austrian division; but he only wanted to have information on the movements of Chasteller. In this particular case he could, moreover, have full confidence in Lieutenant-Colonel Lubienski, whom he knew well and whose talents he appreciated.

The emperor loved always have his forces concentrated at the points where the most important events were to take place. He knew well that when a great battle has a happy outcome, the results of lesser business mean nothing. In this case, Napoleon was convinced that Chasteller would not advance his division, knowing that an army of 80,000 French was near to Vienna.

Part of the Imperial Guard arrived from Spain and came to camp south of the city. The entire army exceeded 80,000 men, but Marshal Davoust's corps still remained in observation of the army of Archduke Charles. The Saxons, commanded by Bernadotte, were still on the march in the north of the Bavaria, and the Bavarians, under the orders of Marshal Lefebvre, were fighting in the Tyrol, by that time in full insurrection.

In reality, Napoleon had no more than 80,000 men on hand in Vienna, and so many engaged in different places. He didn't want to frighten Chasteller by sending against him greater forces, for he saw with pleasure this general was remaining in a country where he was occupied with nothing serious. He preferred to see him wasting his time rather than letting him join with Archduke John, who could have halted the progress of the Army of Italy with this reinforcement.

Finally, it was of great importance for the emperor to communicate with Prince Eugène's army; because, although the army of the Archduke John approached, it had further to go through Hungary and Moravia to join that of Archduke Charles, whilst that of the Viceroy of Italy had just moved from Udine to Hungary to come closer to the emperor's army.

Chapter 20: Aspern and Essling

That same day, the 18th, the emperor sent me to Ebersdorf, to inspect the pontoon crew, which I found in good condition, and I made my report accordingly. The emperor, arrived in the evening and sent two companies of *voltigeurs* on to the island of Lobau. On the 19th, the entire Molitor division had already passed over the bridge. Another bridge was soon built on the other channel of the Danube. On the 20th, three bodies of our troops occupied the island of Lobau. On the same day, at noon, two bridges were thrown on the last channel of the Danube, under the protection of batteries placed on the bank of the river; this last channel is not very wide. Around 4 a.m., the light cavalry division of General Lasalle passed over in its entirety by order of the emperor.

When we emerged from a little wood which was close to the Danube, the Austrian artillery fired shells at us, which did not prevent the division, composed of five regiments, from forming into two lines on the plain, between Aspern and Essling. Around 7 o'clock in the evening, after a fairly strong cannonade, the Austrians launched a fierce cavalry charge. Their hussars attacked in front the first brigade commanded by General Pire, composed of the 8th regiment of Hussars and 16th regiment of *Chasseurs a Cheval*. The charge of the enemy hussars was very lively, on their left a regiment of *uhlans* advanced at a gallop. But when the Austrian hussars arrived 200 or 250 paces from us, at full speed and shouting with all their might, General Lasalle's cavalry came forward to meet them, first at a walk, then at a trot, and finally at a gallop whereafter it fell on them with the greatest vigour.

The *uhlans* were received by a regiment of the second line which executed a change of front to the left. There was a general *mêlée* and already becoming quite dark. The *mêlée*, the cries and the tumult lasted for at least an hour. The artillery had been previously silent. Finally, the Austrian cavalry withdrew and the Lasalle division reformed on two lines a few hundred paces backwards from its original place; so, we had lost some ground. A short time later the Austrians sent us about ten cannon shots in the dark. I don't know where the balls fell, because we did not hear them pass above our heads.

The night became clearer again. When the guards were placed, Generals Lasalle and Pire moved forward. For such a fierce fight, there were not so many casualties; however, there were many more losses on the side of the Austrians than there were of ours; I can positively say that there were twice as many, though I did not count them. This disproportion was due to the fact that the Hungarians gesticulate too much while slashing, whilst the French simply apply the point and yet the Hungarian cavalry have more manageable horses than the French cavalry.

The French, on heavier and less agile horses, cannot manoeuvre at will, but must be more attentive, looking carefully on which side their opponent attacks them, have time to parry his blows, and finally deliver a good thrust directed through the chest of their enemy. Hungarians do not slash from the flat of the blade, like the English, but with a sharp edge, but they are at the full gallop and then turn their horses aside as they employ their sabres as if they had lost their nerves and thus their blows fell by chance.

In this encounter, they attacked us many times; some mingled with us, others crossed our lines on their way back to their own lines after charging, but still at the stampede. The French on the contrary, even if they lost their ranks while charging, always tried to reform and at every moment we noticed their efforts to resume their formations. In truth our cavalry owed their superiority to the handling of their weapons, but also because they were possessed of experience that was lacking among the

Austrians, all of which had been acquired in so many battles and under excellent officers.

What I written about the Hungarians and their light horses and Frenchmen on their heavy horses, does not lead to the conclusion that heavy horses are more practical for light cavalry.

If you could have old soldiers mounted on light horses, commanded by more experienced officers, skilled in handling of the sabre especially at the point rather than than to slash, the result would still be better. An experienced rider knows his profession, knows when to close ranks, knows how moderate the vivacity of his horse when needed, how to take advantage of this liveliness when it charges at a canter, and in all cases where he has to act alone. I relate only the state of things existing at that time and their results. I want to show that the Hungarians, relentless in their attacks, found it hard to reform when they were dispersed and to reform their lines, while the French, knowing that their horses had not the same speed, only attacked in close order so they managed to keep their ranks until the end, and after the charge, were reformed quickly on the designated line.

The Hungarians cutting at full gallop, or attacking isolated horsemen, do not sabre well unless it was their intention to slice the wind; in the worst cases they only caused less serious wounds. The French, are more sober in their gestures, absorb blows and at the same time thrust to pierce their opponents with a killing strike. I had some personal experience of everything that I have written about, because I once received a sabre cut from a Hungarian hussar above my knee; his sabre spun as it fell and consequently the wound was not deep, but the blow was a violent one and I felt the pain of it for several years thereafter.

When calm had returned, I returned near the emperor, whom I found in a small hut constructed of branches which had been erected near to the bridge built on the last channel of the Danube. I reported to him that General Lasalle had taken position in the plain between Aspern and Essling.

During the night the emperor again sent infantry and artillery to occupy these two villages and ordered them to establish themselves there strongly. All night from the 20th to the 21st, the infantry crossed the bridges and took position between Aspern and Essling. At dawn the emperor inspected the positions and gave orders for the placement of his troops. He placed his left wing at Aspern; a double infantry line extended from the wood located near this village towards that of Essling; the cavalry advanced 1,000 paces forward; the walls of the cemetery near and to the left of Essling were loop-holed. The right wing stretched from Essling to Danube, almost at right angles, *vis-à-vis* Enzersdorf, village which was not occupied, probably so as not to extend the line too much. The Grenadiers and *Fusiliers de la Garde* were placed on the right wing, the *chasseurs à cheval* and the two squadrons of Light Horse in reserve. The Dragoons, the *Grenadiers à cheval* and the *élite gendarmes*, as well as the artillery of the Guard, were still on the other side of the Danube.

There were on this side of the Danube only the 60 guns from Marshal Masséna's corps; we placed them in batteries between Aspern and Essling. During the three days that the battle lasted, we had only these 60 guns. The emperor made this defensive disposition while waiting for the passage of the rest of the army. We had barely 30,000 men on this side of the river; on the other bank lay the whole of Davoust's three *cuirassier* divisions, half of the Imperial Guard, a large part of the artillery and the large park, in all about 60,000 men.

Around noon, the Austrians re-engaged the battle all along the line by opening fire from a few hundred guns. Our cavalry, placed in front of the infantry, was forced to withdraw and came to stand in tight columns a few hundred paces behind it. The artillery answered the enemy artillery, but at the rate of only one blow for three or four in reply. We could see the lines of Austrian infantry, but they did not approach that day upon our centre; their attacks were concentrated on Aspern, where besides the fire of the cannons, we heard several times a heavy firefight. From the place where the emperor was situated, one could not see this attack, because the forest hid it from us: but I was sent several times to Marshal Masséna, who was defending Aspern, and I could see the Austrian columns, so deep that it was clear that the Austrians concentrated a great deal on this point with most of their strength. They approached several times upon Aspern and each time were repelled by fire delivered from houses and gardens.

On one of these missions, I found Marshal Masséna seated and resting near a house as I handed him the emperor's despatch. He immediately mounted his horse, but realising that his right stirrup was too short, he called upon his equerry to let it down, whilst he sat on the side of his saddle, passing his leg over of his horse's withers. At that moment a cannonball killed the equerry outright and broke the stirrup; the horse threw itself aside and the marshal fell into my arms, without suffering so much as a bruise. We replaced the stirrup, the marshal climb back on the same horse and away he went.

The shells set fire to several houses; almost all the roofs were on fire, but the most of the houses and stables were built of bricks and our infantry was in good shelter within its positions. Many times, the Austrian columns approached so close that it seemed that our bullets would no longer stop them; every time the French reserves attacked them with bayonets and not once did the Austrians stand to resist, they were routed, though they were advancing in columns whilst our soldiers fought and charged them in line with bayonets as though in a foot race. They should have attacked us without fear, because each enemy column had several guns to support its attack. They must have known that we had little artillery at our disposal to oppose them.

Despite everything, on this first day, the enemy not once succeed in taking Aspern away from us, our defence proving the superiority of the French foot soldiers over all other infantry.

About 5 o'clock in the evening, the emperor was informed than the bridge over the first channel of the Danube had been broken during the passage of the division of *cuirassiers*. It had been broken by a collision of rafts and boats laden with stones, abandoned by the Austrians at Stadelau in the rapid current of the river swollen by the melt of snow.

We managed during the night to repair the bridge; the rest of the *cuirassier* division completed its passage, as well as two divisions of Oudinot's grenadiers and half of the Imperial Guard. As a result, we had in the morning put across near to 60,000 men, but still had only 60 guns. At dawn the emperor mounted his horse and returned to the line of battle; he gave the command of the whole centre to Marshal Lannes, and gave the order to form in columns all infantry, except Marshal Masséna's corps at Aspern, and the infantry of the Guard held in reserve.

The 60 guns were placed between the columns; behind the columns stood two light cavalry divisions and two divisions of *cuirassiers.* Before the attack was begun, the emperor passed in front of the columns, saluting with his hat and showing the direction of the enemy. At this sign from the emperor, the troops responded with loud acclamations, raising their hats in the air on the tips of their bayonets. A thousand paces ahead of us were the vedettes and Austrian cavalry scouts, behind them stood their infantry. At the sight of our marching columns, all these troops disappeared.

The enemy then unmasked a large number of artillery who opened fire on us, and soon the whole Austrian Army was revealed. It advanced on us in columns, which soon deployed, and a few hundred paces from our troops, fired volleys of battalions, so fast that one could think which they fired in companies. The cannons rained a hail of shot upon us, but nothing could stop the momentum of French columns, they rushed with bayonets thrust forward upon the Austrian lines which disintegrated even before the arrival of the French.

The artillery hastily withdrew, stopping at every moment to saturate our infantry with projectiles. Several hundred soldiers fell, but the others still ran forward, and the Austrians rushed away in retreat. Finally, the whole line of enemy infantry was covered by their cavalry. Our *cuirassiers* broke this line several times; other Austrian regiments were coming, supported by numerous artillery which covered our attacks with grapeshot. The Austrian lines withdrew further and further. Several times their cavalry retreated behind their infantry then reformed; ten times our *cuirassiers* swooped down on them, destroying battalions; regiments of fresh Austrian cavalry reappeared, ready to dispute with ours, but were obliged after each response to retire and reform.

Our light cavalry divisions, commanded by Generals Lasalle and Bruyère, also charged the enemy cavalry several times. Until 11 a.m. our infantry columns and our cavalry advanced, gaining near to a league of ground. The cavalry, sometimes in front of the columns, sometimes behind them, were always there. Our troops reached the town Breitenlee, where, it seems, the remains of the Austrian Army had assembled, for they could see enemy troops behind it to the right. Our line of battle was more restricted than that of the enemy. By advancing in the plain the enemy constantly received reinforcements, so it became more capable of surrounding us.

When I came near to the emperor, coming at that time from Breitenlee, with the news that Marshal Lannes had seen masses of enemy troops that could envelop him, he placed in echelon two battalions of the Old Guard before Aspern, but far enough behind the left wing of Marshal Lannes' force, to cover his flank. After the bridges had been repaired, our troops continued to arrive. The emperor was counting on the whole corps of Marshal Davoust, with 60 guns, on the 3rd Cavalry Division, and on the artillery park. Marshal Davoust's corps, arriving at this moment, could have supported the forces of Marshal Lannes.

But around noon, two pieces of bad news came to the emperor's attention. First, the two bridges across the river were broken yet again and then, a little later, he learned that Marshal Lannes had been mortally wounded. He had one leg blown off and the other broken. General Oudinot soon arrived; he had received several injuries which, without being serious, had forced him to leave the battlefield. With the greatest calm, the emperor ordered a retreat on the position we had originally occupied between Aspern and Essling.

The retreat took place with the greatest order: the enemy cavalry attacked us on several points, but was always repelled with great losses by Lasalle's light cavalry, supported in the second line by the *cuirassiers*. The enemy could nowhere break through our lines, and our infantry never had to stop to deal with an attack alone; not once did our *cuirassiers* seek shelter behind them. Around 3 o'clock, our entire army had regained its first position between Aspern and Essling. The artillery, however, was forced to conserve a lot of ammunition.

It was then that the two divisions of *cuirassiers* intended to support our artillery, which was still firing at the enemy, retreated behind rear of the infantry, in two lines in the presence of the emperor: the enemy cannonballs continued to fall among us, and passed often above our heads. Soon they fell upon the fringes of the Danube behind us and killed many of our wounded who were lying near the bridges over the second channel of the great river. During the preceding two days these unfortunates had been taken to this place, from whence they could be transported to the island of Lobau.

When the infantry had resumed their first position between Aspern and Essling, the emperor sent the Grenadiers of the Guard back to the right wing, in front of Enzersdorf, because he had seen Austrian columns marching towards this ancient town. At this time the Austrian Army was forming in an arc around us. Feld–Marshal Bellegarde was leaning on the Danube and occupied the ground in front and behind Aspern, Archduke Charles stood in the centre with the bulk of the forces, and Prince Lichtenstein formed the left wing, directly opposite our wing and almost behind it. This wing of ours was composed of only four battalions of *chasseurs* and two battalions of Guard Grenadiers, having behind them two squadrons of Polish light cavalry and two of *chasseurs à cheval*, also of the Guard.

These six battalions and four squadrons impressed themselves so much on Prince Lichtenstein, that he dared not attack them with sufficient vigour. These troops covered the retreat, and the activity of the Polish Light Horse, despite the losses it had suffered, deserved the admiration of all. In this situation, the cannonballs and shells fired by Bellegarde passed over Aspern, and arrived as far as our right wing, those of Lichtenstein, were usually shot too high, though almost reached our left wing.

The emperor, situated in the centre with his *état-major*, was exposed on three sides. Happily, the projectiles passed over our heads. But their splinters reached our *curassiers*, placed behind the infantry, 500 paces ahead of the emperor. During this time, we could not respond to the Austrians: we only had 60 guns with us, and almost all were dismantled, but not a single one fell into enemy hands though their munitions were completely exhausted.

The emperor remained in his place like a statue, leaving the reins floating on the mane of his horse, telescope in hand, giving his orders and sending us in different directions. But almost none of us had any more horses and mine was so tired, that when I was sent on my next mission though it was only to Marshal Masséna who was not far away, I preferred to go on foot dragging my horse behind me. The emperor had just noticed that a strong column was starting from the position of Archduke Charles, that is to say of the centre, and was marching on Aspern. He ordered me to go notify Marshal Masséna and warn him to be on his guard, advising him to form its reserve column to receive the enemy. The marshal was seated under a tree near ruins of a burnt-out house; one of the few half-intact dwellings. He immediately mounted his horse, and formed his columns in the gardens, just in time to receive the Austrians who were approaching the village with very superior forces.

The French infantry, posted in the houses and in the gardens, welcomed the Austrians with a deadly fire shot from very close quarters, but on this occasion, it was insufficient to halt this inexorable mass of troops advancing under their yellow standards who before long took over houses and gardens. Marshal Masséna, drawing his sword, took his place at the head of the reserve column he had just formed and to which had joined the soldiers driven out of the houses. This reserve column fell upon the enemy without firing a shot and drove them back in disorder killing a large number of them with the bayonet.

Returning to the emperor, I saw so many corpses strewn about the village street that my horse was obliged to trample upon them with almost every step. There were also a great many French bodies, previously killed by cannonballs or enemy bullets. I came to inform the emperor on behalf of Marshal Masséna that Aspern was saved, and that the marshal had said he hoped to hold out there until evening. I was then sent again to Essling, then again opposite Enzersdorf; it was only much later that I learned that before evening the Austrian infantry had taken Aspern three times and had been driven out of it three times by our men.

At the same time the Austrian Army of the centre was forming columns to attack Essling.

General Durosnel, *aide-de-camp* of the emperor, who commanded at this point, mounted his horse and set off to reconnoitre, but his mount was so tired that he could not escape an attack by Austrian *cuirassiers* and was made prisoner.

A double salvo from Austrian guns directed at Essling warned us of the attack on the town.

The Hungarian grenadiers, flags flying, with their mounted officers in front of them, advanced furiously in columns. Shooting from part of the cemetery and the houses did not stop their momentum. Essling was taken and the French were forced to withdraw.

The emperor ordered General Mouton, his *aide-de-camp*, to take to the right wing the four battalions of *Chasseurs de la Garde* and to retake Essling. It was achieved without firing a shot. As in Aspern, the Essling cemetery was strewn with the corpses of Hungarians. Essling remained in our hands until evening.

Again, towards evening, the Austrian Army launched four columns of infantry upon our centre, between Aspern and Essling. Our hungry soldiers were lying in the ditches on both sides of the road between these two towns. When the Austrian columns approached, all of them, at the signal of the drum, rose as one man, shook their ranks, and threw themselves so promptly with their bayonets upon the enemy that its columns buckled and retreated. Our *cuirassiers* passed between our battalions at a slow trot, for their horses could no longer move faster and put themselves in a position to charge, but the enemy cavalry immediately advanced, placed themselves in front their infantry and stopped 500 paces from us though without attacking. Darkness, by this point, was beginning to fall.

Chapter 21: Lobau and Raab

The emperor first sent the *cuirassiers* and the light cavalry to the island of Lobau, by the bridge, which was still used for the passage of wounded. Then it was the turn of the cannons and caissons that were still on their wheels; though some of them were hitched to no more than two horses. I counted 40 guns, so we had been compelled to leave 20 of them on the ground, for lack of attachments. The emperor placed himself near the bridge, which he only crossed at 10 o'clock in the evening with the Guard. It was to the island of Lobau that we transported the stricken Marshal Lannes. Napoleon went to his side and kissed him several times, and as the night was clear, I distinctly saw that he was crying.

Towards midnight the infantry of Massena, then the grenadiers and *voltigeurs* of General Oudinot crossed to the island; immediately afterwards, the bridge was demolished.

In this great battle had taken part 60,000 men, of whom 30,000 remained under arms on the island of Lobau. So, we had lost half the strength of our forces, counting the dead and injured. In the history of the wars of the French nation to this date, this battle transpired to be the bloodiest and one which did the most honour to the French Army. The battle itself, in reality, was lost, because we had to withdraw and the enemy remained in control of the battlefield.

At 2 o'clock in the morning, the emperor crossed the Danube by boat; we followed on two other boats but the strength of the current pushed us half a league from Ebersdorf, where we arrived on foot at 5 o'clock in the morning. Marshal Davoust's force was in this village. The emperor ordered him to march on Presbourg, to occupy the suburbs there and prevent Arch-duke Charles from crossing the Danube at that point. Indeed, if Charles had been master of the bridge at Presbourg, he could potentially cross over to the right bank, defeat Marshal Davoust, and seize the island of Lobau. This would have been a catastro-phe because, in fact, the rest of the army was upon the island together with all our wounded.

The next day, the emperor sent me to Marshal Davoust who had marched for three days and upon the the third day, he at-tacked the suburb which is located near the village of Engerau, captured and occupied it. I returned to Ebersdorf with this news; immediately after the emperor made his headquarters at Schoenbrünn. During the following days, we brought the Impe-rial Guard back by boat from the island of Lobau, who took to their cantonments, the infantry at Schoenbrünn, the cavalry in the neighbouring villages.

After our arrival at Schoenbrünn on May 28, an *aide-de-camp* to Prince Eugène de Beauharnais came in to bring the news that the prince was following Archduke John; and having beaten him several times, the enemy was in retreat, whilst the prince was now fifteen leagues from Vienna. Along with his *aide-de-camp*, named Bataille, Prince Eugène sent to Neustadt detach-ments of his cavalry, to announce his approach to the emperor and ask him for his orders. This *aide-de-camp* was immediately redirected to the Prince Eugène, who marched by Odenburg and Steinamanger (in Hungarian, Szombathely) and pursued Archduke John into Hungary.

The archduke, having joined the troops newly formed in Hungary, chose a very advantageous position at Sabadeggi, three hours from Raab. Prince Eugène immediately attacked him there and forced him to leave this position after a full day of bat-tle. In the evening, the Army of Italy advanced as far as Raab, a city surrounded by old ramparts. Archduke John left a garrison of 3,000 men, to detain the prince's army, while he retreated three leagues further on and passed the Danube at Komorn.

Before this Battle of Raab, the emperor sent me to Marshal Davoust, who was not yet in Presbourg, to announce the march of Prince Eugène in Hungary on Raab, and advise him to connect with the prince through his right wing. I also had to go back on the field by the most direct route to bring back news to the emperor. I arrived with Marshal Davoust in a post cart; he gave me a horse, upon which I went to find his light cavalry which had already arrived in Hungarian territory, on the way from Sheinberg to Raab. I took with me fifteen of the best mounted *hussards* and I started from Kitsee on the right of the high road, thinking that I would still find Prince Eugène in the vicinity of Pápa, as the emperor believed on the map from which I had noted the route of Kitsee to Pápa.

Arriving in the evening at the first village to seek a guide, how surprised and happy I was to hear the peasants speak the Slovak language; they were also happy to invite me to speak Polish. They brought me a guide who had come from Raab the same day. Before the arrival of this man, they had already informed me of the defeat of the Austrians at Raab, and the arrival of the French in this city. I asked them if one of them could take me there; several men immediately offered me their services without asking for any remuneration: the Slavic character is everywhere the same.

They regaled me, as well as my hussars, with bread, wine and ham. They showed their satisfaction with the defeat of the Austrians, saying that they had once belonged to Poland, as their fathers had told them, and that they would be very happy to be reunited with it; This feeling was all the more evident when they learned that the Emperor of the French wanted to reinstate Poland as an independent country. Legends and traditions live on for a long time among peoples. How far back goes this tradition of their union with Poland, not one of the old peasants could tell me. Was it at the time of King Louis of Poland? Was it in an even earlier time? In any case, there is no doubt that the Slovaks of this country were very well disposed towards the Poles. There were no Magyars among them.

I wrote to Marshal Davoust with the news that I had just

heard, asking him to send this report immediately to Schoenbrünn by one of its officers; I assured him that we had to give credence to the new information given by the peasants since they were Slovaks, whose every sympathy was for us; I added that I had full trust in them myself and that I was sending him back his hussars who could testify to the warm welcome that we had received from them. As for me, so as to move quickly onwards towards the Army of Italy, I left by carriage in the night. I arrived in Raab at 10 o'clock, when Prince Eugène was entering the city, which had capitulated after two hours of cannonade.

The prince stopped there only a short time, and went to a castle outside the city where they had prepared his quarters, and where there was already the Italian Guard: two battalions of grenadiers and two of infantrymen, with 100 Lombard mounted honour guards. During lunch I learned from Prince Eugène and General Macdonald, and particularly in detail from General Gifflenga, *chef d'état-major* to the prince, of the incidents of the Battle of Raab, upon which I took notes to bring back to the emperor. I then went into the city, but I could not find a single carriage at the post office. I decided to leave on horseback, when a rotund gentleman in Hungarian costume, approached me and offered to rent me a carriage until my arrival in Vienna.

"But how,'" I said to him, "do you want me send it back to you?"

"It doesn't matter," he went on, "I'm happy to serve you."

Hearing him say those words in good Polish, I asked him:

"Are you Hungarian, sir?"

"No, sir, I am a Slav. I have learned that you were Polish, therefore a compatriot; finally, I learned that you occupy a position with the Emperor Napoleon, and we hope he will rid of us soon of the foreign yoke."

"Thank you very much, but can you tell me someone who I can return your carriage to?"

"Actually, I don't know anyone there. Do with the carriage whatever you want, when you don't need it anymore."

As we exchanged these words, the postilion harnessed his

horses; I said goodbye to my compatriot, I shook his hand, took my place in the Hungarian carriage and I left. Halfway on my journey, during the night, I meet the outposts of the *avant-garde* cavalry of Marshal Davoust. In the afternoon I arrived at Schoenbrünn and reported to the emperor of all that I had learned.

Soon after the Battle of Essling, the emperor had the bridge rebuilt on stilts over the first channel of the Danube, and two other bridges also on stilts on the channel that separates the island of Lobau. The third arm was the least as wide: the materials were prepared on the island needed to build six bridges. Columns of marches made up of entire companies and of battalions, coming from the depots of their regiments arrived with the army. We also received recruits from France, as well as the recovered wounded from the hospitals that we had settled in various towns and villages between Regensburg and Vienna. The greater part of these troops were transported by boat to the island of Lobau, to complete the units found there who had lost the greater part of their complements. Three bridges were built in the month of June. During all this time the emperor remained at Schoenbrünn, but he rode out every day, most often near Ebersdorf, to push forward the construction of the bridges. He also inspected—one by one—all the camps established around Vienna.

In this period several officers belonging to the Armies of our Allies came to Vienna; Once there came two Russian officers: Major Gorgoli, a decent man, and Lieutenant Czerniszeff; then a Swedish officer. We also in Schoenbrünn had living with on several occasions Polish officers, sent by Prince Poniatowski. The visitor who interested me the most was not an officer, but Mr. Ignace Potocki, who was summoned by the emperor, though I do not know for what reason. He was a very modest man, very intelligent, very kind and a complete contrast to his brother Stanislas that I had known in Warsaw and Paris. Ignatius Potocki was received several times in audience by the emperor, but without witnesses. It seemed that he was not very satisfied with these interviews and so he returned to Poland with very little hope in his heart.

We often went to Vienna, but the emperor sometimes contented himself with crossing it when it was his shortest way. Players of the Vienna Opera played several times a week at the Schoenbrünn theatre. Outside officers, civil personalities of Vienna came to attend these performances, with the tickets they had requested. I went once at the theatre in Vienna; I met a number of elegant carriages, filled with those who seemed perfectly indifferent to the occupation of their capital by the French. It had not been the same in Warsaw during the occupation of that city by the Austrians; mourning had been general, from the richest down to the poorest. But you don't have to lose sight of the fact that the Austrian aristocracy had mostly departed from Vienna before the arrival of the French Army, and that the inhabitants who remained in the town, whom I had seen at the theatre and at the promenade, were mostly trades people, probably from the Jewish community. However, I was told the names of several ladies of the Austrian aristocracy who had stayed in Vienna and were giving the French officers the warmest welcome.

Vienna and the surroundings presented the appearance of complete peace. The purchases of the French occupiers paid the wages of many workers, especially valets, and they were accordingly very happy. I bought a small carriage for myself. During this period, I was sent again to Raab, and I had to complete several missions to Marshal Davoust and Prince Eugène. The orders I gave them were dictated to me by the emperor himself.

Leaving Davoust to go to Raab, I found everywhere our light cavalry which was living harmoniously in the best understanding with the inhabitants. In several places I saw French soldiers dancing under the trees with the young Slovak girls and employees of neighbouring farms, dressed in French uniforms, having fun with them. Our riders lent their uniforms to these young people who enjoyed these costume changes. I found gaiety everywhere and the Slovak postilions, hearing me speak Polish, employed their zeal to lead me quickly from one post station to another.

Chapter 22: Wagram

On July 1st, the bridges, solidly built on stilts, were completed. On the 2nd, the emperor arrived at the island of Lobau and settled in his tent. On the 3rd, Prince Eugène arrived with his command. So that the Austrians did not notice of this great movement, three battalions only left during the day for Komorn, in very elongated columns; Marshal Davoust performed the same manoeuvre; he sent some battalions to the east, along the Danube, but both returned to their principal bodies.

The island of Lobau looked superb: it was covered with large woods and huge meadows, but does not harbour a house or a single inhabitant; you could see, however, everywhere at that moment, pretty sheds built by the soldiers. On the 3rd, an absolute deluge of rain fell on the island. The emperor did not go out all day. The imperial tent consisted of three tents linked together. The first was intended for our department, and that is where we slept. In the middle tent slept the emperor on a folding bed; it contained a table equal in size to the folding bed, a few chairs, and a stand with rings to which we hung our cards. The third tent was for a secretary and some servants of the emperor.

The rain fell all night. Next morning, when the emperor came out, he approached an old grenadier placed to the right of the door (there always had two grenadiers on duty, who presented arms when the emperor came out silently), and said to him:

"My friend, bloody weather!"

"Better than none at all!" replied the grenadier.

The fine weather returned in the morning at 4 a.m. In the evening 6,000 grenadiers and *voltigeurs*, wearing on their left arms white armbands so that they recognise each other better at night, embarked on boats assembled for this purpose, and passed from the right of the island to the opposite bank of the Danube. They landed on the right of Enzersdorf, without resistance from the enemy, who had been ready to oppose our passage at the point where we had thrown the first bridge when marching to the Battle of Aspern. Opposite this place, within cannon range, the Austrians had built a battery: it is for this reason the emperor, who was informed of it, had decided to move three quarters of a league further to the right, on the last channel of the river.

Immediately after the landing of these 6,000 men, we threw open the six bridges we had prepared and at two o'clock after midnight, our army began to cross them, the infantry on two bridges at once, the cavalry on two others and the artillery on the last two. The departure of the column heads had been regulated so that the crossing took place in perfect order, and at six o'clock in the morning, six corps had crossed to the other side of the Danube.

Marshal Davoust's corps formed the wing right, including General Oudinot, the Saxons, commanded by Bernadotte, and the Army of Italy (three corps, but quite weak) formed the centre. Finally, Marshal Masséna was on the wing left. The Imperial Guard, the Bavarian Corps, and 10,000 Illyrians commanded by Marmont formed a very strong reserve.

On the same day Baraguey d'Illiers, who had remained near Pressburg, and the three battalions left at Raab marched to the east. Deceived by this manoeuvre, Archduke John marched from Pressburg to Komorn, thus moving away from the army of Archduke Charles; this manoeuvre was the reason 50,000 men of the Austrian Army did not arrive in time to take part in the Battle of Wagram on July 6th.

After the passage of all the army corps, the emperor, believing that the Austrians were going wait for him in the redoubts they had built between Aspern and Essling, deployed two lines of troops on the right of Enzersdorf, for an attack on the left wing of Archduke Charles. But the archduke, following our passage from Danube on a point other than that where the enemy was waiting for us, had abandoned its fortified lines and taken position on the heights behind Wagram, pressing his right to the Danube.

At 8 o'clock in the morning, all our lines began their forward movement. We only saw the enemy cavalry, which was slowly retreating ahead of us. We advanced slowly, still deployed, all day, not knowing where we would find the Austrian Army. It was not until five o'clock in the evening that we saw enemy infantry lines to the right and left, on the heights of Wagram.

Bernadotte's Saxons marched directly on this village and entered it at the moment when darkness was beginning to fall. At the same time the grenadiers and *voltigeurs* of Oudinot, who advanced on the right of the Saxons, approached Wagram, and deceived by the uniforms of the Saxon troops, began to open fire upon them. Before their officers realised their error, several Saxons, unrecognised by the French, had been killed, the rest broke ranks and began to flee, thus the main body of the Saxons was so dispersed that we could not gather it back together in the darkness.

Before evening Marshal Davoust came forward with the right wing facing the Austrian left and immediately began the attack. The emperor, seeing now before him all the army of Archduke Charles, sent the order to all army corps to halt in their places and light their cooking fires. The imperial tent was erected on a dozen drums placed three by three one on the other, the emperor slept there and we, all around him, slept under the stars.

On July 6th, we were awakened at half past three o'clock in the morning; the valets of the emperor came to invite us to lunch! A few steps from the imperial tent, we found a meal laid out on *schabraques* stretched upon the ground; it was a real dinner as if we were dining in Paris, a soup, a dozen dishes and various wines. The day before, none of us had eaten anything but that which we had in our pockets or what the emperor's servants had been able to give us by chance: so we ate with the greatest appetite, joking between us, and telling each other that we would probably not all be able to have any manner of a dinner the next day.

We were lounging, Roman style, around this meal, when the Austrians attacked Davoust, that is to say that their left wing attacked our right wing, starting with a terrific cannonade. Our army forthwith took up arms to the sound of the bugles, a sound which was repeated from regiment to regiment all along the line. Soon the roar of the cannons became deafening.

At dawn, we were all finished with thoughts of dinner and waiting on the spot for instructions. Before us grew the most magnificent canvas that I have seen in my life.

For a league across stretched the Austrian Army, the right to the Danube, the left far beyond Wagram: our left approaches flowed to the Danube, our right also far behind Wagram. Our army kept the same order as it had the day before: Marshal Masséna on the left wing; on his right the Army of Italy; behind it a single Saxon brigade, for the rest had been sent back; Oudinot was placed at the right of Wagram, and Davoust formed the right wing; much further on was the light cavalry; a *cuirassier* division followed Davoust's command.

Behind the centre, the whole Guard stood with the emperor, and a little farther on the right, behind General Oudinot, two divisions of *cuirassiers*. Behind the guard could be found two Bavarian divisions (the third was occupied in the Tyrol), Marmont's corps and the Saxons who had been reformed after their stampede of the day before. The emperor was probably counting on these troops in case of the approach of the Archduke John; also, he had placed them far enough behind the bulk of the army.

The attack of the Austrians on the right wing and on Davoust was only a feint: the real attack comprised of most of the enemy forces was directed to our left wing, commanded by Masséna. At six o'clock in the morning, on the whole front of a league in extent, the detonations of the artillery of both armies were making a racket such as I had never heard before. You could see the fires from the two lines, the first in the plain, from the Danube to the right of Wagram occupied by Oudinot, the second on the heights coming from the artillery of Marshal Davoust.

The emperor stood in the centre, behind the Army of Italy; he was mounted upon his white horse and held his telescope in his hand; next to him stood only Marshal Berthier; close behind, two of us, and two *chasseurs a cheval*, one with a map and the other with strong glasses. When the emperor sent away one of the two orderly officers, another was taking his position. All the others, as well as the *aides* from Marshal Berthier's camp, were placed in the rear about 150 paces distant so that the view of a large group of officers did not particularly attract the shots, which passed over our heads.

The two main lines of combatants were always becoming closer. Around 8 a.m., our right wing with Davoust was visibly progressing, and the Austrian left wing, commanded by the General Rosenberg, was already retiring. On the right wing Austria, on the contrary, was gaining ground. It was here that Archduke Charles delivered the most important blow. After the most violent cannonade, deep columns advanced against Marshal Masséna and threw themselves boldly on his troops so that these, inferior in number, were forced to withdraw in the direction of Enzersdorf. The Austrians pursued briskly, covered on their left flank by a large cavalry force. The head of this cavalry, composed of eight regiments of hussars, dragoons and *cuirassiers* (the *uhlans* were deployed in front of us), rushed towards our light cavalry commanded by General Lasalle: who since the morning had lost a lot of people, so was forced to retire.

General Lasalle was killed during the charge. It was obvious that the enemy was leading the largest part of his forces against our left wing with the aim of cutting us off from our bridges, and by a decisive blow, to destroy our army or to make a large part of its prisoner. But in this great movement turning on his right wing, he had extended his line too far and weakened his centre.

★★★★★★★★★★

The editor is aware, and takes this opportunity to remind the reader, that this book is not a work of qualified history, but prin-

cipally one of personal recollections written by a soldier who witnessed the events recorded within its pages. Any such account is of incalculable value and all of them put together on any given subject of this vintage make an almost certainly rarely expanded and modest body of source material. Any reader who has studied quantities of the memoirs of old soldiers knows that they often vary in consideration of the same event. One can never assume that these kinds of accounts are going to be impartial or accurate according to the broadly accepted views of most contemporary historians on the same subject. However, whilst it may be possible to frequently do so, this edition is not littered with corrections to Chlapowski's text though, in fact, the editors of the French edition have appended some corrections which have been retained for reader's interest in this edition. The present editor has contributed a few others for context, but proposes to limit them for the sake of the continuity of the author's story because this is, after all, the author's story. We are fortunate to have it and should give him free rein to tell it without interruption. That having been said, Chlapowski's perspective of the death of Lasalle, for example, is somewhat at odds with several other accounts which have reported that death under different circumstances and as something of a pointless waste of his life brought about by unnecessary personal recklessness.

★★★★★★★★★★

When the emperor saw the troops of the marshal in disorder, he galloped to meet him. We found the marshal near his last column in retirement, he was sitting in his carriage, because he was sick; though in spite this he remained in the heart of the fire. The emperor only gave him the following order.

Retreat to the bridges if the Austrians don't stop; if they advance further, they will lay down their arms.

After uttering these words, he returned at the gallop towards his place of observation. He rode along the lines of Lasalle's cavalry, who stopped every moment to face him. Between this cavalry and the Italian Corps, the Saxon cavalry brigade was also in retirement, having lost many men to shells and grapeshot. The emperor stopped before this brigade and made it face him; he pulled out his watch and said to the commander of this cavalry: "I ask you to stay another half hour under this fire; beyond half an hour, the fire will cease". Then he returned to his original place.

Thence the emperor sent the following orders to the Polish Light Horse and *chasseurs à cheval* of the Guard, to trot in front the Army of Italy, to the Artillery of the Guard of follow them at a trot, to deploy to the left behind them and cannonade the flank of the Austrians.

General Macdonald was ordered to form columns and move forward to the left of Wagram; two divisions of *cuirassiers* advanced behind him; the order was given to Marshal Davoust to send the third division to following the other two.

When the emperor entrusted the command of this cavalry to Marshal Bessières, the latter's horse was struck in the shoulder by a cannon ball; we believed the marshal killed instantly, but he only suffered bruises. When Marshal Bessières fell from his horse, the emperor turned, summoning the General Nansouty, and repeated to him the order that he had just given to Marshal Bessières. This order was, when Marshal Macdonald broke the centre of the Austrian line, to complete the victory with two divisions, and with the third which was soon to arrive, throwing itself at left of the enemy lines which had pursued Massena. The emperor added that these columns would soon begin their retreat to the shore of the Danube, and that he would have it supported by the Guard cavalry.

While the Guard Artillery fired, in the space of half an hour, about fifteen of salvos from its 60 guns, we heard the fiercely returned fire of the Austrian artillery. It seemed that nothing could stop the momentum of Macdonald, who found himself already far away, together with the *cuirassiers* who were following him.

The emperor gave me a sign and sent me to carry to the *chasseurs à cheval* of the Guard an order to support the Polish Light Horse, and to these troops the order to charge on anything they encountered in front of them. When the emperor gave me this order, I lifted my hat as it was my habit upon receiving an order

This detail from a painting, by Horace Vernet, of Napoleon at Wagram is particularly interesting since it appears to show a moment that is fully chronicled in Chlapowski's eyewitness narrative.

Marshal Bessières is shown to the right of the painting on the ground, moments after—as the author reports—falling from his horse after it was struck by an enemy cannon shot.

Of note is the slight figure on foot who is either giving or receiving one of the emperor's special maps. Across his back this young officer is carrying a large telescope in contrast to the smaller one Napoleon is employing. With his right hand this person is raising his hat just as Chlapowski informs his readers was his habit whenever he addressed the emperor. Moreover, this figure is wearing the uniform of an orderly officer similar to that seen in the Chlapowski portrait in the frontis of this book.

This figure is, based on descriptions of him, therefore likely to be Chlapowski in the moment before the hat was knocked from his hand by another cannon shot.

from him, a cannonball hit my hat and threw it into the air for some distance.

This incident is reported in le Journal du Maréchal Castellane— "July 26, 1831.—The new the news from Poland is bad. General Chlapowski has been forced to take refuge in Prussian territory. I have known him when he was Napoleon's orderly; he is a small man, very witty, who narrowly escaped in my presence at Wagram, a bullet which shaved the top of his hat."

★★★★★★★★★★

The emperor smiled and said:

"It is fortunate that you are not taller!'" and he added that after carrying his orders to the cavalry of the Guard, I should move onto General Macdonald to inform him that the Austrian right wing had halted, and was beginning to retreat, as he was pushing hard at everything in front of him. He ended with these words:

Stay with Macdonald and come back to triple gallop (it was his expression to say very quickly) and tell me everything you see.

One of my comrades dismounted to pick up my hat, wiped the dust off it and commented there was no mark made by the ball, whose speed was probably spent. I mention this incident here, to show the emperor's *sangfroid*, finding the time to joke at such a critical moment. I arrived near the *chasseurs* of the Guard, then with the Polish Light Horse; I then gave General Krasinski the emperor's order. Immediately the Poles charged the *uhlans* of Schwarzenberg with the dragoons of La Tour. I did not accompany this charge, for I was already galloping to Marshal Macdonald's side, but I learned later that it was perfectly successful.

During this charge an incident took place which could have had an unfavourable result without the *chef d'escadron* Kozietulski's presence of mind. The first two squadrons were commanded by the French Major Delaître, the other two by Kozietulski. Delaître had poor eyesight and wore glasses. Seeing that Austrian *uhlans* were ready to attack us and presuming their strength was overpowering, prepared to fall back on the Guard *chasseurs* behind him. He therefore ordered: "U-turn to the right". As senior officer in the regiment, Kozietulski perceived the danger of this movement which could allow the Austrians to fall on the flank of the Poles: he immediately made the same command again, and as he had a stentorian voice and possessed the confidence of the regiment, our Light Horse executed *two* U-turns in a row, and once again presented their front to the enemy, in a single line. Kozietulski immediately shouted: "*Garde à vous! Pointez! Marche! Marche!*" ("On your guard! Point! March! March!") The charge succeeded and Delaître cordially thanked Kozietulski for his timely intercession.

150 *uhlans* were taken prisoner, including a few officers, among them Prince Auersberg, the colonel of the regiment. But our officers affirm that the *uhlans* let themselves be caught rather easily, after having recognised their compatriots in the opposing ranks. Had it been otherwise, it would have been impossible for a regiment to take prisoner 150 cavalrymen in a charge on the battlefield between two lines.

The situation of the two armies was now changed: our left wing was completely turned back, our centre at almost three quarters of a league ahead; artillery and cavalry the Guard between the left wing and the centre and finally the right wing had noticeably progressed. Archduke Charles, saw that although the attack of his right wing on Masséna would have succeeded, this wing could be flanked by our centre and so he was obliged to order a retreat. We must not forget that when we want to envelop the enemy, one exposes oneself to being enveloped oneself, because the enemy is always presented with one flank, that is to say that we uncover ourselves.

In reality, the archduke possessed a strong reserve behind his centre, which greatly hampered McDonald; but he either did not want to expose this reserve excessively or else Macdonald's vigorous progress had made a significant impression upon him. Still, when I arrived at General Macdonald's side, he told me that the Austrians had not once been able to resist his bayonet charges, and I had always seen them in retreat myself, although they had to hold out and keep their position in the centre at all costs, until their right wing, which we had already seen in retreat, could have been released. Macdonald was still pushing vigorously forward, although the enemy endeavoured to hold him back with fire from its cannons.

I stayed over an hour with Macdonald, always hoping to be able to bring to the emperor decisive news; but eventually knowing that he was waiting for news, whatever that might be, I went back to tell him that we saw the retreating Austrian columns along of the Danube, which could not be seen from the where the emperor was stationed, because our artillery, our cavalry and that of the enemy masked the view from almost the entire left of the field of battle. On the other hand, from this place, one could hear the sound of the shooting and that of the cannon advance from Enzersdorf towards Stadelau, best proof that the Austrians were in retirement.

One of my comrades came back from Marshal Masséna announcing that the Austrians had withdrawn completely and that Masséna continued to manoeuvre as instructed. This was around 6 o'clock. I believe that the emperor could not have imagined that Archduke John would allow himself to be deceived by the diversion of some battalions manoeuvring on the side of Komorn. That is what motivated him to keep in reserve 40,000 men, that is to say his Guard, Marmont's corps and the Bavarians.

At 6 o'clock the fire from the enemy reduced all along the line, the cannonballs no longer reached us, directly nor by ricochet, although the cannon still rumbled very loudly as before for an hour. About 7 o'clock the emperor ordered me to return again to General Macdonald, but only to return to him when it was time to begin to set up camp. There was no need to rush on that mission; all my horses were in any event tired; I could see how very many dead soldiers there were strewn upon the ground in the fields and among the wheat. I also came across many wounded who could not rise from the ground and begged me for rescue. Here and there surgeons came help these unfortunate people, but they could not rescue them all.

When I changed horses, one of the emperor's servants had filled my bottle with wine. I carried this gourd in one of my saddle holsters, thinking that in Germany one pistol would be enough for me. I dismounted several times from my horse to give a drink to a few unfortunates; I also shared between them the bread and the ham that I had in the pocket of my *schabraque*.

I came to General Macdonald's side, after passing the three divisions of *cuirassiers* which walked quietly behind his infantry. Macdonald told me he wasn't happy with the performance of his cavalry, and asked me to relate to the emperor that, if it had done its duty, we should have taken 30,000 prisoners!

When night began to fall, the infantry set up camp near Stammersdorf. I returned to the emperor towards 10 o' clock and found him taking his supper with Marshal Berthier, in front of his tent, which was now strongly constructed and not placed upon drums as it had been the day before. I made my report and I was obliged to repeat what Macdonald had told me about his cavalry. The emperor made no reply. My comrades were already at supper and so I could take something to eat myself. When we counted each other, there was only one of us that had been killed, poor Alfred de Noailles, and only one other of us injured. Half of our horses, however, had been killed.

Chapter 23: Aftermath

The next day we were rid of one of our comrades, the Prince of Salm-Kyrburg. His aunt was the Princess of Hohenzollern-Sigmaringen, who raised Prince Eugène de Beauharnais and his sister Queen Hortense when their mother abandoned them. The Princess of Hohenzollern had lived in Paris for long time and the care she had taken of the son-in-law and daughter-in-law of the emperor had earned Napoleon's favour and opened the way into the imperial court.

It was at his own insistence, it was said, that the emperor had taken as orderly officer the youngster from Salm-Kyrburg. He was twenty years old, very proud, and wore a star and a grand Bavarian cord: he displayed this grand cord in the slightest circumstances and as a German prince imagined himself to have the right to be honoured by elevated positions, never failing to explain the importance of his dignity to officers on duty, who naturally were completely unimpressed by such fripperies and made fun of him.

During the Battle of Wagram, the emperor sent him on a mission carrying an order. Napoleon used, when he employed a new orderly officer, to make him repeat his orders aloud to ensure that they were well understood. Did Salm become confused while doing so, or did he report the Imperial Order in the wrong way to one of the marshals or was it that the emperor sent him away because he had had enough of this service? In any event, he was obliged to promptly leave us the next day and in short, we never saw him again. He was replaced by Watteville, an officer who was already well experienced. It was the first time that the emperor had taken into his intimate service a man like Salm, who had never served with a weapon in his hand. Most of those he employed came out of the artillery or the engineers. Prior to their appointment, the *aides-de-camp* of the generals had to have served two years in a regiment and be able to transmit orders and report accurately all they had seen.

At midnight we were awakened by a loud noise and cries coming from the right, rear of Marshal Davoust's corps. The emperor rode out on horseback to discover the cause and so did we to various locations. After three quarters of an hour, we were all back where we started, one after another, with the news that a mass of our soldiers had fled unarmed, shouting alarms that Archduke John was advancing upon them.

The emperor had sent a division of light cavalry early in the morning, immediately after crossing the bridges, in the direction of the March (Morawa), near Presbourg, to observe whether Archduke John sought to approach and make a conjunction with Archduke Charles. Napoleon had his whole Guard behind him, so he was confident, calm and readily returned to his bed. The cause of this noise, in fact, came from soldiers who had dispersed during the night in search of provisions for themselves and for their horses; they had met Bavarians marauding like them, and hearing them speak German in the darkness, had run back to their comrades spreading the panic that had reached us.

After an hour, however, order was restored everywhere. The lesson to be drawn from this incident is that, while at night and in the vicinity of the enemy, soldiers must not be allowed to disperse to go in search of provisions. If there is absolute need, *i.e.,* if the soldier has nothing to eat out of his pocket, it is essential to form search detachments commanded by reliable officers. In this respect, there always reigned a great disorder in Napoleon's army. Only one corps was an exception, that of Davoust, which always distinguished itself by its order and discipline.

The army certainly needed a rest after the battle, I was, none the less, astonished that at 7 in the morning, the emperor did not order an immediate pursuit of the enemy, as he usually did. He mounted a horse at 8 a.m., followed only by Fodoas and me, and by Roustan naturally, together with two *chasseurs à cheval*. He paced through the battlefield, strewn with an enormous quantity of dead; we also met many our seriously wounded soldiers. The emperor stopped several times near to them and distributed wine, bread and brandy served by Roustan, who always carried some. Ambulances arrived to remove the wounded, and we saw the surgeons helping these unfortunates. Soon Roustan informed the emperor that he no longer had any supplies to distribute to the wounded.

Napoleon then took to the gallop towards, a league distant, General Macdonald's corps. Macdonald, seeing from his bivouac the emperor was approaching, mounted his horse and rode out to meet him. Napoleon quickly took his hand and pressed it against his heart, saying:

"Macdonald, you are here now: I appoint you marshal!"

There had long been, it is said, a misunderstanding between Napoleon and Macdonald, probably since Moreau's trial. Now reconciled they rode together before the front of the 10th line infantry regiment, if my memory serves me well. Marshal Macdonald presented this regiment to the emperor, announcing that on the day before the regiment had marched so bravely on the Austrian reserves, that, after an hour and a half, he had overthrown with the bayonet all the enemy regiments who wanted to withstand him. As a reward for its bravery, the emperor authorised this regiment to carry on its *fanions* (the little flags used to hold the line), the following words: "One against ten!"

★★★★★★★★★★

According to the Journal de Castellane this motto would have been given to the 84th regiment and not to the 10th. It is a fact which is indicated in the history of the 84th regiment. The 10th regiment did not take part in the Battle of Wagram: it spent the whole year 1809 in the kingdom of Naples and in Abruzzo.

★★★★★★★★★★

On leaving Macdonald, the emperor rode onwards towards Stammersdorf, where our outposts were situated. This village was the first post stationed from Vienna on the road to Prague; it was positioned on a mound from which the view extends all around. The emperor dismounted and looked out on all sides with his glasses. He shortly saw a small detachment of cavalry accompanied by a few soldiers on foot who were pointing at us. The riders were an officer and a troop of *chasseurs à cheval* sent to reconnoitre at dawn who had been approached by the soldiers on foot, coming unarmed out of the bushes and waving a white handkerchief. These soldiers were Poles, deserters from the Austrian Army.

The emperor told me to ask them what regiment and what corps they belonged to, where that body was the day before, because they had remained hidden at night in the darkest woods close to them. They told me that there must still be many more of them hidden, because together with other Gallicians from another regiment, they had agreed to run away and go over to the French. The emperor asked them if they wanted return to service:

"It's precisely for that reason we have come," they answered, because we know that there are Polish regiments in the French Army."

Actually, during this campaign, there was only the Polish Light Horse regiment in the army, and no others. The emperor asked me who was the most prominent former Polish officer who had arrived from Poland to Vienna and where he was in the general neighbourhood. I replied that it was General Bronikowski, but that he was no longer in the active service: he had only accompanied his friend Prince Joseph Poniatowski. He had served under the orders of Kosciuszko, but did not know, so far as I knew, the current infantry regulations. Finally, I said to the emperor that there was in the regiment of Polish Light Horse of the Guard a very intelligent officer, Henri Kaminski, who had previously served in the infantry. I knew he wasn't in good favour with its leader, General Krasinski, and that he wanted to leave the regiment.

I also made known to the emperor the name of an officer

of the Gallician noble guard, who served under the Emperor of Austria and who had recently been dismissed, probably because they didn't have much trust to him; I told him that I knew this officer, Krasicki, and that I believed he was no stranger to the details of military service. The emperor had the *chasseurs* bring forward a table and some chairs; each of the orderly officers had pen and ink in his portmanteau.

It was there, in Stammersdorf, on July 7th, 1809, that the emperor dictated the decree of formation of the 4th Infantry Regiment of the Legion of Vistula, (the first three were in Spain). He appointed General Bronikowski head of this regimen, Lieutenant-Colonel Kaminski Colonel, and Krasicki Lieutenant, in the first company. He designated Augsburg as the place of formation of this new regiment. Soon 3,000 deserters were assembled; the officers were sent to them from the depot of the Vistula Legion, which was at Sedan.

After having dictated this decree, the emperor sent the orderly officer, Fodoas in search of the general staff.

Chapter 24: Znaïm

When the escort squadrons arrived, who were not far away, the emperor took to to his horse, and sometimes at a walk, sometimes at a gallop, so that they might follow us, we arrived at Wolkersdorf, two leagues further on the Brünn road. A fairly large castle stands in this village, and on the arrival of the general staff, the headquarters was installed there. The Imperial Guard placed its self all around, and the command of Marshal Davoust, who arrived the same day, crossed the Brünn road and established itsself in front of us. Marshal Masséna's left wing marched to Stockerau. The emperor had also appointed Marshal of France, General Marmont, who put himself on the march with the Bavarians ahead of us.

The Army of Italy was sent to the March *vis-à-vis* Presbourg, to hold against the Archduke John, who was now coming forward to make his junction with Archduke Charles. The move was three days too late. It is likely that upon hearing the news of the Battle of Wagram, he stopped on the march.

The emperor learned at Wolkersdorf, by a report of Marshal Masséna, that he had before him the army of the Archduke Charles, who withdrew from Stokerau to Znaïm, *i.e.* towards Bohemia, and that the only corps of General Rosenberg, who had formed the left wing during the Battle of Wagram, withdrew to Brünn. The emperor then sent Marshal Davoust towards Nicolsburg against Rosenberg, and Marshal Marmont to Znaïm by Laa, by the small left road. Napoleon himself followed this last body of troops.

From Laa Napoleon sent me to Marshal Marmont, who I

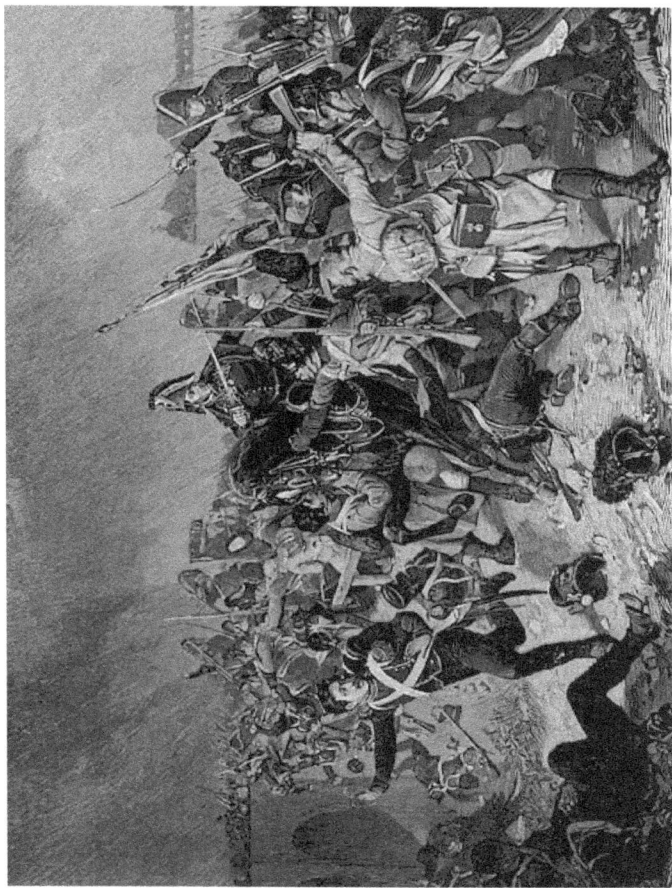

Battle at Znaim, July 11, 1809

found already installed in a good position opposite Znaïm. Marmont, therefore, commenced an attack on the whole army of Archduke Charles, on whose flank he had placed himself, and upon which he had cannonaded during its retreat on Znaïm.

The Archduke Charles deployed on the right a part of his army, and tried to dislodge Marmont from his position. His plan would succeed, if a French division did not arrive to support Marmont and replace the already hesitant Bavarians. A heavy rain that had fallen since the morning advantaged the attack of the Austrians, because the fire of the defending infantry was diminished, but the French division coming from Illyrie with Marmont showed the greatest bravery and did not allow the enemy to approach the heights. Marshal Marmont sent me back to the emperor, asking him for help.

I rode flat out, pushing my horse for as long as he could go, and soon I came near to the emperor, whom I found in his hot bath, complaining of violent pains. He told me to draw him a sketch of Marmont's position: but, when I began to draw in pencil the positions of the French and the Austrians, he abruptly took the pencil away from me, telling me that he well knew the ground and that he only wanted me to quickly show him on my paper, which I had leaned on a book, troop locations.

He was starting to designate by perpetually taking his arm out of the water and before long he had soaked the paper so that it was good for nothing. He ordered me to go to Marshal Berthier which instructions that he must set out for Znaïm without delay with all his command; he then told me to change my horse and go back and tell Marmont that the Guard was on its way to help him.

When I returned to the marshal, I found him in his same positions, the French division in the first line, the Bavarians behind, and a Bavarian brigade on the left wing, where the danger was not so great. Fire had already ceased; the Austrians had given up their attack; you could see their close columns marching on Znaïm, and further on, to the left of these columns, a large baggage convoy retreating through the fields.

The rain was still falling, but not as hard as it been in the morning, and so we could see all the movements of the troops of the archduke. Part of his cavalry had crossed Znaïm and deployed in front of our right wing, where our light cavalry also deployed. The two cavalry forces faced each other without moving. The earth was so soaked as a result the rain that it was difficult to manoeuvre. Around 4 o'clock in the afternoon, we heard a heavy cannonade from the side of the road which went from Stockerau to Znaïm. It was the rearguard of the Austrians who were fighting against Masséna's *avant-garde* advancing on Znaïm.

Marshal Marmont ordered the firing of the guns of the battery placed in the highest position, but they were shots without consequences for the Austrians who were already far away, but their true purpose was to announce to Masséna's *avant-garde* that we were on the enemy's flank. Around 6 o'clock Marshal Berthier arrived with the light cavalry of the Guard. Napoleon also arrived, but in a carriage. He stepped down, surveyed the surroundings with his telescope for a few minutes, and exclaimed; "Forward!"

Chapter 25: Armistice

The movement of the Illyrian division had already started; it began to descend from the heights and to march on Znaïm, when a cavalry officer rushed up with the news that Prince John of Lichtenstein had come to present himself before our cavalry and asked that it be announced to the emperor that the Emperor of Austria sent him. A quarter of an hour later, the emperor received him in his tent, which had been pitched on the highest mound, under a stand of superb cherry trees. After a quarter of an hour, Marshal Berthier came out of the tent, and sent orders to stop all movement.

When the Prince of Lichtenstein came out of the central tent, where he was with the emperor and Marshal Berthier, and thence entered the tent where we stood, tightly packed together, because that there were six French generals with us. He greeted them, calling each one by name since he probably knew them from preceding wars and so cordially shook their hands.

The prince, accompanied by Marshal Berthier, then went to the tent of the latter, which was 100 paces from that of the emperor. On the other side was a third tent of the same size as that of Marshal Berthier, but both of them were smaller than that of emperor that I have already described. This tent was that of General Monthyon, his chief of general staff, who had his quarters with many with many officers of the general staff of the army. The armistice treaty was drawn up in the tent of Marshal Berthier, and signed only by him and by the Prince of Lichtenstein.

★★★★★★★★★★

Mr. Casimir Chlapowski, son of the author of the Memoirs tells us the following anecdote that his father told him told:
"When, after the Battle of Znaïm, we made an armistice with General Lichtenstein, we came to talk about the battles that had just taken place; Masséna addressed the Prince Lichtenstein in a rude way. The prince replied: "Monsieur le Maréchal, you speak like a cab driver"—"That's what I was," Masséna replied— "Well, if you have the experience, you should do it again!", responded the prince.

★★★★★★★★★★

We immediately made several copies, signed by the same dignitaries, and orderly officers were sent to carry them to the distant corps. The emperor called me, gave me a copy, and ordered me to go to Iglau, headquarters of Archduke Charles, so that the latter would give the order to his troops to let me pass through Brünn, Olmütz, Krakow and Warsaw.

According to the latest news from Poland which had arrived with the emperor, the Austrians had left Warsaw and were in retreat on Sandomierz.

The armistice was concluded on July 12th. The last line of the article I carried ran as follows:

As for the Army of Poland and Saxony, the troops will stop to occupy the positions where they are.

But it was not explained literally if these troops were to hold the positions that they occupied on the day of the armistice, that is *i.e.* July 12th, or the day of receipt of news of the armistice. The emperor recommended me to tell the Prince Poniatowski that if he did not at that moment have what he wanted for Poland, it was because he didn't want to offend the Russians, but that he would never forget the help that the Poles had given him, and, relying on the last article of the armistice, the emperor added:

If Prince Joseph Poniatowski has advanced since the 12th, he will have to rely on the article of the armistice, saying that this is the position occupied the day of the reception; if on the contrary he had to withdraw, he will be asked to take over the positions where he was on the 12th of this month.

I left with my comrade Septeuil, who had to take the news of the armistice to the Saxon corps and to the Westphalian corps in Dresden. We came level with the Austrian vedettes who were infantry sentries posted near a wood. We were challenged: "*Wer da?*", but Septeuil, who was very lively in temperament, put his spurs into the belly of his horse, exclaiming: "He will miss his shot!" and took off at a fast gallop. My horse also galloped. Two infantrymen fired on us but missed us. We passed them, but the guard had heard the bangs and tried to stop us.

At this time an Austrian general of the *état-major* was finishing his inspection of the main guards; he stopped, recognised our uniforms, and let us pass.

Two officers, one of hussars, the other of *uhlans*, broke away from his suite, approached and greeted us kindly; one of them asked me about the General Krasinski, Lieutenant-Colonel Kozietulski and some other Polish officers of the Imperial Guard. I asked who he was to be so interested in the Poles and he replied that he and his brother served in the regiment of *uhlans*, that they were called Wojna and were themselves Polish. I was young and lively then, and the Austrian uniforms worn by Poles made a painful impression on me, so that instead of answering him kindly, I exclaimed:

"Well! gentlemen, your place should be with us and not here"... I saw tears in the eyes of Wojna, although he had done no harm in taking service in the Austrian Army, since his father lived in Austria. Youth must serve everywhere, to be active and learn. Maybe I did not understand that necessity fully at the time.

We arrived at headquarters; I announced to General Wimpfen, Chief of Staff of the Archduke Charles, the purpose of my visit, from whence I had come and where I had to go. He sent immediately to Rosenberg the order to let me pass by Brünn and Olmütz to the Army of the Archbishop Duke Ferdinand d'Esté. Septeuil took the road to Prague. I returned by

Znaïm and from there to Brünn. I took to reach Znaïm a post carriage and stopped the next day near Pohobitz. Not far from this place, I met our outposts, then later those of the Austrians. A hussar descended from a small eminence and stopped me: a non-commissioned officer came next, he conversed with me in German and went away to the guard, from whence an officer came and took me away. The captain of the hussars gave me a sub-officer who accompanied me to the General Rosenberg's camp, which was at Medryce.

When I arrived in front of the post office, I saw several Austrian officers walking towards me; I gave my non-commissioned officer some Austrian coins and asked him to be kind enough to pay for the carriage and the horses at the next station, and to wake me up when the carriage was ready; I told him that I was sleepy and wanted to rest a little in the carriage that had brought us, while our postilion was feeding his horses. I only pretended to sleep, because the trip was a short one, but I wanted to avoid having to tell these officers of the events of the campaign and details of the armistice, such as I had been obliged to do with the officer of the guard and his captain. I had to later tell the same story at even more length to General Rosenberg or his chief of staff, I don't know which one it was, for I dared not ask to whom I had the honour of speaking.

I finally arrived at Brünn: an officer led me to the governor of the place at my request, who was called Lazanski, he replied that he did not know Polish. Dinner was just been served, he invited me to take part; there were several officers present and I had once more to recount details of the Battle of Znaïm and the following armistice. Shortly after dinner the post carriage arrived in front of the house; I took my place in it accompanied of an officer whom I had asked the governor to give me, because I was wasting a lot of time in explanations with the commanders of the various detachments. He was a polite and very amiable, named Bredow. We quickly became true friends, and I entrusted him without ceremony with the money to pay for the carriage and the tips for the postilions.

We arrived at Olmütz at midnight; the gates were closed. M. Bredow went alone to the guard, but two hours passed before his return. He finally came back with a new carriage, a postilion and horses, which led us through the fields around the city. I don't know if my officer had received instructions to Brünn to do so, or if the commander of Olmütz was stupid enough to prevent me from crossing this stronghold in the night, when it was impossible to distinguish anything of military value. Finally on the 15th, at 11 o'clock, we arrived at Wadowice, the headquarters of Archduke Ferdinand, who soon arrived. I was taken up to the first floor, where one of his officers showed me to his rooms.

The archduke read the copy of the armistice which I given to him; he invited me to lunch, asked me my name and told me that he felt very unlucky to be designated to fight against the Poles, because it was a nation with a cause for which he would have liked to fight. He added:

> As much as I wanted to fight against the French that oppress us, as much as it is against my heart that I accepted the command of troops against you, Poles, whose cause I consider to be fair: I'm out of luck with your country!

There was only with us at lunch, Colonel Neuperg, who replaced the chief staff, sick or perhaps killed. I was obliged to tell the archduke all the incidents of the Battle of Wagram, of which he was already aware in broad outline, but he knew nothing of the battle at Znaïm and so he asked me all the details. Colonel Neuperg always spoke much more than the archduke and seemed to me to be a great braggart.

Archduke Ferdinand d'Esté was a modest man, simple and very well mannered. After lunch, and after giving all the explanations that were asked of me, I wanted take leave of the archduke and begged him to issue an order, accompanying officer or written instruction for his patrols to let me pass on my way to Krakow. He told me himself that Prince Poniatowski had entered this city on the same day as the Russians, or a little before them, and had occupied it. However, the archduke hesitated, asking me to wait longer. Finally, I told him that the Emperor of the French would not allow his officers to lose time, despite the pleasure I would have had in staying and the benevolence with which he had honoured me. He then told me bluntly that he couldn't permit me to go further; although he saw the signature of Chief of Staff of the Archduke Charles and that he would keep me until an officer of the Austrian General Staff brought him official armistice order.

Four hours after my arrival an officer came from Archduke Charles bringing the same orders as I carried. So, Archduke Ferdinand dismissed me; the officer who was to accompany me was already designated, the carriage ready for two hours. The archduke said to me as he bade me farewell: "You see, sir, I believed in the truth of news that you brought me, because I had given the order to prepare everything for your travel. But I couldn't let you go without having received the order from my superior. Come to see me please, when you come back."

I immediately set off with my new companion. In the fields to the left of the town, two Austrian *cuirassier* regiments were setting up their camp. They appeared to be in very good condition. Behind them was a regiment of hussars. I noticed that the *cuirassier* regiments were less numerous than the hussar regiments. The infantry, already encamped, was lighting its fires. The last squadron of these hussars was posted in Izdebnik; my companion communicated his orders to the leader of this squadron, and soon we passed the Austrian vedettes.

Half hour later, towards Mogilang, to the right of the main road leading to the village, we saw Polish peasants on a path together with some Austrian infantrymen after having taken their guns. I noticed that this display made a painful impression on my companion. Soon afterwards a Polish lancer of the 6th regiment arrived at full gallop and stopped near our carriage. The evening was already coming on; I let my coat slip off my shoulders, so that he recognised a French uniform. I had the idea of leaving my companion at the last Austrian grand guard, but he asked me to keep him until Krakow and take him back with me, if that did not bother me. I had consented, thinking that this was authorised by the archduke. But when we arrived at Podgorze, a suburb of Krakow, commanded Colonel Dziewanowski, he did not want to let my Austrian officer pass into the town so I had to bid him farewell and leave him.

Chapter 26: Krakow

It would be impossible for me to describe the feelings that seized me as we approached Krakow, free now of foreigners. In the *faubourg* of Podgorze, we could see our soldiers walking the streets arm in arm with the inhabitants and all of them embracing. I was also happy to see Wielopolski there, my mother's cousin. When I stopped in the marketplace, which was as well lit as the rest of the city, I learned that Prince Poniatowski was present at a ball given in his honour by the inhabitants, in a large hall in Sukiennice. I preferred to see him in Krzysztoporg, and I asked an officer who was there to go tell the prince that I was coming from the Emperor Napoleon.

The prince arrived without delay. I had to tell him for two hours of the incidents of the battles of Wagram and Znaïm. He related the details of his march on Krakow and his entry, the morning of that same day, into the city. The prince told me that Archduke Ferdinand had sent him a parliamentarian, begging him to wait two days, that is to say to ask him for 48 hours of armistice, so that he could remove from Krakow his wounded and his baggage.

The prince consented to spare the city the suffering from an occupation by his main force. He therefore stayed for two days at half a league from Krakow, and at the end of the second day, that is, on the very day of my arrival, the Polish Army formed up in full dress with the prince at the head of his entire staff, and with no escort before him, advanced towards the city. However, on arriving at the gate of Saint-Florian, he found some Cossacks who proposed to block his way.

The archduke, obliged as he was to abandon Krakow, had informed the Prince Galitzin, who was on the march, coming from Tarnow with 30,000 Russians. He was supposedly coming as an ally of Napoleon, but the archduke had no qualms on that score, because the Russians did not fight against the Austrians, since they were actually their allies. It is more likely that the archduke, announcing his retirement from Krakow to Prince Galitzin, was actually offering him the opportunity to occupy the city.

The Russian general accordingly sent on forced marches a light cavalry brigade together with a Cossack regiment. This same general had agreed with Prince Poniatowski that the Polish Amy would advance to the left bank of the Vistula, whilst the Russian Army would move to the right bank. By virtue of this arrangement, the prince had withdrawn his detachment which was already occupying Lemberg; therefore Galitzin, on entering Krakow, had faithlessly broken these conventions.

So, Prince Joseph called upon the chief of the Cossacks who occupied the gate to forthwith withdraw. On his reply that he could not do so, having received the order to occupy it, the prince drew his sabre from the scabbard, set off at a gallop with his staff at his heels and rushed to the gate and into the middle of the Cossacks, while his following infantry, was advancing at the double so quickly that the Cossacks were pressed against the walls of the passage. The regiment of the Mariampol Hussars was stationed in the market place, but it offered no resistance and our army therefore entered the city. The hussars retired against the houses on one side of the market and a bloody conflict was thus avoided.

After two hours of conversation, the prince retired to his room, and I, taking advantage of his permission, fell asleep for a few hours on a couch in the reception room. Early in the morning, I went to visit General Dombrowski, who was staying in the house of Madame Michalowska, *née* Wielopolska. I also found General Mielzynski there, who gave me one of his shirts so I could change mine, because on leaving Znaïm I didn't have time

PONIATOWSKI AND AIDES DE CAMP

to instruct my wardrobe to be put in my carriage. I also found there, Prince Henri Lubomirski, with whom I accompanied to Madame Wielopolska and the margraves Wielopolski. An officer sent by Prince Poniatowski came to collect me to go immediately to attend the prince. I found Generals Fiszer at his house, Rozniecki and Sokolnicki, as well as officers of the prince's staff.

The prince had just received by the express posts a letter from Archduke Ferdinand asking him to evacuate Krakow under the article of the armistice document which required him to halt in the positions he had occupied on the 12th. The prince and his generals were very embarrassed by this request and did not know which side to take. The prince did me the honour to ask my council, because, having been present with the imperial staff at the time of writing the armistice, he thought I must know how this article had to be interpreted.

I replied that the city of Krakow was so important to us that we had no right to abandon it without the formal order of the emperor. I didn't want repeat the instructions that Napoleon gave me about this article. I preferred keep silent, the emperor not having ordered me to repeat them in a precise manner to Prince Joseph; I only told him about my personal appreciation of the situation, especially after having noticed that he was less hesitant than the generals who were present.

The prince gave the instruction to write immediately to the emperor to ask his orders; but, judging that the Austrians would not let one of his own officers pass by the direct route, that is by Olmütz and Brünn, he asked me if I could return immediately to the emperor. I consented willingly, but I begged him to keep copy of the armistice and send the example that I brought him to General Galitzin in Tarnow. I had no orders in this regard, but I was convinced that if the emperor had known Galitzin and his Russians were so close, he would have sent an officer with a copy of the treaty. The prince immediately had a copy made which he sent to Galitzin by one of his own *aides-de-camp*.

Dinner was announced, but I asked the prince to excuse me and allow me to go dinner at my cousin Madame Vincent

Wielopolska's house. Thanks to the care of an *aide-de-camp* of the prince, a carriage was soon at the door of my cousin's house. I left at three o'clock in the afternoon and arrived at 8 o'clock in Wadowice in front of the headquarters of Archduke Ferdinand. During the journey, I noticed that the Austrian troops that had been camped between Izdebnik and Wadowice were already closer to Krakow.

When I found myself before Archduke Ferdinand, I represented to him that if he attempted entering Krakow, Prince Poniatowski would defend the place, with the assistance of the inhabitants, whom he trusted and who would support him vigorously. The Cracovians had warmly received the Polish Army and so, I added, that they would defend themselves at all costs. It moreover, I told him, would only be for them a question of defence of the Podgorze suburb, for the archduke could go no further. In the most unfavourable case for the Poles, if they had to abandoned the suburb of Podgorze, they would assuredly destroy the bridge over the Vistula as they withdrew.

Finally, I added it would be very probable that the engagement would take place on this side of the Vistula, because Prince Poniatowski, considering the treaty with Galitzin as broken as a result of the arrival of the Russians in Krakow, had placed his army on the right bank of the Vistula. In closing, I said that I carried for the emperor a letter from Prince Poniatowski, which stated he could not abandon Krakow without an order from of the emperor.

It seemed to me that the Archduke was not displeased with my explanations, whilst Neuperg, on the contrary, seemed to me quite angry. After half an hour, another carriage arrived in front of the archduke's quarters: I climbed in and set off again. I had to wait two long hours in front of the glacis of Olmütz, where the grand guard was stationed; finally, the officer arrived with the post carriage, and I was still driven around the place, though this time it was during daylight. If you want, in a very short time, an idea of the state of a fortress, it is easier to bypass it on the outside rather than crossing it within. The officer who accompanied me agreed with me on this point, and found the precaution quite unnecessary. Olmütz is an old fortress, and the emperor, who in 1805 was actually in the vicinity, would in any event, be in possession of a detailed plan of it. At the last post station, Stammersdorf, I couldn't find a carriage, and so I then was truly glad that I didn't have to take care of luggage.

I mounted my horse, and crossing in haste the Vienna bridges, I arrived at Schoenbrünn.

"Where is the Polish Army?" asked the emperor.

"Within Krakow, Sire," I replied.

"Oh! how the motherland rejoices!" he replied in answer.

Then the emperor questioned me in detail; but when I told him that the Russian brigade had entered Krakow, he thought only of Galitzin's Russian corps. I had to confess that I had not gone to General Galitzin personally, but that a Polish officer had brought to him a copy of the treaty of armistice. The emperor, very displeased, admonished me severely and put me under arrest, repeating several times:

> When I send an officer, that's why he knows everything. Especially in this case you had to to know what interest it would have been for me to have a report on the state of the Muscovite Army.

I left him and returned to my room very crestfallen. I was so tired that I fell asleep immediately. The next day, around 10 a.m., one of my comrades came to fetch me for lunch. I reminded him that I was under arrest, and asked him to inquire of General Savary, who replaced Caulaincourt (upon whom we were administratively dependent), whether I was under 'ordinary' arrests or 'forced'. General Savary put the question to the emperor, and soon my friend Talhouët returned to me to say that the emperor had lifted my arrest. In ordinary arrest, the officer keeps his weapons, but only goes out for lunch and dinner; in forced arrest, he gives up his sabre and he is forbidden to go out at all.

During my trip, I had eaten very little; back in Schoenbrünn, I could barely eat anything at all even though everything was available. It seemed to me that I could not swallow anything without pain. The irregular life that I had carried out for several months, the food always cold, especially during my travels, had debilitated my stomach. I had to ask Ivan, Ordinary Physician to the emperor for his advice. He ordered me to drink a cup of linden tea before each meal then, when the stomach attack had subsided, take a donkey's milk cure. I followed this treatment in Paris after the signing of the peace.

Chapter 27: Peace and Promoted

We stayed at Schoenbrünn for four weeks, throughout the duration of the preliminary stages of the peace treaty. Life there was a little dull. The most important event of this period was the attempt on the life of the emperor by a German student, not as one might expect an Austrian one. He came from northern Germany to accomplish his purpose, entering in the middle of a crowd of spectators who were allowed access from the castle courtyard to see the magazines that took place there every day. An *élite gendarme* apprehended him just as, coming out of the crowd, he was heading towards the emperor, his right hand hidden in his coat where a large knife was discovered. He confessed that he wanted to kill the emperor who was, he said, 'the tyrant of Germany'. After a few days devoted to the investigation of this affair, he was shot or hanged.

Then we were finally back in Paris. At the end six weeks my health recovered and I departed to find the emperor at Rambouillet. This was where he had resided since his divorce from Empress Josephine; he wanted to remarry for the purpose of leaving an heir to the throne of France. Two of us were always on duty at Rambouillet. One day the emperor informed us both:

"I am sending you on a mission to Saint-Pétersbourg," he said to me, "and you", he added, turning towards Fodoas, to Madrid.

I was surprised that he proposed to send me to Russia, and I ventured to make the following observation to him,

"What! Sire, I, a Pole, at Saint-Petersburg?"

"You are right," replied the emperor. "Go to Madrid to my

170

brother!" I received, for this mission, a detailed instruction, written under the dictation of the emperor by his secretary, Fain. The emperor only changed my name upon it but, a moment later, he gave me further instructions verbally. I went back to Paris to pick up my wardrobe, because my mission was not absolutely urgent. Nevertheless, that same night I was on my way to Spain. From Bayonne, Vittoria, Burgos and Madrid, I sent the emperor, directly by couriers, military reports on the state of our forces wherever I passed.

I told King Joseph that the emperor would not be coming to Spain at the moment, but that he wanted to give his orders because the Spanish Army was approaching Madrid. This army was subsequently defeated at Ocana. It was the Polish division, made up of the 2nd, 7th and 9th Infantry regiments of the Duchy of Warsaw, which decided the happy outcome of this battle for Napoleon. The colonels of these regiments were Potocki, Sobolewski, and Prince Sulkowski of the 9th regiment, in which I had served myself in 1806 and 1807. The Polish Lancers Regiment of the Vistula Legion, with Colonel Konopka, threw themselves on to the flank of the Spanish infantry in retirement. I don't know if it was this regiment that made so many prisoners, or if we gathered together all Spanish prisoners, but in any event, a detachment of this regiment led into Madrid nearly 10,000 Spaniards captured at Ocana.

On my return, I did not find the emperor at Paris, but at Compiègne, where he awaited the arrival of the Archduchess Marie-Louise; Marshal Berthier had married her by proxy in the name of the emperor on the Austrian frontier, and went to Compiègne, accompanied by the Queen Caroline Murat. I was constantly on duty at Compiègne. One week after arriving in this city, the wedding ceremony of the archduchess took place in Paris with the greatest pomp, in the Louvre gallery. The train of the dress of the young empress was carried by six crowned princesses: the Queen of Spain, the Queen of Naples, the Queen of Westphalia, daughter of the king of Württemberg, the Queen of Holland, the vice-Queen of Italy, daughter of the

King of Bavaria, and the Princess Elisa Bacciochi, the emperor's eldest sister.

German kings and princes were also in Paris, including the King of Saxony, and at the same time Duke of Warsaw, the most honest and the best of men. The balls of the court, the balls of the grand dignitaries of the Empire, followed without interruption. The Ambassador of Austria, Prince Schwarzenberg, raised a superbly decorated ballroom in the garden of his hotel. The ball started at 11:00. At midnight a hanging gauze took fire, and the room was in flames in an instant. Prince Schwarzenberg and the diplomatic corps surrounded the emperor and empress, and managed to get them out, but the guests rushed to the doors in disorder, several were knocked down, so that some ladies and the Russian Ambassador Kurakin were badly burned. Princess Schwarzenberg perished, and many other people died a few days later from their injuries.

Prince Kurakin was an extremely rich prince. He had been chosen as ambassador because of his fortune which allowed him to represent his nation. The diplomatic affairs of the ambassador were led by Nesselrode, who I met almost every evening in the lounges. The Russian embassy further included Krüdener, the son of the famous Madame Krüdener, and Boutiakin, from Ukraine, both of whom I knew well. They weren't typical Russians, since they judged cases calmly and lucidly. I also knew the priest of the embassy; I don't know if he was a good theologian, but he seemed to me to be a good man; I begged him to give me Russian lessons and he came to my house three times per week. I then often saw the Russians, as I saw them later in the second period of my life, and I studied the Russian language, thinking it might be useful to me during the war which could surely not be long in coming.

A month after his marriage, the emperor promoted his orderly officers to be lieutenant-colonels, and gave us all commands in regiments. I was appointed to the Polish Light Horse Regiment of the Imperial Guard. The emperor preserved for us the privilege that we previously had as ordinance officers, to be able to enter his house in the morning, during the time when the emperor gave the orders for the day. After having received my certificate for the Imperial Guard, I went the next morning to the emperor, and asked him to allow me to serve in the Polish Lancer Regiment of the Vistula commanded by Colonel Konopka. The emperor asked me why? I replied that it was because this regiment was in the field, whilst the Light Horse regiment was at Chantilly. He answered me thus,

"The Guard will have to fight and I want you to be not far from me."

I had nothing else to do but thank the emperor and to return to Chantilly. General Krasinski, commanding the regiment, was very kind to me throughout my stay in this city. We did our regimental duty a week each, the two of us only, Kozietulski and me, because at this time Thomas Lubienski was in Sedan, organising a new regiment of Polish Lancers of the Vistula Legion, which would be No. 8 in the Lancers in the French Army. Stokowski was appointed colonel replacing Konopka who was promoted to general.

Six regiments of French dragoons were transformed into lancers; Konopka's regiment took number 7, that of Lubienski number 8. Usually, I spent a week in Chantilly and another in Paris: often, during the winter, Kozietulski replaced me during my week, so that I could stay a longer time in Paris. I was staying with the Caramans, my good friends, I had my horses and my Guard uniform, and when my regiment came for a review in Paris, I went to meet it at the the barrier so as to enter the city with it.

This was how the winter of 1810 to 1811 was spent. At the beginning of Spring the drills and manoeuvres began again, and I never left Chantilly. In the month of September, 1811, I received the order to take 150 light horsemen and 150 *Chasseurs* of the Guard and to go with them to Boulogne-sur-Mer, where the emperor was soon to arrive. A division was stationed in Boulogne, in the camp from which the army left in 1804. It is this army, ready to embark to invade England, which changed destination and left instead for Ulm and Austerlitz, and in 1806 found itself at Jena. There were always a few hundred troop transport vessels at Boulogne.

The division manoeuvred in front of the emperor. Then he embarked on a boat, ordering me to take with me 50 *chasseurs*, and sent the whole flotilla out to sea. Since in the morning the sea was absolutely calm the transports could row, but towards noon the west wind rose; three ships English showed themselves, a frigate and two brigs; they spread their sails, and advanced on Boulogne so quickly that they arrived behind the last of our last transports and captured two of them, each loaded with 40 men.

We were already in port with the emperor when this occurred, for as soon as the French vice-admiral saw the English ships, he had given the order the entire flotilla to return to port.

Twenty-five horsemen escorted the emperor from Boulogne to Flushing, where there were at anchor fourteen ships of the line and four frigates. We stayed on the coast. The emperor passed one night on the ship of the line, *The City of Warsaw*. The next day he visited all the vessels and after dinner left for Antwerp, where we arrived two days later and we stayed for two days, then we left for Amsterdam, ahead of the imperial procession. Meanwhile Kozietulski arrived with his detachment; I joined him in Utrecht, and he handed over command, as the oldest senior officer.

The emperor, escorted by our squadron and that of the *chasseurs a cheval*, inspected the coast as far as Texel and Helder, whence he returned to Amsterdam. We continued our journey through Nijmegen to Dusseldorf where the emperor stayed a few days; then he returned to Paris. We also returned *via* Aix-la-Chapelle and Liège. Throughout this trip, except in Boulogne, the emperor was accompanied by the empress, who had come directly from Paris to Antwerp.

The winter of 1811 to 1812 passed for me like the previous one; I was almost always in Paris.

We talked a lot about a war with the Russia, but it was not decided until the month of May.

We received the order to leave, and we set out for Posen, *via* Reims, Verdun, Mainz, Dresden and Glogau.

Chapter 28: Before the War of 1812

We spent the winter very cheerfully in Paris from 1811 to 1812. On his return from Holland, the emperor wanted to entertain his wife, who was considerably younger than him, so there were many balls, either at the Tuileries or at the sisters of Napoleon, or with Queen Hortense, who still wore the title of Queen of Holland, although that country was already reunited with France. By a peculiar order of Napoleon, this kingdom had been deleted from existence: it was indeed a strange calculation, because how could the inhabitants have any esteem for monarchs that the Emperor named today, but whom he expelled the next day from their thrones, or moved upon other thrones as mere officials?

After the balls at the emperor's residence and at the members of the imperial family, the evenings and the most beautiful *soirées* were given by French ministers and foreign ambassadors. This is how the grand ball of Russian Ambassador Kurakin came about, although we were already talking about the war with Russia. The Emperor Alexander did not want or could not observe the conventions of the Treaty of Erfurt, whose most important article was the closing of Russian ports to English trade. I knew several of the members of this embassy: Prince Kurakin was a wealthy *boyar*, charged only, as I said, with the representative side: the real head of the embassy was Nesselrode, with whom I often met in intimate gatherings. He was an intelligent, witty man who represented to everyone that Russia absolutely had need of the commerce of England, and that it was impossible for the Emperor Alexander to close Russian ports.

Another member of the embassy, of whom I have already

mentioned by name, Mr. Boutiakin, was younger than Nesselrode; he was very kind to me, and assured me that he belonged to an old Lithuanian family, that his parents had property in Ukraine and that he considered himself rather as a Pole than as a Russian. I had also the best relations with the young Krüdener, of the same embassy; it was the son of the famous Mrs Krüdener, who had such a great influence on the Emperor Alexander.

I must not forget Czerniszew, because he was much talked about at that time; he managed to pervert two poor secretaries of the Ministry of War, and bought from them, at the price of silver, the states of all the corps of the French Army. In possession of these documents, he fled so quickly that the dispatches sent to stop him at the border only arrived when he was already on the other side. He was very skilful to conduct such business. Czerniszew, who we had only seen for a moment in the fire at Aspern in 1809, left among us sad memories which were very unflattering for an officer.

To conclude my recollections of the Russians I knew in Paris, I still have to talk about the priest who gave me Russian lessons. Certainly, his government, having to send a Russian priest abroad, had chosen one of its best. He had a natural mind, but was absolutely ignorant of culture.

By May, war with Russia seemed quite certain. We left our garrison at Chantilly in the first days of May, and we returned to Reims, then to Verdun, where the English residence in the city had contracted a such friendship with our officers, that they wished victory to the French and not to the Russians, and that our fatherland would be reconstituted. I made the acquaintance of Lord Blanche, Lord Bogle, and several other Englishmen.

From Verdun we went *via* Longwy to Luxembourg, a very important stronghold, which required a large garrison. It was there that General Konopka joined us. From there the country became very beautiful, especially around the environs of Treves. At Mainz I took the post. I went to Dresden where my sister lived and we two left for Turwia where I stayed ten days. I joined my regiment at Glogau, and we went to Wschowa. The *état-major* and all the officers of the regiment went down to Turwia to be with my father, and we danced all night.

We arrived in Posen in the first June days. I thought it was already too late for starting a campaign against the Russians this same year; indeed various armies were just beginning to come together. The Prussian Corps marched on the Baltic side, therefore on the left side of the army, and the Austrian corps formed the right wing. An expedition started so late in the season, and the locations of the various bodies of the army, all indicated that the emperor only wanted to scare the Emperor Alexander, by presenting him with these 400,000 men, opposing his 200,000 Russians.

This is also why he had placed the Prussians and Austrians with the wings of the army, because he knew that he could not will not count on their sincere support during this campaign. If he had really wanted war, and if he had believed it, he would have kept these dubious allies in the centre, framed by French and Polish corps. When we arrived at Wilna, we had proof that Napoleon did not want the war, because he kept negotiating with Alexander. We stayed two weeks in Wilna, without undertaking any movement. It was only when Napoleon was convinced that the Emperor of Russia did not want to make peace with the conditions that he proposed, that he saw himself obliged to go to war, and found himself drawn into heart of Russia at a time which was late in the year.

Chapter 29: Württembergers

The entire Imperial Guard was quartered in the surroundings of Posen. In our brigade, the *Chasseurs à Cheval* were encamped at Oswinski, and we were at Murowana Goslina.

Balls were given in the neighbourhood; one took place at my aunt's home in Lopuchow. It was there that I received the order to take 150 *chasseurs à cheval* and 150 Light Horse Lancers, and to go by forced marches to place pickets from Thorn to Danzig. I started out without delay. The first day I arrived at Gnesen, the second beyond the Mogilna, the third, I stopped two leagues beyond Inowroclaw.

Almost all of my detachment was quartered in villages near the road. For me, with the captain, two officers and a troop of Light Horse, the village of Kaczkow was designated for our lodgement: it was comprised of a *château* and a few houses. On my arrival at the castle, I found waiting in front of the door one of our quartermasters who told me than a Württemberg major with five of his officers were lodged at the *château* and that an entire Württemberg company was housed in its out buildings. Furthermore, he told me, the major had told him that he would not let us establish our quarters there.

I entered the yard, despite the presence of two Württembergers who were posted in front of the door. I dismounted and my troop did the same. I entered the *château* and introduced myself in the room where the Wurttemberg officers were situated. The officers of this army wore epaulettes signifying the rank higher than the one they actually held, for example, a captain wore major's epaulets: I knew this was the case, so addressing myself to the one who had upon his shoulders the rank of major, I called him: "Captain", and I politely explained to him that we were arriving by forced marches to place high guards for the service of the emperor, and that we had to leave the next day at 3 a.m.

Consequently, our horses needed shelter to rest, and I prayed him to give us the stables and sheds for our horses. I added that we did not need anything for ourselves and that we wouldn't disturb them in any way. Not only did this captain not stand up when I addressed him (as he should, given I was a superior officer) but he replied that he would not do anything I asked.

"So," I cried, "send your men to fetch your horses, because otherwise I will bring them out of the stables myself and let them loose!"

I went out, I ordered some of my men to bring out the Württemberg horses, and having learned that the *châtelaine*, Mrs. Dambska, was in the castle on the upper floor, I went to her, and found her with her daughter huddled as if captive in a small room.

She greeted me kindly saying: "How can I receive you? The Württembergers have taken possession of my pantry, their soldiers cook for themselves downstairs, and it is only in secret that my servant can bring me bread. I still have some coffee and tea, with which we have been living for five days and we are in constant fear of a house fire, for they make their own fires on the floors of the kitchen and bedrooms."

I reassured these ladies as best I could. I had with me a young cook mounted on horseback, who led in hand a second horse laden with everything we needed to eat. He had bread and meat he had purchased in Inowroclaw for us. I addressed myself to these ladies, saying to them: "Ladies, I invite you to supper."

Soon Lieutenant Lubanski entered, who informed me that the horses belonging to the Württembergers were outside, whilst ours were settled in the stables. Some Württemberg soldiers were mounted on the thatched roofs of the stables and began to demolish them. On seeing this desecration, one of our Light Horse troopers mounted a ladder behind them, and grasping hold of one of these wretches threw him off the roof to the ground; he hurt himself when he fell and began to scream. The captain then left the castle, sabre at hand, and threw himself on the Light Horse trooper; but Quartermaster Smolski, who had been busy with the distribution the fodder, came to confront the captain, snatched his sabre from him which he then broke over his knee, saying to him in German: "*Apprenez, monsieur*, use your sabre for a better purpose!" 'Captain Württemberger', thus humiliated, returned to his room and we saw him no more.

After this incident, I was afraid that after our departure the Württembergers would want take their revenge on the Polish ladies who would be left behind alone in the castle and possibly go so far as to burn the farm. Passing through Inowroclaw, I had noticed that the village was occupied by French *cuirassiers*, and I knew that their leader was General Sebastiani. I sent him a report on the behaviour of the Württembergers and on our business with them, and asked him to send to the *château*, before 3 a.m., a French squadron, to prevent the Württembergers taking against the inhabitants.

Mrs. Dambska and her daughter had been not out from their small room for five days. She consented to letting her daughter go for a walk with us in the garden. Everywhere the Württembergers had built huts under the trees, they had lit fires on which they were cooking their favourite dishes, from which escaped a penetrating and unpleasant odour. In the room where their officers were, the odour was no less horrible; we felt they were cooking or grilling something in fat.

Mrs. Dambska's cook joined with mine, and they prepared between them a pretty good meal. We were at the table and it would be 9 o'clock at night, when Lawoestine, *aide-de-camp* to General Sebastiani, entered the dining room, just four hours after the departure of my letter to the general. Lawoestine was a young and handsome officer, very cheerful, who had known me in Paris; that's why that he was in such a hurry to reach us; he had covered in one hour the two leagues which separated us from Inowroclaw.

He told me on behalf of General Sebastiani that a squadron of *cuirassiers* would be in Kaczkow before 3 a.m. so that the Württembergers would do nothing wrong: the general had already sent a report on this affair to Marshal Ney, on whom the Württembergers depended for patronage.

Lawoestine spent the night with us, for his horse was too tired to start the return journey straight away. We stayed till midnight with the ladies Dambska, and the gaiety of Lawoestine succeeded in ridding them of all their fears. When I was certain of the arrival of the *cuirassiers*, I called together fifteen peasants who were in Kaczkow. Most had not wanted to part with their carts and or to have their horses requisitioned by the Württembergers and were hoping that they would be given back to them. Others had been obligated to chop wood for the fire, and be made to do different chores for these strangers. I ordered them to go to the villages where the Württembergers had taken horses or cattle and to bring their owners to Kaczkow, telling them that everything that had been taken from them would be returned.

At midnight, after bidding farewell to these ladies, we left the dining room and we lay down to sleep for two hours, but long before dawn our trumpets signalled to us the approach of our detachments quartered farther away and that of the French *cuirassiers*. The peasants of the surroundings also arrived during in the night; each placed himself near that which belonged him, and before I had given the signal to ride a horse, they fled with their property in all directions.

The *cuirassier* captain arrived first and said, greeting me: "Be certain, my colonel, that I will not allow any abuse", and he then lavished epithets upon the Württembergers that need not be repeated here.

Chapter 30: The Advance

We left for Thorn and it was only when we reached Chelmno that we fed our horses; in the evening we arrived at Graudenz. The countryside is absolutely flat and we crossed it almost entirely at a trot. The cavalry of the Guard always went at a trot if the road was good, even if there were not too many steep ridges: but in descending hills, we always took the lead; often dismounting while leading our horses in hand. In general, we started at a walk and kept like this for an hour.

After this first hour we made a stop of 10 minutes; we dismounted to let our horses relieve themselves, and for a re-girth, because after an hour of walking, the horses deflate, the girths become too loose and need to be tightened. Then we got back on horseback, set off again at a walk for a few hundred steps, then we took up the trot when the road was good enough and we kept at the trot until two o'clock. This was how we conducted our forced marches.

When several squadrons marched together, it is necessary, during the trot march, that they keep between them an interval of at least 100 steps, so that each unit walked as if it was alone and can trot without ever being stopped. By trotting on the road, firstly we saved time, then we had the advantage of preventing riders to fall asleep as they would at the walk. While sleeping, the rider leans to the right or on the left and so overheats and can injure his horse.

At the place where we had to stop, our quartermasters came to meet us and told us where our marching lodgements were whilst we were still mounted. The riders could thus go directly to their billets with their horses and no one was left behind. The same process was used for the start. Everyone gathered on the road at the exit from the cantonment on the side where one was supposed to walk, so that, once again, no one was left behind. The same cannot be done with young soldiers; it is necessary to arrive with them on the place designated, distribute the lodgements to them there, and the next day bring them together on the same spot. In the Guard, almost all the men were old soldiers who could be left behind alone, and still they were always found at the meeting point indicated. By walking, as I have just said, the men and horses fatigued very little, each one did nothing more on the journey than he would have had to do had he been travelling alone.

It was in the evening that we arrived in Graudenz to stop there. I took off my *kurtka*, and keeping only my overcoat and my police cap, I went towards the fortress. The captain of *chasseurs à cheval* was lodged near me; we met and went together to visit this fortress behind the left city gate, on the banks of the Vistula. Approaching the glacis, we found two sentries who blocked our way. One of them called his sergeant, who came to the spot, and told us that we needed special permission to visit. I made myself known, and begged him to announce me and request this permission for me and for the captain who accompanied me.

After five minutes, we heard the drums beat, and the commander, with another officer, approached us. I noticed that he was a little surprised to see us in police caps; he himself had his coat on with the epaulettes and the sword at his side; nevertheless, he bade us come in and promised to show us everything that we would like to see.

When we passed through the rampart gate, the guard stood to arms, and I saw that the garrison was gathering in the square. On my request for the reason behind all these movements of troops, the commander replied that he had received the order to always put the garrison under arms when a superior officer entered the fortress and that he was complying to this order. I apologised to him for our behaviour especially without weapons, because I had intended to visit him the next day, thinking that in times of peace the access of the fortress was open to us without special permission. The next day, in the morning, I put myself in full dress, together with all my officers, and went with them to the commander; he was visibly flattered by this step and gave us a kinder welcome.

Graudenz Fortress forms a half-circle on the Vistula; it is composed of three bastions and two demi-bastions leaning on ramparts forming an enclosure in the system of Montalembert. There is also a rampart on the side of the city These fortifications are very well built and the pillboxes excellent. All this constituted a very strong place and made Graudenz a first order fortress perfectly fitting the Vistula.

On the 3rd I was at Kwidzyn, where I found some Prussians, I had known before. On the 6th, I escorted the emperor to Sztum. We caught up with our detachment at Kwidzyn; only one troop remained there, the other four, that I commanded, left for Malborg, Dirschau (Tczw), Pruszcza and Dantsig. They were ordered to return to Kwidzyn after the passage of the emperor. Our regiment set out from Thorn directly for Heilsberg and Gumbinnen, and we reached only a few leagues before Kowno, when at the same time the emperor, coming from Kœnigsberg arrived in this city to go to the bridge over the Niemen. The next day he crossed the Niemen and we crossed after him.

Kozietulski was on duty that day. The emperor ordered him to cross the Wilja swimming with a squadron, because we could see Cossacks on the other bank. Our men threw themselves into the river, where some were actually drowned; the Cossacks, however, fled. There were three squadrons of Light Horse left commanded by General Konopka; the emperor ordered them to also cross the Wilja behind Kozietulski, and to reconnoitre as far as Czerwonidwor, a village located on the banks of the Niewiaz.

The owner of this village, Mr. Zabiello, received us with his daughter, and came to spend the evening with us in our bivouac. We had forded the Wilja, barely fifteen paces from where Kozietulski had swum it; though our horses had water only up to their stomachs and we barely got our *schabraques* wet.

The next evening, we were back at Kowno: during our absence, the emperor had gone to the outposts at Wilna. We left after him and two days' march brought us there. I was on duty in this town for a week. Every day the emperor set out on horseback to visit the attractive surroundings of the city: Large numbers of French troops were still marching towards the Dwina, because the enemy was said to be retreating behind this river and were organising a fortified camp in Drissa, because that it was there that the Emperor of Russia wanted to defend the ancient borders of his empire.

The second Russian Army, commanded by General Bagration, withdrew by Minsk on the Borysthènes (Dniéper). This Russian Army was followed by the corps of the King of Westphalia; but this prince, despite to the orders of the emperor, often stopped in his pursuit so he was sent back to Cassel, and command of his troops given to Marshal Davoust.

Count Pac gave in honour of the emperor a grand ball in his palace at Wilna, where Count Tyzenhaus also lived. Although gaiety reigned in Wilna, we often had news about the horrors of war caused by indiscipline and disorder in the French Army and our hearts would break to see our homeland in such misfortune. During my stay in Wilna, I often went to visit the Princess Gedroïc, where I met Miss Sophie Tyzenhaus who I already knew; I also went to Mme Kossakowska's, *née* Potocka. I never thought we'd stay so a long time in Wilna. The manoeuvres of this campaign were an enigma to me, both on our side and on that of the Russians.

A deputation from the Diet of Warsaw came find the emperor at Wilna to beg him to proclaim the reunion of Lithuania to the Duchy of Warsaw. The emperor gave them an ambiguous answer, which produced on several of us a painful impression. We only had one hope left, which was that the approaching events of the campaign would oblige Napoleon to decide clearly in favour of our cause. We were quite certain that emperor wanted to force Russia to peace, by uniting with him against England.

If he reconstituted Poland, that was going to against his goal, because Russia, by losing its Polish provinces, would lose more territory; allied to England it would never have concluded peace with Napoleon, and on the contrary would have fought against him to its last resources. The emperor would therefore have had to fight at the two extremities of Europe, in Spain and Poland, and could never have achieved his goal, which was the lowering of England. The Poles had never been for him more than convenient instruments. It was in Wilna, while these events were taking place, that I remembered the words of our famous Kosciuszko, and his advice: "Learn your trade, while you are with the greatest captain of our time!"

Chapter 31: Cossacks

We left Wilna with the emperor for Witebsk, by Glebkie. A few leagues before Witebsk, we had a bloody fight entering the village of Ostrowno, between our vanguard under the command of Murat and the Russian rearguard. One of our squadrons which was near Murat, lost a few men: it was well known that Murat never exposed anyone to danger more than he did for himself. The emperor arrived on the battlefield when the cannons that had been heard for the last few hours ceased to rumble. Murat's cavalry must have been very tired, for the emperor made our brigade advance.

But the Russian cavalry also suffered, because approaching Witebsk we met with the Russian rearguard the Cossacks and the hussars of the Guard, which did not stop to charge us, but retreated, scattering with their scouts behind them. A few Cossacks, dressed in red, fell. They were tall and vigorous people.

When we entered Witebsk, we did not find anyone there. They had retired on the Dwina by the Wielkieluki road, that is to say, by the road to Petersburg. The bridge over the Dwina was not destroyed. You could also cross this river by a ford, and it would have been very easy to build a bridge there because of the abundance of wood, of which all the houses are built. We learned in the first village that the Russian Army had not moved on Petersburg, but had turned right towards Smolensk.

General Bagration's Russian corps was always withdrawing before Marshal Davoust and crossed the Dnieper at Rogaczew. The Russian rear guard had fought fearlessly against Davoust to this point, and stopped our vanguard long enough to allow the entire Russian corps to make its passage. The emperor, moving quickly from Kowno to Wilna and from Wilna to Witebsk, succeeded in cutting the Russian Army into two sections, of which one, under the orders of General Barclay de Tolly, with which was also the Emperor Alexander, retreated to Drissa crossing the Dwina, and the other, commanded by General Bagration, withdrew by Minsk on the Dnieper.

Napoleon soon saw that after shearing the Russian Army in two, neither side was inclined to stand to give him battle. He decided to give them time to come together again, because he realised that Barclay de Tolly, in marching from Witebsk on Smolensk, and Bagration walking from Rogaczew on Mscislaw, were not looking to join together. However, Napoleon favoured their junction for his own purposes. The French Army encamped at Witebsk and in the surrounding area, resting in the villages and in its cantonments. The emperor finally received the news of the junction of the two Russian generals: we set off towards the Dnieper to join Marshal Davoust, who had under his orders the Polish Army.

We crossed the river at Dombrowna. The Dnieper is winding before arriving in Smolensk; the largest loop being at Katany. Headquarters learned that a Russian corps was in Katany, on the other side of the river, on the side of our left wing. The emperor sent four squadrons of our regiment, out of the six that we had under the command of Kozietulski. We set out after midnight and arrived half a league from Katany, under the guidance of two old peasants who still spoke Polish. We soon saw the Cossacks. We stopped behind the last village, and then pursued them with a single squadron; they withdrew to the left towards the Dnieper. The sun was starting to rise and we could see all around us clearly. We saw on the height before us a line of Russian cavalry, preceded by a few hundred Cossacks.

Kozietulski ordered the first troop of our Light Horse, already grappling with the Cossacks, to withdraw, and the whole squadron began to form in line. From the height where they were placed, the Russians had certainly seen our other three squadrons, and kept quiet, but the Cossacks that had scattered in front of us approached every moment to unload their guns towards us, and as we had not sent our skirmishers to meet them, they came closer and closer, shouting to us: "*Lachy!*" (word used by the Cossacks to designate Polish), because they had recognised our nationality.

A Cossack officer, mounted on a grey horse, approached to 100 paces or even less, and challenged us in Polish to fight with him, but Kozietulski did not allow anyone to move. This same Cossack dismounted shouted, "Now you can take me!", then he began to remove the saddle of his horse: finally, seeing that he could not urge us to leave the ranks, he went back to his horse and returned to his family. They fired on us more than a hundred shots without killing anybody.

The Cossacks would not engage with a squadron in line, even if it was alone; they only wanted to fight against dispersed soldiers, seeking to draw them out, laying a trap for those who advanced too far and make them prisoners. So, we must never allow our soldiers, bloodthirsty and courageous, but imprudent as they may be to engage as skirmishers against the Cossacks.

Soon after, when the day was quite clear, we saw on the other side of the Dnieper a strong column of cavalry marching on Smolensk: these Cossacks and hussars found themselves heading to the same shore as we were, so broke off following our column. We returned to Dombrowna. The emperor, who had imagined that the conjunction of the Russian Armies would take place there, and that these armies would stop to deliver to him battle at Dombrowna, Lady or Krasnoè, was then convinced that it would only be at Smolensk that Generals Barclay de Tolly and Bagration would come together.

Chapter 32: Smolensk

It was August 15th, the birthday of the emperor, who wanted the battle to take place upon this day. We advanced by Lady and Krasnoè and stopped before Smolensk. A league and a half from this town, on the side of Mscislaw, the Polish Army (V corps), commanded by Prince Joseph Poniatowski, joined the Grand Army: it formed the *avant-garde* of Marshal Davoust's corps. The cavalry division, commanded by Prince Sulkowski, made a very good impression on me.

The men were handsome, their dress militarily precise with excellent horses. I saw that day only the first brigade of this Polish division, it was composed of the regiment of 'Silver Hussars' no. 13, Colonel Tulinski (thus named to distinguish them from the regiment of Polish hussars no 10, Colonel Uminski, who had the same uniform with trimmings of gold), and of the 5th regiment of *Chasseurs à Cheval*, Colonel Kurnatowski, a superb and superior regiment, carefully mounted.

Smolensk is located on the left bank of the Dnieper. The Polish Army took up position on this side, the Polish V corps, formed the right wing of the army. The Imperial tent was erected on the same line with the Imperial Guard encamped behind it. From the emperor's tent the view stretched over the entire city of Smolensk, surrounded by towers and walls on which one could distinguish Russian infantry and guns, whilst Cossack patrols circulated in front of the walls.

Between the French lines and the ramparts there was a ravine in which were ambushed by the Cossacks. I was on duty that day: I received the order of the emperor to take a squadron of Polish Light Horse Lancers and to hunt the Cossacks on the other side of the ravine, for the emperor wanted to approach the city and examine the potentials for undermining the ramparts; he rode in that direction and we followed on behind him.

When we descended into the ravine, the Cossacks fled; coming out of the ravine on the side of the city, I deployed my squadron, because I foresaw that the Russians were going to shoot at us from the top of the ramparts. Indeed, that proved to be the case because several shells fell on us, one of them burst in the middle of the squadron; some horsemen were thrown down, some horses galloped away. This chaos was an ideal opportunity for the Cossacks to rush at us and they came on so quickly that I had to counter with a sabre stroke the lance thrust at me by a Cossack who was ahead of the others; I did not cut the lance shaft, it slipped on the head of my horse scratching it from the top of the ears to the nostrils. Captain Skarzynski slashed several of these Cossacks with his sabre.

The Cossacks have lances that are too long, so they can't handle them as well as our lancers can. The squadron moved forward and compelled the Cossacks to seek shelter right under the city walls. The emperor, behind us, recognised the position and saw everything he wanted to see so he returned to our lines and immediately made arrangements for our attack on Smolensk.

When the assault commenced the Polish infantry, with great intrepidity, advanced as far as the ramparts despite a terrible carnage; but found no breach so could not enter the city and lost a lot of people. General Chlopicki was injured there in the leg. The French infantry also made several attacks against the ramparts, on the left side; but could not enter the city.

I don't understand why the emperor had not brought forward our guns, and did not use them to make a breach before these attacks commenced though they continued without result until night time. The next day, at dawn, we placed batteries for breaching; but before the day had fully begun it was learned that the Polish infantry was already in the city. I was looking for in vain for evidence of the enemy, but the Russians had withdrawn by the bridges during the night.

The Polish infantry brigade, made up of 15th and 17th line

regiments, had entered into the city through a hole in the wall that they had discovered, and which was barricaded only by large pieces of wood: this is where the Poles had entered. They brought in through this same breach two guns of their artillery commanded by Lieutenant Chrzanowski.

In the agenda, or as it was called, the "Bulletin" it was announced that the French members of Marshal Ney's corps had been the first to seize the ramparts and enter into Smolensk. That was a lie, but the emperor wanted to flatter them for the sake of their self-respect. Marshal Davoust's corps crossed the town at once, crossed the bridges and continued to pursue the Russians on the road to Moscow. The emperor, accompanied by the Guard, entered Smolensk. We stayed there for two days.

During the second night the emperor was informed that a mass of Cossacks, forming the vanguard of all the Russian cavalry, had appeared on the side of Mscislaw, intending to pounce on the part of our army which was encamped on the left bank of the Dnieper. The Polish Army had not been moved, because it had lost a lot of people; all other corps, except the Guard which remained in the city, were already on the right bank of the river. The emperor summoned me and ordered me to go with a squadron of Light Horse lancers, from the side of Mscislaw, to be sure of the accuracy of the information he had received concerning the approach of this body of Russian cavalry.

I left the town with my squadron; we fed our horses in the street on newly mown rye; the men had slept on the pavement, for there was no straw. Half a league away, Prince Poniatowski was bivouacking. He slept in a hut, and I was obliged to ask one of his *aides-de-camp* to wake him, so could tell him that I had to cross his high guards and to ask him if he possessed any further information about the enemy. The prince slept fully clothed; he came out and gave me an officer to accompany me through the grand guards and the Polish vedettes.

The night was clear. We arrived at the Polish cavalry camp, to the division of Prince Sulkowski. The prince also slept in a hut, but he rose immediately and when I told him the goal of my mission, he assured me that a few moments previously a patrol had just returned from the road to Mscislaw, and that the officer who commanded it, after talking with the peasants of the surrounding countryside who spoke a language which was half Russian, half Polish and who brought provisions and fodder to the Polish cavalry, had reported that they had not heard any talk about Russians nearby.

The horses of my squadron and, indeed, my own personal mounts were starving, so I took advantage of the fodder that I was offered, and thinking that we could have full confidence in the officer who had led this patrol, I gave the order to feed the horses, and then returned to Smolensk in the morning. It was only at 8 o'clock in the morning that I made my report to the emperor, not judging it necessary to wake him up to inform him that there was nothing to worry about and that the news he had received was false.

We left Smolensk at noon. Marshal Davoust sent to warn that the Russians were in position on the road to Moscow and that his vanguard, formed from the division Gudin, was already engaged. When we arrived around 4 o'clock on the battlefield, the Russians were already withdrawing. We saw a mass of corpses strewn over the land, including several Russian officers. General Gudin was wounded in both legs and died soon after. We learned that the Russians were fighting with great courage and stubbornness, sheltering behind clumps of fir trees. This battle was called by the French 'The combat of the 10th *Verst*', for such was the distance to Smolensk; it was later called the Battle of Valoutyna.

Three days after this fight we stopped in front of Drohobuz (Dorogobouje). The whole country, from Smolensk, was sad and deserted, covered only with brushwood fir trees and from time to time complete woods of the same trees. It was quite different to Lithuania, where one sees simple but clean villages, cultivated ground, where one sees everywhere plough marks and evidence of the human hand at work. Between Smolensk and Drohobuz there are two leagues from one village to another.

The Russians almost always burned the villages as they withdrew, and obliged their inhabitants to ride on their *kibitkas* (carts), with the little they had, to take their cattle and move beyond Moscow. Yet from time to time some Russian peasants came back. As far as Mojaisk, we encountered peasants, speaking Russian, but understanding the Polish language.

This wasteland extended to Wiazma. Around this town the land was a little better, and in front of the town one could see a few trees and a few gardens, as can be found in the poorest Polish villages. There is in Wiazma, on the market place, only a dozen one-storey brick houses; The same is true in Gracz (Gjat).

On September 5th, we finally arrived in front of a Russian position which had been fortified by entrenchments; so, we understood that the Russians had accepted the battle. The same day the 5th Corps (Polish) stormed a great redoubt which was on the front of the Russian position as a great vedette. The Polish infantry covered themselves with glory in this business, but lost many of its brave soldiers. The Imperial tent was erected very close to this conquered redoubt. The cavalry of the Guard had already placed itself on the left in a hollow; the infantry and the artillery of the Guard took up position in the rear. It was already dark when the cavalry drove their pegs into the ground to picket their horses for the night.

Since Smolensk we no longer fed our horses on anything other than green rye. In Lithuania and in White Russia we gave them more oats that we found in the villages among the peasants. But, from Smolensk, Russian troops captured everything, and forced the peasants to flee before us; this devastated country only changed in appearance a few leagues before Moscow.

I don't understand how some writers have been able to say that the old province of Moscow is densely populated and the peasants who inhabit it are comfortable. It is a mistake. The Muscovite peasant wears a coarse dirty shirt, tied at the waist with straw or a rope. He sometimes wears a straw hat, but is mostly bare-headed; his hair is thick, he wears a beard: all these peasants are barefoot and without pants. We could see at first glance that these were people of burdened with misery. I can certify these details having them seen them personally, because we made reconnaissance in several directions, to several leagues distant, and

195

we found peasants in the villages, outside the zone about two leagues around the road, in which the Russians forced the peasants to leave.

Chapter 33: Borodino

After setting up our camp, Kozietulski and I slept on two *schabraques* stretched out on the ground, and we fell asleep wrapped in our coats. A light rain began to fall during the night, and as we were at the foot of a mound, a little stream made its way between us, wetting my whole left side and we woke up. It was a very unpleasant feeling. We had to get up, give up sleeping and dry off next to the fires that our men had lit for their cooking.

We stayed in this position the whole day of the 6th. The emperor travelled on horseback along the whole line, making a reconnaissance of the enemy positions. Before dawn on the 7th, infantry buglers sounded the reveille, regiment by regiment, from the right wing. They had chosen the nicest pieces from their repertoires, because the music made a great impression on hearts of men before a battle. No one then doubted the imminence of a great conflict.

When the day was bright enough, we began proceedings by reading to each battalion a short proclamation from the emperor, then the guns of our left wing began to fire. It was the command of Prince Eugène de Beauharnais that was beginning the attack. I do not intend to describe this battle, called by the French the Battle of Moskowa, and which the Russians call the Battle of Borodino from the name of the river which crossed the plain. It has been told many times, first by Ségur in a somewhat romantic way, then by Chambray from the military point of view, and also by Boutourlin in a way fairly accurate, for an officer of the defeated army.

On the other hand, I could not see myself what was happening down the line as well as I had in previous battles from where I was placed near the person of the emperor, who always chose the position from which one could see best.

We were placed in a ravine, and we saw the smoke from the cannons all over the line.

Only once were we placed for an hour on a height, while the *cuirassiers* advanced to charge the infantry enemy defending itself in the great redoubt of the centre. The emperor had ordered the regiment of Polish Light Horse Lancers to come forward and charge without delay if the *cuirassiers* failed in their own attack and were repulsed. This order is the best proof of the perfect trust that the emperor had in us.

This great central redoubt was so riddled and overthrown by the shells that the emperor had rightly judged that it was possible for cavalry to seize it. We were witnesses to this magnificent spectacle of the attack executed by four regiments of French *cuirassiers*, a regiment of Polish *cuirassiers*—the only one in the Polish Army, commanded by Colonel Malachowski, and a regiment of Saxon *cuirassiers* commanded by Leizer. Malachowski and Leizer, covered with wounds, fell from their horses. After taking the redoubt, we returned to our old place, where the enemy cannonballs did not reach us. While we were waiting outside the great redoubt, several Russian balls passed over, whistling above our heads.

We constantly saw the emperor walking in front of his tent, on the height, his telescope in his hand; but he couldn't see all the line, because the right wing with Marshal Davoust and the 5th Corps with Prince Poniatowski were in the forest and behind it on the old road to Moscow, and the left wing with Prince Eugène was behind the heights: he could not see the corps of Marshal Ney and almost all the cavalry united under the command of Murat.

Every moment generals arrived from battlefield to see the emperor, and, as we learned of it, begged him to send a part of his Guard to decide the fate of the battle and enjoy the favourable results. But Napoleon stubbornly refused and with the exception of 60 guns of the Artillery of the Guard, no troops of the Guard took part in the battle. Napoleon, 400 leagues from France, wanted probably keep the Guard intact: as its main purpose was to frighten Emperor Alexander of Russia to force him to agree to peace, he wanted him to know that he had won the battle without engaging the Guard, and he pointedly mentioned after the battle in his Bulletin: "the Guard did not take part in the Battle of the Moskowa".

Around 4 p.m., an orderly officer came to the emperor and in returning to us we realised that the Russians were in full retreat. They withdrew in the greatest order beyond Mojaïsk, retaining this town that night under their control. Contrary to his habits, the emperor did not order a pursuit. Assessing the movements and attitude of the emperor that we saw from afar, we realised that he was in physical pain. Sometimes he was walking, sometimes he sat on his field chair, but at no time did he mount a horse.

Chapter 34: Moscow

The day after the Battle of the Moskowa our regiment and that of the Dutch lancers, also of the Guard, put themselves in marches, under the command of General Édouard Colbert, to the right on the road to Moscow, with the order to cut the road from Moscow to Kaluga. At a league's distance from the camp, we began to meet peasants in the villages. There were in our regiment several Light Horse troopers and some officers coming from the provinces of Podolia, Volhynie and Ukraine, all of whom spoke the Russian language. Our vanguard always had one of these men in it and some of these riders; when they met peasants, spoke to them, in the Russian language of course, so that they took us for Russian horsemen. They knew that there was also in the Russian Army a regiment of lancers, coming from the provinces conquered by the Russians; so they took us for soldiers of their army.

In the small towns in front of which we were often placed, the inhabitants formed several classes, some of which were more cultured than the peasants. In the beginning we were taken, as I have told you, for Russian troops; but later, when we were heard using the Polish language and with the Dutch lancers using the French language, they knew well who we were. In these villages there were enough provisions and fodder and since our soldiers had an excellent discipline, the inhabitants, far from fleeing, made us welcome. Several of them complained of their government. These same peasants warned us several times of the appearance of Cossacks in the surrounding countryside.

However, we always kept ourselves well protected, placing high guards and vedettes around us: the outposts were supplied by the Polish lancers, the rear guards by Dutch lancers to whom we added one or two of our own men as interpreters. During our stay in the large village of Fominskoïe, where we spent two days, the Cossacks, advancing through the brushwood with their usual silence and precaution, managed to completely overwhelm a large guard formed of Dutch lancers; only one was able to escape at full gallop and bring us the news at camp.

General Colbert with two squadrons chased after them, but the Cossacks fled so quickly with their Dutch captives, to whom they had left their horses, that we only saw by their traces on the ground, in the woods and in the countryside. Our riders, after a pursuit of an hour and a half, could not catch up to them and had to return to our camp.

Following this incident, General Colbert composed the grand guards of half Poles, half Dutch; the vedettes were doubled and formed of Polish troopers beside the Dutch. General Colbert always slept in a tent, which he had carried by a horse during the marches, and which was spacious enough so that twelve people could find a place within it. His two *aides-de-camp*, Bro and Bragues, sang extremely well, and possessed between them the entire repertoire of Martin and Elleviou, from the Vaudeville theatre in Paris. Each day a few of us spent the evening with the general.

Being on the march from Fominskoïe to Wereia, we found a well-built village, in the middle of which was a sugar refinery, containing a large amount of sugar formed into loaves. All our riders helped themselves to a good provision and ate it for several days following. Severe dysentery reigned in the army, as a result of bad food and probably also poor water quality. Several of our Light Horse troopers suffered from this illness: two days of "sugar cure" got rid of almost all of it.

It is also during this journey that one of our patrols seized a post carriage on the main road between Kijow and Moscow. In this carriage were the Russian minister Gouriew and his secretary; General Colbert sent them under escort to the emperor. We finally arrived at the village of Podol on the road from Moscow to Kaluga. I left for Moscow, to replace the squadron leader

Jerzmanowski, who had been on duty there since Mojaisk.

During this isolated march of our brigade, we had frequent contact with the Russian peasants, and we were convinced that nothing could be easier than to initiate an insurrection among these people, who suffered severely from the yoke of their government, but it is probable that Napoleon did not want to use this means of action. During this march also, I noticed everywhere that the inhabitants of the old Moscow province were not nearly as rich as the Russians abroad claim they are. They certainly have a lot of cattle, because the pastures there are without limits, but traces of ploughing can only be seen in the immediate surroundings of the villages. Perhaps there more favoured regions; but I always heard that it is precisely to the surroundings of Moscow that the peasants are most rich and I confess that I did not get that impression anywhere.

However, in some very remote villages in the vicinity of Moscow, we saw houses of peasants that were well built and painted: these were houses built for their peasants by wealthy lords, who owned palaces. We have seen in passing palaces of different styles and nice gardens, very well maintained; where those palaces were, there too the peasant houses were pretty enough; but very often, near the same village, we saw poor and miserable cottages, with a very small courtyard, surrounded by huts for the livestock and almost never a shed.

In the houses of Russian peasants there are no chimneys; windows are replaced by holes through which smoke escapes as well as through the door; it is impossible to stand up in the room, you have to sit down or go to bed, except here are no beds either, they sleep on benches and the children in the fireplace. We often entered these houses, but we always spent the night in our camp near the village, which was a good and natural way in an expedition like ours.

We were 7 leagues from Moscow when the city was burnt down. All night, despite the distance, we saw the glow of the flames; the fire lasted several nights. The peasants watched with us and said that it was Moscow that was burning.

Arriving in the city, I relieved the squadron on duty. I received the order to leave only 25 men and an officer in the Kremlin, where the emperor had his quarters, and to go with the rest of the squadron in the Rue de Twer, by Bialogorod and Kitajgorod. I was lodged in the palace of Prince Labanow. Opposite my lodging was General Krasinski's quarters, in the house of the banker, Barisznikow. These two houses were well furnished, everything was perfectly installed on the ground floor as on the first; the rooms had large beds with mattresses covered in Morocco. Behind the palace we found the stables, sheds, gardens with an orangery, finally the vegetable garden with adjacent large fields. The *façade* of the palace was in the city: on the opposite side we seemed to be in the country. Buildings behind the palace contained about a hundred Muscovites, servants, workers, peasants, who came to the aid of all our needs. Among them were cobblers and tailors, which happened to be very useful for us. Our soldiers commissioned them do everything they needed.

It was said that three quarters of Moscow was burned and only a quarter remained intact. This seems exaggerated, because the Kremlin in its entirety remained intact, Bialogorod and Kitajgorod also, as well as the Rue de Twer, the greater part of the suburb near Mojaïsk and almost everything the suburb of Kaluga was untouched. Colonel Morawski, who was ill, came to see us in our neighbourhood and spent a few days with us.

Caraman was then in command of a horse artillery battery in the corps of Marshal Davoust: he often came to see me, although his lodging was in the suburb of Kaluga, at least a league from mine. I had as orderly one of my light horsemen, named Marcin, who spoke Russian well, and procured at a good price everything we needed.

When I arrived in Moscow, the fire had burned out; our troops were lodged in the houses; there were no bivouacs. I was told what had happened during the fire, which had lasted six days; everywhere there was in a big mess. All the officers agreed that if, at that time, the Russians had thrown themselves upon us even in small numbers, they would have won a victory. But now order was restored. In the houses that weren't burnt, as in shops and cellars of those that had been destroyed by fire, were found wheat and provisions in such abundance that these supplies of food and fodder could, it was said, have sufficed for the army throughout the winter.

However, I had the painful experience of seeing French soldiers selling all kinds objects looted from shops. Our troopers bought wine and provisions from them. There were enough vegetables in the city and in the surrounding gardens. We also found large fur and pelt stores.

Before leaving Moscow, we provided our entire regiment of sheepskin *pelisses*. Hay and straw were brought to us by parish priests as we sent detachments to the surrounding villages, starting with the closest and ending with those furthest away. We created, for the cavalry of the Guard, fodder stores for the entire winter. The French cavalry, under the orders of the King Murat, camped some distance from Moscow, around the village of Woronowo, where also camped the 5th corps (Polish) of Prince Poniatowski.

After a few weeks the Cossacks began to attack our detachments sent to gather forage. I was sometimes sent on reconnaissance, but as soon as our squadrons showed up, the Cossacks disappeared.

The French officers found in Moscow French actors, and theatrical performances were held every evening; naturally only the officers attended. I visited some Russian churches. During a service, I heard a sermon in which the priest rose up violently against his government proclaiming that it was lying. I think this was done at the instigation of French officers and without the knowledge of the emperor, who certainly would not have tolerated it, for he had rejected the idea of insurgent peasants.

Chapter 35: The Retreat

The French Army, entered Moscow on September 14th and stayed there until October 20th.

Thereafter, the army marched on Kaluga taking, after crossing Malo-Jaroslawetz, the road on the right which leads to Mojaisk.

We only entered the campaign in the first days of June; if we had left two months earlier, the retreat could have been operated on the frontiers of Lithuania during the right season. And even with this entry late in the campaign, entering Moscow on September 14th, if we had left it on October 1st after two weeks of rest, we could have arrived on the Dnieper when the autumn weather was still mild. But the emperor allowed himself to be deceived by the Russians, in the hope of the peace that he longed for could be achieved.

A kind of armistice was concluded during the duration of our stay in Moscow between the Russian supreme general, Kutusow and King Murat, because the emperor had sent General Lauriston, his *aide-de-camp* to Emperor Alexander with a view to negotiate a peace. This armistice could be broken by notifying each other party three hours before the resumption of hostilities.

While we occupied Moscow, the Russian General Kutusow gathered reserves as much as he could and insisted upon the mobilisation of all possible conscripts. It was also said that 12,000 old Cossacks of the Don, who had already done their military service, came to rejoin the ranks which altogether elevated the number of men in the Russian Army to 120,000 men, while the French Army in Moscow had barely 86,000 men, following its losses at Mojaisk and during the marches.

On October 18th, the emperor learned that Murat, impatient

to see that the Cossacks constantly attacked the flanks its detachments of foragers despite the armistice, had denounced the armistice himself; three hours later, Kutusow pre-emptively attacked Murat, with such superior forces that the King of Naples would have been beaten if Prince Poniatowski had not rescued him with the Polish 5th Corps. Once again 5th corps covered itself with glory!

The order to leave Moscow was given on October 19th. On the 20th, the whole army left the city, except for the Young Guard, which remained there with Marshal Mortier. He had received from the emperor the order to blow up the Kremlin and the arsenal, in which the Russians had left sufficient guns to arm at least 60,000 men. The Russians, leaving Moscow, knew well that we would not need these weapons ourselves; but that proved that they had not dared to distribute them to their own militia, which was only armed with spades. This militia, called *"Druzyna"*, was employed in guarding the food stores and ammunition, and during the fight to remove the wounded.

Four days after the departure of the army from Moscow, Marshal Mortier also left the city, covering the large convoy of wounded headed towards Mojaïsk, by the crossing of Wereia.

From Moscow to Malo-Jaroslawetz our brigade served as the rearguard, but during the first three days we did not see the enemy. Even when the Army of Italy fought the Battle of Malo-Jaroslawetz, the Cossacks did not attack us, but then they suddenly threw themselves at us from the right side on to the headquarters of the emperor, between Borowsk and Malo-Jaroslawetz.

The escort squadron was comprised of Polish Light Horse Lancers under the orders of Lieutenant-Colonel Kozietulski; in the twinkling of an eye, they rushed on this band of Cossacks. According to reports, they were thousands of old Don Cossacks, newly arrived with the army, and that the *hetman* Platow commanded them in person. Kozietulski received a lance strike which crossed his arm into his chest. (He continued the retreat by carriage, then by sleigh.) The Horse Grenadiers of the Imperial Guard were not long in arriving. Their black horses and high fur-caps made such an impression on the Cossacks that they fled into the forest, but soon afterwards, half a league further on, they rushed towards our brigade again.

General Colbert sent me to meet them with two squadrons. I walked 500 paces, and, seeing some French soldiers (who were following their regiments as stragglers) racing away on our side in front of the enemy, I picked up a hundred of them which I established in cottages to our left. My scouts skilfully brought the Cossacks in range of these hidden infantrymen who opened fire upon them: the Cossacks dispersed and withdrew, leaving our brigade time to ride on unmolested.

General Colbert sent me the order to rejoin the brigade, leaving to the fore only a squadron of Dutch Lancers commanded by a captain. The Cossacks soon saw that they were Dutch and emboldened attacked them vigorously, surrounding them on three sides. At this sight, General Colbert charged them with the whole command. They withdrew to the side of the forest, but from there ten times as many Cossacks threw themselves at us. Our horses were tired from their long charge, we were attacked at both our front and on our two flanks; we lost from our regiment about 20 men and the Dutch lost about a further one hundred.

It was the fault of General Colbert, who, seeing in front of him one of his squadrons in danger, assaulted the enemy thoughtlessly with all he had at hand. He would have avoided the loss of his horsemen if he had charged with a few squadrons, keeping the others in reserve and moving them forward slowly. One must never instantly commit all one's forces; this rule must be applied even more strictly when dealing with Cossacks. In the march on Moscow and during the retreat something like this never happened to us as a regiment.

We would have certainly lost even more men in this affair if our Polish Light Horse had not been experienced old soldiers, each of whom defended himself with the greatest bravery. The Dutch, less skilful, did not know defend as well against the Cossacks. During the retirement, whenever they were in the rearguard, they lost a few men and the Cossacks always attacked them boldly.

General Colbert, attempting a subterfuge, once ordered a squadron of Polish Light Horse to give their white coats to the Dutch lancers, taking and wearing their blue coats in exchange and then he ordered these decoys to hang back before the day began to rise. We waited for what was to come. When the Cossacks arrived, they saw the blue coats and believing they were dealing with Dutch lancers, they boldly attacked them as usual. But our men had hardly advanced in front of them with their usual business-like attitude than the Cossacks recognised their mistake and forthwith fled shouting, "*Lachy! Lachy!*" (Poles! Poles!)

After the Battle of Malo-Jaroslawetz, the emperor, convinced that Kutusow's army had doubled in size during the armistice, decided instead of taking the shortest route and through territory not yet devastated, by Medym, Mncislaw and Orsza, to go by Borowsk, Wereia and Mojaïsk, following the main road by which we were come to Moscow, crossing countryside which had been totally devastated. This resolution of the emperor was very difficult to understand, because the road to Medym was shorter and rich in resources. Because of this change, the Russian *generalissimo* took this last road, and stopped in front of Wiazma when the emperor passed through this town with his Guard.

The Grand Army left behind the Italian Corps, that of Marshal Ney and that of Davoust which was compelled by force of arms to cut through a passage to cross Wiazma, and so lost many people. They succeeded to join us in Smolensk, where the emperor stayed 48 hours, and we left this city in the same order for Orsza. Marshal Ney, forming the rearguard, walked a day's distance from us. We reached Krasnoye in two days. Russians attacked the Young Guard near this village and cut off our communications with the Corps of the Viceroy of Italy, of Davoust and of Ney. The emperor ordered General Durosnel, his *aide-de-camp*, to take a battalion of the Old Guard and two of my squadrons, and to open a road to Davoust.

The night was clear. The Cossacks retreated immediately in front of us, but a league away we caught sight of the fires of the Russian camp. General Durosnel judged the enemy too strong to attack him in his camp. He ordered me to select a skilful and intelligent sergeant, to send him with two Light Horse troopers to the two corps which were separated from us, to announce to the two marshals that the emperor would not move from Krasnoye until they rejoined us. We were back in Krasnoye at 3 o'clock in the morning.

Chapter 36: The Grand Army Regrouped

The next day at dawn, the emperor, with the vanguard, took the road to Smolensk, but after half a league, he stopped, because we heard the sound of cannon and musketry shooting, which approached nearer and nearer. The emperor rightly judged that they were our columns that had opened a passage through the Russian Army. Indeed, we saw from afar a few cavalry detachments, and soon afterwards Marshal Davoust with his command, appeared though much reduced in numbers. Around noon the Italian Corps of the Prince Eugene also arrived, though once again much depleted and without artillery; all their guns had to be abandoned.

The emperor ordered the 5th Polish Corps, which, so far had not lost a single cannon, to give 30 guns, half of what it had, to the Italian Corps. The Polish Corps, which had lost many men in the Battle of Woronowo, had enough with the 30 guns which it had left, and it happily brought them all back in the end, though, as we will see later, it would have to fight once again with courage and dedication at the Battle of Bérésina.

The emperor waited another day for the arrival of Marshal Ney, and stayed once more with us at the same point, but instead of seeing to arrive the marshal, we saw on the side from Smolensk the deep columns of the Russian Army who were beginning to surround us on the south side, while the Russian cavalry showed itself both beside us and behind us. The Russian skirmishers advanced in numbers towards the ravine where we were, and had already taken a small village on our right flank.

I was with four squadrons of Polish Light Horse behind and to the right of emperor. King Murat rushed towards me and ordered me to follow him at a trot with a squadron. Going to the trot was very difficult for our horses, because the snow was deep. The King of Naples stopped with us in front of the small village occupied by the Russians saying to me: "Enter inside!" It was an extraordinary order to give to the cavalry, but I had to obey. This fact shows why Murat lost in this campaign almost all the cavalry that was under his orders. Following his order, I threw myself into the village by the street that crossed it. From the courtyards of houses, the Russian *chasseurs* fired at us at close range; 4 Light Horse troopers fell and Murat has them on his conscience; we had besides 6 wounded, as I learned later.

The Russians did not flee, in fact they could not because they would not have had time to save themselves by sheltering behind the hedges. I was not going at a walk through the village, but the snow, which reached almost to the belly of the horses, did not allow them to gallop. I left the village by the other side and came back to form my squadron between it and the emperor, who was about 600 paces from us. At this moment I saw a company of Grenadiers of the Guard, probably sent by the emperor on seeing the extravagant order given to us by Murat, to seize the village. The grenadiers occupied it without firing a shot and the Russians barely had time to fire once; some of them were able to withdraw by crossing a ravine, but others were taken prisoner.

The emperor was on foot before his guard. I went back to take my place next to him, he was furious with Murat. Addressing me, he said, "How could you listen to that madman?"

Russian shells began to fall more numerous at each moment and threw to the ground several of our men. The Guard remained motionless like a wall. Our guns placed in position on the edge of the ravine barely answered. The emperor did not allow any shooting in response, saying the Russians were shooting at us from too far distant. But their *unicornes* reached us, notwithstanding.

★★★★★★★★★★

The "unicornes" were howitzers or guns with a chamber, the handles of which represented unicorns or horns—They were also called cannons à la Schouvalow, from name of the field-marshal who had invented this system of artillery during the Seven Years' War.

★★★★★★★★★★

A shell fell close to the emperor. Napoleon struck out at it with his whip saying: "Oh! I haven't received one for a long time between the legs!" The shell burst covering the emperor, with snow, but without hurting anyone. Noting that new Russian troops kept coming, Napoleon concluded that Marshal Ney had been taken prisoner or that he made a massive detour around the Russian Army to join us, and so he ordered a retreat.

We marched in tight columns, led by escort squadrons, the infantry of the Guard in two columns, artillery of the Guard on the road, then the infantry, and finally all the cavalry of the Guard. We arrived before night at the small town of Lady, followed to the south by the Cossacks, behind whom we could distinguish the uniforms of the regular Russian cavalry. These Cossacks were constantly firing at us with their small cannons, the balls of which came as far as the emperor, who walked on foot among the Grenadiers of the Guard. Our squadrons were very often obliged to drive away the Cossacks during this hard march.

The next day we continued our walk in the same order to Dombrowna. The Cossacks caused us alarm there during the night: our guards and our vedettes had well placed, but too close to some cottages that were outside the city, which was already quite a Polish town. Their habits were so similar to those at home, and we distributed all the supplies they could give us. It was the end of our great misery.

From Dombrowna to Orsza our march was much quieter, we could no longer see the enemy.

When we had arrived at Orsza, a short time after our installation in the city, the emperor ordered me in the evening to leave with a squadron on the road to Witebsk, to discover if Marshal Ney had arrived from this side. We set off and soon we saw horsemen in the distance which the light of moon allowed me to recognise as Cossacks: on seeing us they dispersed. Two leagues further on, we heard gun shots. Towards Taube we saw approaching near to us first a few horsemen, then infantry. We soon recognised Polish cavalry in the lead.

Marshal Ney, unable to pierce the line of the Russians on the main road, had thrown himself to the North, led by a peasant who spoke Polish. He had crossed the Dnieper, sacrificing guns and horses which could not pass over the thin ice on the river, and constantly walking upon the right bank they eventually joined us. We saw the brave marshal mounted on a horse, followed by a few hundred armed men and a column of almost as many unarmed soldiers, for whom exhaustion and fatigue had caused them to abandon their weapons. The marshal was very happy to meet us and to learn that the emperor was waiting for him just 3 leagues away, at Orsza. The officers of the marshal told us what had happened during in their painful march. Near Marshal Ney were some Polish officers, who the marshal himself said that he owed his salvation.

After our return to Orsza, one of my light horsemen who was on patrol at night, on the other side of the town, recognised an artillery officer who was warming himself with a few other gunners around a fire. It was my friend Caraman, in a pitiful state. All our light horsemen knew Caraman very well, because he came see us very often, when his post was not too far from ours. When I heard this news, I immediately went to join him; I found him very weakened.

Unable to stay away from my squadron for a long time, I returned to Orsza and immediately sent him one of my horses in the care one of my orderlies who he knew well. They both came back to us, as we were leaving Orsza. From that time Caraman remained with us throughout the whole retreat until we arrived at Posen. At the start of the campaign, Caraman commanded a horse artillery battery in the corps of Marshal Davoust; it was lost at Wiazma, the horse he was riding was killed under him, his servant and his other horse were taken by the enemy. Since that time Caraman had made his way on foot.

It was also in Orsza that I met my old comrade Tascher, cousin of the Empress Joséphine, who had lost his horse and was also forced to follow the army on foot. I gave him a horse with all its harness, it was the one that had received a battle-scar in Smolensk. I had 9 horses: There were still 7 left, all in good condition as were the horses throughout the regiment, because our light horsemen always daily rode the small horses of the peasants which we kept with us during the retreat so as not to tire our own cavalry mounts in the event of action.

The officers ordered a search for forage in neighbouring villages and the searchers rarely came back empty-handed: they brought us Russian *kibitkas* filled with oats and other provisions: our foragers had crept up on a small village where Russian horsemen were ensconced, who, fearing no attack from us, slept quietly in the houses, after putting their horses in the stables; the "*kibitkas*" were all harnessed: the Russians thought they were so safe that they had placed neither guards nor vedettes. So, because of the great cold, they had taken refuge in the houses without taking the slightest precaution.

Chapter 37: Bérésina

From Orsza we took the road to Boryssow, which passes through large forests; this road in several places is built on large wooden logs that could be seen under the snow which covered them. We no longer suffered from famine: inhabitants of the surroundings, the *Lètes*, made us very welcome.

The emperor wanted to continue his retirement by the main road from Boryssow to Minsk where he knew there were great stores of everything needed, but he received the very disheartening news on the day of our departure from Orsza. General Dombrowski, pressed by the army of Admiral Tchitchagow, had been forced to abandon the vicinity of Bobrujsk and to retire on Boryssow: he had fought bravely to defend and save the bridge over the Bérésina; but overwhelmed by very strong superior forces, he had to cross over the river and burn the bridge.

Other news no less unfortunate followed. The Lithuanian Brigade newly formed under the command of General Kossecki was destroyed and the town of Minsk was now occupied by the Russians. Then the Austrian General Schwarzenberg and General Reynier withdrew to Warsaw before General Tormansow; at Slonim the Polish General Konopka had imprudently let himself be engaged in an unequal combat in command of a single regiment, the 3rd Lithuanian Lancers of the Imperial Guard and had been taken prisoner with a large part of the regiment by the division of General Czaplic's Russian cavalry.

Finally, to make matters worse, Marshals Victor and Oudinot, beaten by the corps of Wittgenstein, withdrew from Polock, and the Bavarian General de Wrède beat a retreat before the Russian General Steindel, who had arrived with the Finnish corps to support Wittgenstein.

It seemed impossible that the Grand Army could escape by crossing the Bérésina, because the Russian plan was obviously to reunite the corps of the North and South Russians to stop us making the passage. The plan would certainly have succeeded if the *generalissimo* Kutusow had rushed straight on with the army following us, and if the Polish corps, united with the troops of General Dombrowski, had, by dint of bravery and of intrepidity, succeeded in repelling Admiral Tchitchagow. The emperor, on arriving at Boryssow, was convinced that the passage was impossible on this point. He sent engineering officers to 2 leagues above the city and ordered them to throw over bridges at Zembin.

The 8th Lancers of the Vistula, commanded by Colonel Thomas Lubienski, was the first regiment which forded the Bérésina and chased away the Tchitchagow's Cossacks who were ranging on the opposite bank. After them, the corps of Dombrowski, the Polish divisions of the generals Kniaziewicz and Zajonczek, the Legion of the Vistula and the brigade of French *cuirassiers* of the General de Berckheim passed over the bridge which had just been built and started immediately on the left in front of the troops of Tchitchagow who were opposite Boryssow, and who, at the news of the French passage and the construction of bridges, were heading towards us.

Half a league from Boryssow, the Russian admiral was defeated by our troops, so that the rest of the Grand Army and the Imperial Guard were able to calmly cross the bridges (the second bridge had been completed during this time). The Polish General Turno joined us during the passage.

The Battle of Bérésina, the last of this campaign, was won by the Poles alone; there was with our troops only one brigade of French *cuirassiers*. Generals Dombrowski, Kniaziewicz and Zajonczek were all three wounded during the battle: the General Zajonczek had to undergo amputation of a leg in the open air. Prince Poniatowski sprained his foot in the Woronowo fight; the emperor had entrusted the command of the Polish troops to Marshal Ney.

The remnants of the French Army, followed by a multitude of wounded and sick, crossed the bridges when Marshal Victor, who withdrew to defend against the attacks of Wittgenstein, came to them. Russian cannonballs were already passing over the bridges, reaching the wounded on the other side of the Bérésina.

Chapter 38: The End of the Retreat

The emperor continued his retreat, marching with the Guard on a narrow road, through completely frozen marshes, crossing several bridges which was necessary to get to Malodeczno. Behind marched the Polish troops who had defeated Tchitchagow. Finally, Marshal Victor formed the rear guard. We arrived at the end of three days at Malodeczno without being harassed. This is where the emperor decided to leave for France in order to oversee the formation of a new army; but he did not leave until the next day, from Smorgoni, entrusting to Murat the command of the whole army.

The emperor's convoy consisted of two carriages: he was in the first with Caulaincourt; in the second, Duroc and, the *aide-de-camp* of the emperor, Mouton. The Polish officer Wasowicz and the Mameluke Roustan preceded in a small sled.

We continued our retreat until Wilna, where we stayed only two days; then after Wilna, we took three days to arrive in Kowno. On leaving Wilna, a frightful disorder arose among the transport which could not, because of the ice, negotiate the Ponary coast. Thanks to my knowledge of the region, I turned right with my riders, we passed the Wilja on the ice and thus avoided this dangerous coast. Acting on the assurances that I gave him that we could cross this river, the regiment of cavalry of Savoy under Prince Carignan followed us and passed over without accident.

At the start of the campaign, leaving for Moscow, the regiment of Polish Light Horse Lancers of the Imperial Guard had crossed the Niemen with 915 men. We had provided cadres for a regiment of volunteers in training at Danzig: three captains were sent to Moscow with executives to organise three regiments of Polish cavalry, that we didn't have time to train.

Despite these reductions, our regiment passed the Niemen after the retreat with 422 men, and found itself stronger than the whole of the three other cavalry regiments of the Guard: I am not talking about the regiment of Dutch Red Lancers, because with the exception of Captain Colqhoun and the *maréchal de logis* his brother, who had become attached to us since Smolensk, I had not seen anyone from this unit. Yet we had been spared nowhere! When arrived at headquarters if a report that there were Cossacks somewhere near the army, always the same order was heard: "Polish, go see!" It was very rare for us to have a quiet night.

The most complete demoralisation reigned in the troops of the Confederation of the Rhine; the best proof of this was my meeting with the General de Wrède, head of the Bavarian troops, the day after our arrival in Wilna. The cold exceeded 20 degrees, it was the coldest day in this icy countryside. I went in the morning to headquarters of King Murat, who was in the *château*. I met a man covered of a civilian coat, a kind of turban on the head, sword in hand, without gloves, and running, followed by about fifteen armed soldiers, crossing without the bayonet as if about to load. By noticing and recognising my *czapka* and my uniform, he shouted to me sharply: "Where is the headquarters? The Cossacks are in the city!! They arrest our men in the street and the Imperial Guard does not come out of its quarters."

Carefully examining the face of my interlocutor wrapped in handkerchiefs, and at the sound of his voice, I recognised General de Wrède, whom I had often seen in 1809, and I replied quietly: "I am just going at King Murat's headquarters and if the general allows me, I will guide him. But we let's go there quietly, because the doors of the town are guarded by infantry, there are guards everywhere, and I affirm that there are no more Cossacks in town." I added: "My general, put your sword back in its scabbard, not to frighten King Murat."

In general, the senior French officers withstood the extreme cold and its drawbacks much better than their allies, and I am

Lancers escorting Napoleon on the retreat from Moscow

Polish lancer on the Retreat from Moscow

convinced that if the emperor had even pitched his tent in the middle of the field chosen to camp, the generals could not have departed to go to houses, their subordinate officers and soldiers would have followed their example and order could have been established. The supplies prepared in the stores could have been distributed with order instead of being wasted.

As for battles fought during the retreat, the French always defended victoriously against the Russians, despite their numerical inferiority. My regiment was still holding up well: the officers always slept in the bivouac in the middle of their light horsemen. The provisions were sufficient, because we were near the headquarters and we met the cattle convoys following us.

When we arrived somewhere to spend the night, our light horsemen occupied any building and ensured that any French people present did not set fire to it for warmth. This was where my cook Garolinski, helped by a dozen riders, was always busy preparing our food as best they could. Our soldiers were tasked with finding meat and flour: when they found them, he cooked the meat, and made with the flour a kind of large pancake, unfortunately salt was missing. Almost every morning, before our departure, each rider received one of these hot patties and a piece of meat, which was enough for the day. It was not surprising that our cook Garolinski was kept by his comrades like 'the apple of their eyes'.

One day, some officers and I, settled in a room to warm ourselves waiting for a piece of meat that was being cooked for us. The chamber was heating up a little when a terrible smell spread through the room. We found under bales of straw the corpse of a Dutch general.

The whole Neapolitan brigade froze to death in only one night, a little before Wilna. They implored the help of their king, Joachim Murât in stretching out their frozen hands towards him. No one took care of them during the night. After recrossing the Niemen near Kowno, we no longer camped anywhere: we always stopped in small villages. We rested a few days at Elbling, and marching by Thorn we arrived at Posen.

It was in this city that King Murat returned to Prince Eugène the command of the debris of the Grand Army. The prince immediately began the reorganisation of the troops, and sent back to the rear all the men who could no longer serve in the ranks. He noticed that there was more than 10,000 men still in good condition, most of the Old Guard, some Italian companies, and by chance 60 Bavarian cavalrymen, who were added to my squadrons. Those Bavarians bothered us a great deal in times to come with their softness.

Viceroy Eugène received the news that the Russian Army had marched from Plock on Kalisz, and so was then forced to abandon Posen. I was angry to leave this town, thinking that I may not see my native soil again for a long time. At four o'clock in the morning, our last Grand Guards and vedettes withdrew before the enemy and returned to Posen, from where the viceroy and his troops had gone out the day before; at dawn I had sent on the squadrons of the rearguard. As for me, I stayed with a trumpeter and some light horsemen on the market place, leaving twelve Bavarian horsemen of the other side of the bridge, so that the Cossacks would boldly attack such a small number.

I soon saw the Bavarians return by the bridge, followed in the main street by Cossacks and enemy regular cavalry. It was then, with a heavy heart, I beat a retreat, passing in front of the Court of Posen: the Russians stopped when they saw in the market square the Polish lances and pennants. I finally left Posen, with twelve Bavarian horsemen, six light horsemen and a trumpeter, and rejoined my squadrons. It was 8 a.m. on February 12th 1813.

We no longer saw the enemy as far as Magdebourg where the retreat from Russia ended.

Marshal Bessières, who commanded all the cavalry of the Guard, sent me to Frankfurt to receive 2,000 horses offered to the emperor to remount the cavalry of the Guard by the German princes of the Rhine Confederation. The marshal joined me with an officer and some old *maréchals de logis*, of the cavalry regiments of the Guard. The accomplishment of this mission occupied me for several weeks, but this task allowed me to rest a little, because I lived in the same house as my old comrade and friend Tascher, who because of his poor state of health had been appointed Governor of Frankfurt.

Prince Dominique Radziwill, who had served as colonel throughout the Russian campaign with the 8th Regiment of Polish Lancers of the Duchy of Warsaw, was appointed by the emperor, major in the regiment of Polish Light Horse Lancers of the Guard. He took his command of the regiment after the Battle of Leipzig. The regiment received as cantonment the town of Grima, but soon arrived at Friedberg, near Frankfurt; where it was supplemented by 500 men chosen from among the best in General Dombrowski's division, and by the rest of the Lithuanian Lancers of the Guard, who had lost so many men at the Battle of Slonim, including their leader, the General Konopka.

In this way, the cavalry regiment of Light Horse Lancers of the Guard comprised ten squadrons instead of five: six squadrons remained at Friedberg, the other four, which were the ones who had returned from Moscow, had already left in April by Fulde and Weimar under the command of the Prince Dominique Radziwill. I commanded the first two squadrons and Jerzmanowski the other two.

Chapter 39: Saxon Campaign, 1813

The Saxon campaign began on May 1st, 1813. The emperor had come to meet us at Naunbourg and it was on the very next day, May 1st, at Weissenfels that we had our first fight. The enemy cavalry line showed itself on the heights before us accompanied by artillery. The emperor sent Marshal Bessières to reconnoitre with our first squadron. The Russians only fired a few cannon shots at us, but one of them fatally struck Marshal Bessières, who was 30 paces ahead of my squadron; the same cannonball also killed my Chief Quartermaster, Jordan, who coincidentally happened to be on the right flank.

The emperor entrusted Marshal Soult with the command of the Guard. He moved forward that same day, accompanied by us. The enemy cavalry and artillery retreated before us on the beyond Lützen, where the headquarters of the emperor was installed. We camped near the city. On May 2nd, the march was continued towards Leipsig. Prince Eugène and his corps formed the vanguard; behind him marched the Imperial Guard; to our right, the corps of Marshal Ney, which occupied the village of Kaja. Behind the Guard followed Marshal Marmont's corps, and finally the corps of General Bertrand, *aide-de-camp* of the emperor.

Around 10 o'clock in the morning we heard a very heavy cannonade and musket fire coming from behind the village of Kaja. Both the Prussian and Russian Armies suddenly attacked the corps of Marshal Ney, which was composed only of young soldiers. These youngsters could not withstand this vigorous attack of the enemy infantry, supported by light artillery and rapidly abandoned Kaja. All Ney's corps was routed, the young soldiers threw down their weapons, which littered the ground over which we had just arrived. The moment was most critical. The emperor was marching mounted on horseback at the head of the Guard; he sent the order to Prince Eugène to deploy to the right; in this way he would approach the emperor. Napoleon then, turning his horse, gave us the order to follow him at a trot, and ordered the infantry of the Guard who were behind (it was from the Young Guard) and the Artillery of the Guard to follow us.

After half an hour we stopped between the road and the village of Kaja, and there we deployed in line, opposite this village, on the fields among the debris of the Ney's soldiers who were still fleeing. The entire French Army, with its one hundred and twenty thousand men, had marched in column towards Leipzig, where the emperor hoped to find the enemy; he had accordingly prepared to deploy it forward, though it was even easier for him to manoeuvre to deploy it to the right.

All the French corps, by a flank movement moved to the right, while the Guard alone made in half an hour a backsliding movement to stand on the threatened point, *i.e., vis-à-vis* the village of Kaja which was by this time already occupied by the enemy. When we arrived in front of Kaja, we were received by artillery salvoes and by enemy infantry shooting at us from the gardens. The emperor gave the order not to allow Ney's fugitives to pass between our squadrons: they were forced to retreat behind our left wing, that is to say between us and the Young Guard which was advancing.

Consequently, instead of dispersing in the plain, they were forced to escape in a mass through this interval from the cannonballs of the enemy. The last of them in retreat, those who had resisted the longest in the village were, for the most part, officers and non-commissioned officers, all old soldiers: therefore, quite straightforward to reform behind us, because they, though few in number did not throw down their weapons like the youngest soldiers had done.

Our artillery finally arrived: the emperor immediately placed two batteries in position, and formed behind us the Young

Guard in columns. The enemy did not debouch from the village, but put all the houses into a state of defence, and then a thick column of enemy cavalry took up position left of Kaja, so close to us that we could recognise in the front line stood a regiment of *cuirassiers* with a regiment of Black Hussars formed next to it. We distinctly heard the commands that were made to them during the very short intervals where the guns ceased to rumble. We could also notice different movements in the columns placed in rear of these regiments.

We were sure the enemy would ere long throw themselves upon us and attack us with cavalry in numbers sufficient to envelop our right. We were well prepared to receive them, but they had wasted too much time in preparations to deploy and the decisive moment for them passed very quickly. In war, an army commander must make his decisions promptly, because a movement which is advantageous at a given time can become impossible to execute five minutes later. Timely decisions and presence of mind are the *sine qua non* qualities of a leader.

The French batteries followed one another every moment on the battle line. The emperor ordered all the artillery to direct its fire on the village, and he also made me advance my two squadrons by troops on the right. The two other squadrons commanded by Jerzmanowski made the same manoeuvre to the left, leaving an interval between us. The emperor drew his sword, placed himself between the two columns of the Young Guard, and launched them at the village which they entered without a shot being fired; the firing from the gardens had by this time ceased. The enemy cavalry did not move at all. The situation had changed: from the defensive we now went to the offensive. Marshal Marmont's corps appeared in line in the distance, on our right wing.

It is probable that at the sight of the corps of Marmont on the march, the enemy cavalry had stopped to prepare some manoeuvre; the enemy's attack to envelop the French right wing would have had a better chance of success if he had usefully employed this cavalry instead of defending with all its forces the villages of Kaja, Rahna and Görschen, which became their grave a few moments later. The emperor sent us the order to follow on and we passed through the village filled with dead and wounded: in several places these unfortunates, French or enemy alike, were laid pell-mell on top of each other.

We noticed a gigantic Prussian soldier of the Guard and a very young French soldier placed as if they were kissing: one would have said a father and his son, remarked General Lefebvre-Desnouettes who was with the head of my squadron. It was him who had been taken prisoner in Spain by the English. He told me that during his captivity he lived in a small town in central England, where he had found a trader who had prepared his escape for 100 guineas, transporting him to the seaside, from whence a smuggler had brought him to the French coast.

After crossing Kaja, we formed behind the Young Guard which pursued the enemy that was retreating on all sides. Prince Eugène had had more difficulties on our left wing. He had in front of him a Russian corps commanded by Wittgenstein, which began to withdraw only when he saw the Young Guard keenly pursuing the Prussian corps and when the artillery attacked it from the flank.

The entire enemy line was then in retreat in front of us; the enemy cavalry, on our wing right, also withdrew, pursued by Marmont's marines, and further to the right by the corps of General Bertrand. We had only 2,400 cavalry left; the emperor did not want to use them, so as not to further reduce their number; but it is very strange that the enemy cavalry, which was so numerous, did nothing to take advantage of the situation.

At dusk, Napoleon ordered all the corps to halt, but to remain under arms. Before it was quite nightfall, we saw the enemy cavalry also halt, while the infantry continued its retreat. The night became dark and the artillery stopped shooting. General Lefebvre-Desnouettes approached me and told me to follow him with a squadron. We walked past our infantry who were 1,000 paces from the enemy; I accompanied the general a few paces before the squadron, when we saw our right something that looked like a line of troops. A strip of sky which was a little clearer on the horizon allowed us to distinguish them despite

THE BATTLE OF LÜTZEN

the darkness.

The general ordered us to stop, and I went further in this direction with Lieutenant Leski of the first troop, to see better. Advancing from 200 to 250 paces, we distinctly perceived this line, and we heard the sound of cavalry on the march, and the commands *"Halte! poste!."*

Having thus assured ourselves that this line was of enemy cavalry, we returned quickly towards the squadron, when we saw, on the left, a rider standing beside his horse. Arriving near him, I recognised him by his helmet for a Russian or a Prussian (both had similar helmets). I grabbed the reins of his horse, and the soldier, who seemed to me a little drunk, shouted at me: *"Wer da?"* These two words sufficed to recognise his nationality, and I ordered him to mount and us. I held the bridle of the Prussian's horse, Leski stood on the other side. This man did not resist, but he wanted to explain why he had left his ranks and dismounted. I told him to be silent, and although drunk, he seemed to understand that he had to be quiet.

When we got close to General Lefebvre, who stood with his *aide-de-camp* at 10 or 15 paces ahead of the squadron, I questioned my prisoner: I asked him what his regiment was. He replied that he belonged to the 1st Brandenburg Cuirassier Regiment.

"Where is your regiment?", I asked.

"It should not be more than a hundred paces away", he responded, "for it was only a moment ago that I left it."

When I translated these questions and these answers to General Lefebvre, he drew his sword, exclaiming quite loudly:

"Oh! Ah! they want to throw themselves on us unexpectedly. Let's go! Let's attack them! They won't be able to see our numbers us in the dark!"

But at the same instant, the emperor, who had followed the squadron with some officers without our knowledge, showed up in front of General Lefebvre, heard him speak, and called him saying:

"Lefebvre, you are always the same, always mad! Let the squadron stay where it is!"

Then he ordered me to question the Prussian *cuirassier* further. The prisoner, who had us finally recognised us, took fright despite his drunkenness and answered us quite clearly "that towards midnight, twenty cavalry regiments were to throw themselves on the French line."

The emperor made us withdraw, and we returned accompanying him behind the line of infantry who was still under arms. The emperor immediately sent the order over the whole line that each division should send 100 paces forward, in the greatest silence, an infantry battalion, which would then form a square and stay in place.

Before midnight we heard before us the sound of enemy cavalry; it lasted no more than five minutes, when one of our squares on the right opened fire. The sound of horsemen grew louder in front of us, but the infantry square on the right was the only one which had fired. The fire in this first square frightened our horses so that it was necessary to reform the squadrons. A cavalry attack at night almost never succeeds, because the slightest line of infantry is enough to stop it, and forces the cavalry to retire in disorder. It's probably what happened to the Russian-Prussian cavalry. Such an attack should be performed one hour before daylight, to take advantage of the enemy's disorder if it succeeds.

That day, the emperor, not having enough cavalry on hand, had been unable to place grand guards and vedettes, nor send patrols ahead of the entire infantry line; that is why he had ordered the entire first line of infantry to remain under the arms; perhaps he had also been informed by a spy of the intentions the enemy. At two o'clock in the morning, he had the first line of infantry rest, because the second line and the reserve had already taken a few hours of rest. The second line remained under arms from two o'clock until morning.

We also left our position in the early hours of the morning and followed the emperor to Lützen: we camped near the town, at the same place where we had spent the previous night. But we didn't stay there long, because at daybreak we accompanied the emperor who was leaving Lützen. We crossed Kaja again, and rejoined the infantry already marching on Pegau by the main road, a shorter to go to Dresden than the road to Leipzig.

Our march on Dresden was distinguished almost every day by small fights between our vanguard and the enemy rearguard. We sometimes found ourselves in a position on heights from which we saw these engagements clearly. These fights were really extraordinary: on our side there was only infantry to fight, on the enemy side that of cavalry. The infantry advanced in columns preceded by its skirmishers, who never saw too far ahead, because of the presence of numerous enemy cavalry and the cloud of Cossacks who were operating there.

The French infantry was still marching in this order almost without stopping, and when the enemy showed his numerous artillery, the column unfolded without ceasing to advance. Between the battalions were guns, which, when the occasion was favourable, deployed to shoot at the enemy who had seemed to change his retreat to an offensive.

It would certainly have been much better to place cavalry in the vanguard; however, this march from Lützen to Dresden, then to Bautzen, proves that it is not necessary to put so much cavalry in the vanguard as usually employed, and where often we lose it by using it too much. It is necessary that the cavalry be always on the alert, the horses always saddled: but it has been demonstrated by the hard work that the cavalry was put to during the Russian campaign how the mounted arm can be readily compromised.

King Murat always had on hand in his vanguard a large cavalry presence, and often it was entirely obliged to stop for the simple crossing of a wood, when it was occupied by a few hundred enemy foot gunners; it was necessary to call upon the services of a battalion of French infantry to clear the passage. During the march to Bautzen, the infantry did not suffer much contrary to the popular conception that it would, although it formed the vanguard without cavalry; it lost a few men as a consequence of artillery fire, but enemy cavalry attacks upon it had no success anywhere.

To conclude these reflections on the vanguard duties of the infantry, I have to anticipate future events. After the Battles of

Bautzen and Hanau, the infantry was not employed by way of a vanguard. General of Division Maison stopped in front of Hanau, instead behind the city, covering itself with a few weak high guards and sentinels, formed the guns in groups and scattered the men to seek provisions in the city. The enemy cavalry, covered by a nearby forest, threw himself suddenly on the sentinels and the main guards, cut them to pieces, got as far as the batteries, slashed their guards and then withdrew. The loss in men was not great, but this surprise had a detrimental influence on the morale of the infantry.

This incident would never have happened if the division had halted behind the town, had sent ahead of it a battalion to occupy the outer houses, covering it naturally by high guards and sentries. When the *avant-garde* cannot settle next to a town or a village, and circumstances force it to cross them and take forward positions, it is necessary to only send men in detachments looking for food, wood and straw. But the French Army never knew how to keep guard.

I repeat here that we must not propose in principle that an *avant-garde* does not need cavalry; during these marches it was necessity which forced the infantry to provide the *avant-garde* duty alone. It is much better to have enough cavalry to employ it as guards, *vedettes*, and especially on patrols and reconnaissances, but for this duty there is no need to have so many horsemen employed.

In my opinion, we should keep in reserve the greater part of the cavalry, to operate in support during the battle and to unleash it for the pursuit after a victory. I do not ask to spare the cavalry; on the contrary, I advise to use it with force, but only when the situation of the fight and the moment is propitious. I do not ask that during the battle we hold far back, we must be behind the infantry, close or to its side if the terrain requires it, so that we are always ready to pounce on the enemy and destroy him at any moment, as soon as the favourable occasion arises.

It is true that cannon and the musket fire costs more cavalrymen if they are on the line. But experience also showed that cavalry which remained for several hours exposed to enemy fire charged the enemy with much more vigour, despite the losses that it had suffered. So, I don't want to put the cavalry under cover from fire, but simply not to damage it by unnecessary exposure and marching. The French have never been able to prudently spare their cavalry. With the exception of the Saxony campaign, they always put too many horse soldiers to the fore-front, sent on patrols and on reconnaissance; thus, they spoiled their horses and lost too many people, especially to the Cossacks, who were accustomed to setting up ambushes and very adept at vanguard warfare.

We entered Dresden, into the old town, on May 8th, without encountering any obstacles. The bridge over the Elbe was half destroyed; on the other side of the bridge, in the new town, the Russians had placed cannons and were firing at whatever ap-peared in front of them.

The emperor ordered his ordinance officer Caraman to bring a battery from the Guard to the banks of the Elbe. It was really a pleasure to see him manage officers and gunners and make their arrangements. Barely had our battery fired three or four rounds from their six guns that great disorder was seen among the Rus-sians across the river. In one half hour their guns and their troops had faded away.

On the left side of Dresden were the French engineering troops; they threw another bridge under the protection of 60 guns which General Drouot put in battery on the heights of Prüsnitz. The same day we repaired the partially destroyed bridge (only one arch had fallen), by means of wooden beams. On the 10th, the corps of Prince Eugene crossed the bridge and set off towards Bautzen; he was followed by Marshal Marmont's corps. The emperor followed the same route with the Guard after the return of the King of Saxony from Prague, where he had gone into hiding upon the arrival of the Russians.

We travelled from Dresden to Bautzen on the same day, the 18th, whilst the emperor rode on horseback and spent almost all the night traversing the line of the main guards and vedettes, to discern the positions of the enemy from his bivouac fires. The emperor thought the enemy would defend the advantageous positions it occupied near to Bautzen, because the city was easy to put into a defensive state. On the left are heights and, on the right, begin the small mountains that separate Saxony from Bohemia.

The emperor ordered all arrangements for the next day's battle, requiring all corps to make a forward movement in concert. Marshal Oudinot advanced on the right, Marmont in the centre opposite Bautzen, whilst Marshal Ney went to Hoyerswerda with the order to debouch on our left wing of the side of Bautzen. All the corps set off, the Imperial Guard in the middle, though we couldn't see the enemy, except for small detachments of *uhlans* and a swarm of retreating Cossacks; their artillery and the infantry remained invisible. We passed Bautzen on the left, crossing the Spree at that time when it was almost dry, and half a league beyond Bautzen we saw the enemy lines near Hochkirch.

Chapter 40: Bautzen

Evening came on ; at sunset the emperor returned to Bautzen where his quarters were established in the Bishopric. As soon as we entered the city following him, we were given tickets to indicate our billets; we settled our horses in their stables, unsaddled, with the exception of the duty squadron, lived thereafter as though we were in full peace. The inhabitants cooked us supper in their houses. It was the first time that we enjoyed such pleasant comfort so close to the enemy; but we had the security of being guarded by our infantry who were in position half a league from the town. At that moment we were employed very sparingly, indeed we were almost pampered since we were among the handful of cavalry that remained in the French Army after the disaster of the Russian campaign.

We were ordered to saddle our horses and have them ready at 4 o'clock in the morning. But we only left Bautzen to escort the emperor at around 7 o'clock. All the cavalry of the Guard, that is to say four regiments of everything, was placed on a dominant height, so that the enemy could see us from Hochkirch. We formed the centre and putting in communication the left wing and the right wing, because the emperor commanded from the centre on the left the corps of Marshal Marmont and the cavalry of General Latour-Maubourg; Marshal Ney had, in fact, sent to inform d'Hoyerswerda that he had encountered bad roads and could arrive on the line only around noon.

On receiving this news, the emperor postponed the attack of the infantry, but the cannonade did not cease, and on our right wing, in the mountains and in the middle the skirmishers' fire continued unabated creating disruption on one side or the

The Battle of Bautzen

other. It was to the sound of this artillery music and of roll of musketry that the emperor lay down on unfolded coat on the ground and gave the order not to wake him until two hours had elapsed; he slept most peacefully in front of us. During these two hours, we heard continually on our right wing, in the mountains, the whistling of bullets and balls from a dozen cannons that the French had brought there. The enemy had on this point more guns than us, for he had plenty of time to prepare them to receive us. In the centre, only the guns in front us were shooting and we also heard a fire weak enough to be skirmishers in the ravines.

From time to time, we received cannonballs from our enemies. About fifteen arrived and could be seen ricocheting, but also rolling towards us without much speed and without doing us any harm. A shell fell near to the emperor. About one o'clock the 7th Regiment of Lancers arrived, members of the Vistula Legion. This was an old Polish regiment, which had taken part in all the campaigns in Italy, and then returned from Spain thereafter after being brought up to strength at Sedan with cadres and horsemen sent from the Polish corps which was on the banks of the Rhine. The leader of this regiment was General Stokowski, former leader of the Light Horse squadrons of the Guard. He had stayed in Sedan to train two squadrons, and at this time the regiment was commanded by Colonel Tanski. We placed it on our left wing, extending the line of the Guard cavalry.

Napoleon was still sleeping peacefully when the orderly officer, Bérenger arrived from Marshal Ney, bringing the news that the corps of the marshal, after having traversed sandy roads, had come out on the right wing of the enemy, which was placed on a height which had been fortified with entrenchments, as we could clearly see.

Marshal Duroc, who was walking near of the emperor, did not want to wake him before the two hours had past, because everyone was accustomed to meticulously execute his orders. He looked at his watch and said, "Another twenty minutes!" Those twenty minutes had not yet passed when loud artillery detonations were made near the Russian positions at our left wing; we could see not only the smoke, but even the flashes of the bursts. This cannonade started so suddenly that the emperor woke up crying: "It's Ney attacking!" He mounted his horse, sent his orderly officers to all marshals with the order to advance, and added: "In an hour, victory will be ours."

But he was wrong in his prediction of time, for after an hour had elapsed the right wing of the enemy still held in place, the fire did not cease and seemed, on the contrary, to increase.

The emperor sent his officers to Ney nearly every ten minutes one after another; none came back. He took up position about 50 paces ahead of us. I walked a little closer, because from this point we could see the situation better. The emperor looked around him, and seeing no more orderly officers but seeing me, he called me, cursing: "Quick, Klaposki! (this is how the emperor and all the Frenchmen pronounced my name), go to Ney, and tell him to hurry up, that he must attack with all his might! Marmont is already close to his right wing to support him."

I found Marshal Ney in the heart of the fire, in the midst of repulsed infantry columns and attempting to form them again. The first columns whom I met were Württembergers, retreating in great disorder, then French columns also in retreat, but in better order. I repeated to the marshal the words of the emperor. Marshal Ney answered me, swearing:

Tell the emperor that I have Russians in front of me. If I had Prussians, there I would have removed the position long ago. Now I only want to employ French soldiers; I am going to send back the allied troops, they are useless against the Russians.

At this moment the four reserve columns were already advancing, composed only of French infantry, and they exceeded those which had been repelled. The marshal went in front of everyone, saluting them with his hat and animating them with warm words. The grenadier companies were placed in the lead columns, bayonets forward, without firing a shot, advancing as fast as they could on higher ground. Many of them fell, but the fire upon them didn't last long. They were about 200 paces from the summit and Russian batteries when the fire ceased; arriving at the top, they found the trenches empty. We immediately went to the summit, from where we had a grand view. We had no more business behind the village of Weissenberg than the last men of the Russian columns; they had left their positions half an hour previously. Their guns followed them at a trot, and in the plain that stretched between us and Weissenberg, the enemy cavalry approximately 6,000 horses, placed on two lines, covered the retreat of the artillery.

The Russians therefore withdrew in time to lose only a few men; their leader, General Wittgenstein, had judged in good time that the French were going to seize his positions, and that the corps of Marshal Marmont, which advanced towards the village of Boschwitz, had gone to fall on his left flank.

In attacking a position, there are two periods. During the first, the attacker loses many people from the fire of the defence, which he would be wrong to answer. In the second, the defender, if he stubbornly defends its position, loses even more people, because the soldiers attacking it, after seizing the position, have such moral superiority despite the losses suffered they overthrow everything that stands in their way. Russians executed the first part of this defence well, and cautiously avoided the second. They withdrew on time, in perfect order, behind a screen a numerous cavalry, against which we had nothing to retaliate.

I returned to my regiment, which I found on the march following the emperor towards Hochkirch. I did not see the necessity of reporting to him; from the place where I had left him, he had seen himself everything that had happened to Marshal Ney. It was already getting dark when we arrived at Hochkirch. We couldn't therefore not easily distinguish the trenches that the enemy had built in front of this village, and that he had abandoned when his right wing withdrew. We stopped to camp on the left of Hochkirch, near a village where we prepared the imperial headquarters.

The next day we set off again to accompany the emperor to Gorlitz. At after two hours we heard before us musketry shots and cannon fire. Marshal Soult soon came towards us, having had command of the cavalry of the guard since the death of Marshal Bessières; he ordered General Walther to march to the right with the cavalry of the Guard, and to advance on the heights where he had found the Russian rearguard, defending the passage of the small village of Reichenbach. Once we arrived on the height, we had to make half-turn to the left and throw ourselves on the flank of the enemy to force him to retire.

Chapter 41: Reichenbach

We immediately set off to the right across fields, riding at a trot as long as possible; at half a league we came to a deep ditch edged with trees on both sides: we had to stop to cross it two by two. When my two squadrons had passed, General Lefebvre-Desnouettes who was marching at our head gave me the order to move forward and to drive out the Cossacks, a swarm of which had gathered in front of us. I deployed my two squadrons, and advanced upon them at a walk: the Cossacks retreated, firing their guns on us as they fled. We thus advanced 300 paces, while Jerzmanowski's two squadrons crossed the ditch.

We came to another ditch, but less deep. The Cossacks stopped there and, sheltered by the trees, directed at us a heavier fire, letting us get close to them; but they still withdrew upon seeing us crossing the ditch in two places. After having crossed it, we saw behind the Cossacks a line of regular enemy cavalry. I carried on for 50 paces, and recognised four squadrons, two of dragoons in the middle, two of *uhlans* on both wings. When my two squadrons, after their passage, had reformed in line, I went forward with them, at a walk. General Lefebvre rushed towards me telling me to charge at once; it was not a formal order, for he added that he had confidence in me.

On a formal order from my leader, I would have ordered: "At the trot!" then "At a Gallop!" without adding the command "March!" because we know from experience that movements are not executed on the field of battle as during a review where, after the preparatory command: "At the gallop", one gives the execution command: "March!"

We were about 500 paces from the enemy. I said to the general: "Allow me, my general, to advance again at a walk for another 150 steps, though I will not immediately make the command: 'March!' and I assure you that I will sink their centre."

He consented and returned to Jerzmanowski's squadrons who were finishing crossing the ditch. We walked in step again for 300 paces, but I warned my squadrons that when I would shout to them: "March! March!" they would have to go 'belly to earth', as we say meaning 'flat out' but not to lower their lances except in the faces of the dragoons. We still marched slowly, and arrived so close to the enemy horsemen that we heard the voices of their officers probably addressing their men, saying to them: "*Szutka*" (It's a joke!).

We weren't 200 paces from them when I shouted, "March! March!" and in the blink of an eye we fell on their line. The captain Jankowski (later he became a general in 1830), was on my right, Gielgud (elder brother of the general of the same name in 1830) rode to my left; the horse of this the latter reared up at arriving on the dragoons, and at the same moment an officer of dragoons brought him such a blow in the stomach that he fell off his horse; he died a few weeks later.

This affair only lasted a few seconds. The dragoons had held up well in the first moment, but they became disorganised and began to flee; the *uhlans* did the same, without having anyone ahead of them. I couldn't see how many of our enemies were lying on the ground, for I passed over them so quickly; my two squadrons did not pursue the enemy, for the best mounted light horsemen had passed the enemy horsemen who rode the worst horses, and brought them down. Soon I saw a second line of *uhlans* advancing on us: I stopped, and I had just given my men the order to reform, when these *uhlans* charged, before we were in line. We formed quickly however and I could command: "Forward, march!"; though other *uhlans* were falling on our halted riders. They fired at us: we barely noticed it, because such a fire, made from horseback, has no effect on old soldiers. So, I moved away and ordered immediately: "March! March!".

The Russian *uhlans*, in their galloping charge, became a little separated, but this time their attack merged with ours; they out-

SKIRMISH WITH HUSSARS

POLISH LANCERS IN COMBAT WITH UHLANS

numbered us and the action was about to turn to their advantage, had not Jerzmanowski arrived at that moment with his two squadrons. He was certainly the most experienced officer in the regiment, full of courage and coolness. He arrived just in time to charge the enemy on our left, first approaching at a walk, then charging it vigorously over a short distance. The *uhlans* immediately turned about and ran away, though fifteen of them stayed in our hands. Some, seriously hurt, groaned and addressed us in Polish which made a very painful impression upon me.

One of them was defending himself with his sword, refusing to surrender, but one of my light horsemen shouted to him: "Brother! we are Poles like you!" He then threw down his sword. We believe that someone had told them we were French dressed as Polish Lancers. In the middle of the fray, a Cossack came towards me, I do not know where from. He was old with a big beard.

Since he was on foot, he seized the reins of my horse with one hand and tried with the other to strike me with the butt of his gun. At the same time, a *uhlan* officer was throwing himself upon me with his sabre in an attempt to kill me. I parried his blow with my own sabre and fortunately the Cossack did not have time to complete his own assault before he fell, pierced by the lance of one of my men, Jaworski, who received the Cross of the Legion of Honour for having saved my life. I met this brave man later on at Maluszyn.

We never saw these *uhlans* again. Our four squadrons then lined up. We were still far from the *Chasseurs à Cheval* of the Guard who were pouring over the ditches to follow us; General Lefebvre made us halt. Suddenly we saw another regiment of Russian *uhlans* who had replaced the one we had bested, and it advanced towards us in line and at 500 steps from us they galloped to attack us.

General Lefebvre, who was talking in front of our squadrons with Jerzmanowski and me, wanted us charge this regiment. Jerzmanowski, who had known Lefebvre-Desnouettes for a long time; told him that it was not worth charging the Russians, that they had galloped from too far distant, would soon become disunited and would consequently not reach us. Indeed, we soon saw their line had overextended; about a hundred of them were galloping ahead of the others and the most part of them actually stopped: none came closer than about 100 paces from us apart from ten of them.

General Lefebvre-Desnouettes launched two troops deployed as foragers upon them, and soon our horsemen brought us six of these *uhlans*, who as usual were probably the worst mounted. We recognised then they were Cossacks from the Ukraine. One of them, with a strong Russian accent, told us in good Polish, that they were four regiments of the same troops, commanded by General Witt, and that this general was not present at the battle.

Seeing these Cossacks disperse, having formed to charge so far from us, we concluded that they were young recruits, probably commanded by officers of the same category; I must add again that they were fighting against us most reluctantly. I learned later that these regiments had been originally formed the previous year by the Polish nobility resident in the Ukraine to make common cause with French Army that had marched on Moscow; but when the balance tipped in favour of the Russians, these same Polish nobles, so that they might be be forgiven by the Russians, offered the Emperor Alexander these four regiments. Willingly or unwillingly, the sons of Ukraine dispersed before us, and we had no more trouble from them later and rarely from any others apart from the Cossacks of the Don.

General Walther, personally offered me his congratulations on the charges we had executed and thereafter we made a U-turn by troops to the left, and walked uphill to the position occupied by the Russian rearguard to prevent infantry from entering Reichenbach. This rearguard was commanded by General Miloradowitch. There were 40 guns there, including those shooting directly down the only street of the town, so that the French infantry could not move from cover behind the houses.

Jerzmanowski moved first to the top of the edge with our left wing, and immediately formed his squadrons in line; I deployed my squadrons on the right. When Jerzmanowski appeared with his two squadrons, the Russians turned a portion of their guns upon him, and also on my men before I could put them fully in position. A regiment of Russian hussars presented themselves at the same time a few hundred paces to our right, which forced me to make a change of front, and face them with my two squadrons.

But, by making this change of front to the right, we exposed our flank, so that the Russian shells were aligned with our ranks, and this cost us in ten minutes more men than had been lost in our previous charges. Jerzmanowski's squadrons arriving on the line to our left, were closer to the guns and lost even more people than us, but we charged without delay at the hussars, who, 60 paces from us turned about, to the right and dispersed backwards at top speed; they probably eventually stopped in front of their kitchen line. Russian *cuirassiers*, then crossed over their front line and formed before it.

The *Chasseurs* of the Guard arrived at their position in front of Russian guns. The dragoons and the grenadiers of the Guard remained in line behind the height, but, as I learned later, they nevertheless lost more people than we did. The reason why this happened can be explained by the fact that the Russians most often shot ricochets. Cannonballs and shells fell to the ground in front of us, but then ricocheted over our heads, and were finally falling most often behind the mound among the troops ostensibly sheltering there.

Before manoeuvring, we had formed our four squadrons in line, not placed on the very top of the rise, but a little lower beyond it, for it stood between us and the Russians upon the plain. I approached Jerzmanowski and had barely left my place before three cannonballs came to fall exactly on the place I had just vacated, one after another, and all of them thereafter ricocheted away, singing away above the squadrons. The *chasseurs à cheval* who replaced us while we charged the Russian hussars, also lost fewer people than the dragoons and Grenadiers of the Guard.

The *chasseurs* of the Guard were not long in coming to our aid, General Walther having probably glimpsed the enemy *cuirassier* line in front of us. First came the Mamelukes, who formed the first squadron of *chasseurs a cheval,* they passed to our left and immediately advanced towards the Russian *cuirassiers*. The commander of these *cuirassiers* could not suppose that a single squadron was going to pounce on a brigade, because it was clear that there were two lines of *cuirassiers*. The Mamelukes advanced at a walk; at 50 paces or even less, they unloaded their carbines upon the enemy; the right wing of the *cuirassiers* promptly fled disrupting the formation of the entire regiment. It was about then that our squadrons came close to these *cuirassiers*, but we didn't have to attack them, for they were already retreating in disorder onto their second line.

We then received the order to return to our first position, that is to say in front of that occupied by Miloradowitch. In our place came the regiment of Saxon *cuirassiers*, with yellow collars, which I did not know. It had to be comprised of newly trained recruits, because their officers could not maintain them in this position, so we had to go and replace them. The guns of Miloradowitch redoubled their fire to cover the retreat of the Russians.

Hardly had we replaced the Saxons, than a shower of cannon-balls and shells fell around us, but fortunately very few of them fell into our ranks. A shell exploded between Captain Jankowski and me; shrapnel struck the captain lightly in the thigh; I was also quite seriously bruised on the right arm, but I did not dismount immediately, I waited the end of the battle. Behind us was placed the cavalry of General Latour-Maubourg, between us and the French infantry and Saxons which had debouched from Reichenbach. This division lost some men from artillery fire, without however approaching the enemy.

General Miloradowitch retired. His guns paraded at a trot in the middle of its infantry. The French infantry was already coming out of Reichenbach. French skirmishers covered the heights. We soon lost sight of the Russian infantry; a few guns, escorted by cavalry, were still shooting at us from time to time, when the emperor, accompanied by us, started towards Görlitz. One of the last cannon shots mortally wounded Marshal Duroc who was close to the emperor.

Napoleon could have entered Görlitz this same day, but Duroc was almost dying; so he ordered everyone to stop where they were, had the tents pitched in that place, and spent almost the whole night with the marshal who died during the night. We were ordered to camp near a forest, close to the imperial tents. The whole cavalry of the Guard was gathered around the bivouac of the emperor.

When I wanted to dismount, gripping my saddle with the right hand, I felt a sharp pain in the arm. The next day I could not shave, and I had to employ a hand foreign to the task, while I had the injured arm wrapped in bandages. But in the evening, I was consoled, because the generals of the Guard, Walther, Lefebvre-Desnouettes, Le Fort, had come to see me in camp, and congratulated me on the charges we had executed. I was really delighted when they addressed me the following words: "If someone is braver than us, if someone fights better than us, it is you!" It is necessary to possess a well-mannered sense of one's own courage, so as to give first place to another.

The Battle of Reichenbach was fought on May 22nd, 1813; it remained memorable because the French cavalry, despite its huge numerical inferiority, transpired to be a principal asset.

The next day we crossed Görlitz, then continuing our way towards Buntzlau, we went into camp near Waldau. On the 25th we approached Buntzlau; the 26th we passed through Hanau, where the Prussian cavalry had assaulted the division of General Maison, who had placed his infantry in a very reckless situation.

Chapter 42: Hanau

General Maison had camped his entire division before the little town of Hanau, and, after letting the infantry pile its arms, allowed them to scatter in the city to look for provisions and straw. There were only 200 armed men left, in full guards and sentinels. The Prussian Army cavalry laid a trap for him, taking advantage that it was covered by the woods to the left of the road to Hanau. The Prussians could have seen from there that the French had not kept watch. They fell on the grand guards and sentries, slashed at them, dispersed them and fled.

This attack would never have succeeded, if General Maison, had placed the camp in front of the city, occupying the outer houses with a battalion, and had placed, in default of cavalry, the grand guards and the sentries at a short distance around his division. We arrived a few hours after this attack. There were about 150 men killed or wounded and many broken guns, because during this attack, the soldiers of the train had been leading their horses to the drinking troughs.

We camped that day in front of Hanau, where the emperor arrived on the 28th. He formed all the infantry into two columns of battalions, that is to say over the width of a front of battalion. The cavalry and the artillery were marching in the centre with him, and it's in this order which we pursued for two leagues our march on Liegnitz. The display was truly magnificent to see these 100,000 men walking on a plain so wide that one can could see both columns perfectly.

As we arrived near Liegnitz, the emperor gave the order to Marshal Soult to put himself at the head of the cavalry of the Guard and to go around the city from the right to capture some enemy troops, if the enemy had made his retreat by this road. So here we were at a trot to the right. South of Liegnitz is a long village that we had to pass through. This village was divided by a stream, which we had to traverse upon a fairly narrow bridge. This obstacle lengthened our column significantly so it was only after crossing the village with my two squadrons and taking the trot immediately after leaving it, that I moved away from our column and noticed a few enemy cavalry, separated from the others, retreating before us.

When we came closer to them, I saw they were four squadrons formed in line. I immediately formed my own men and we had barely stopped arranging ourselves when I saw these four squadrons advancing at the trot, their trumpets sounding the charge. I advanced in step to receive them. The commander of our opponents was surely an inexperienced officer, for hardly had they finished ringing the charge, that his trumpets sounded: Stop! He gave the signal: Turn back, and they were beginning to trot away when we fell on them.

Quite naturally, they scattered. The worst mounted riders fell into our hands: we could have willingly taken more of them if their infantry had not been so close in columns. However, they also did not stop to take issue with us, on the contrary they withdrew with more haste than we had ever seen the Prussian infantry flee before.

These troops were withdrawing from Liegnitz to Javsorz. Perhaps we could have taken this entire infantry division (according to our prisoners), if the rest of our regiment and the *chasseurs à cheval* had been able to cross the village expeditiously. We camped and spent the night where we had made our prisoners, who belonged to the Prussian guard. There was among them hussars, dragoons, and some Berlin Cossacks, wearing beards actually longer than those of the Don Cossacks; in all about 150 men.

On May 30th, we made a reconnaissance towards Jaworz under the command of General Flahaut, *aide-de-camp* to the emperor. Marshal Marmont also led his corps on this village, but by another road to our right. A league from Liegnitz, we saw

Cossacks before us. General Flahaut climbed up a windmill and recognized some regiments of Cossacks, and behind them other numerous cavalry. He had, he told me, an order from the emperor to communicate with Marshal Marmont, but seeing the impossibility of us making our way through this enemy cavalry with my two squadrons, I made him the proposition that he should write in pencil what he had to say to Marmont from the emperor, and that I would send two of my light horsemen who spoke German during the night to Marshal Marmont having first crossed through enemy lines.

Fortunately, these two messengers arrived at Marshal Marmont's headquarters and were back with us at the end three days with a receipt from the marshal; they joined us two leagues from Breslau where the French *avant-guard* had entered under the command of Marshal Ney.

The emperor remained with us at Neumarck. There I received the order to accompany the grand equerry Caulaincourt to the *château* of Leuthen, then to Pleiswitz, where he was attempting to negotiate for peace with General Schouwalow.

Chapter 43: Resignation

We stopped in the yard and dismounted. With General Schouwalow were a few hundred Cossacks, who also dismounted from their horses. We talked with their officers; they told us in which houses they had stopped in during their march through Poland and mentioned some families I knew. I addressed myself to the colonel of the Cossacks and asked him if he would be kind enough to send a letter to my father by post from Russian headquarters, a letter which I would give him unsealed. He promised to do so, telling me to write the letter, to seal it, but not to put upon it an address, that he would put it on himself with his own hand, so no one would open the letter.

Having entered the *château*, I asked the secretary to the emperor (Baron Fain), who accompanied Caulaincourt to give me some paper and so I could write my letter. I was alone in the room with the secretary (Caulaincourt had gone into the next room with Schouwalow and the Prussian General Kleist). So, it came about that Fain showed me the proposals for the peace treaty between Napoleon and Alexander of Russia.

Napoleon's first proposal was to offer to Alexander the whole of the Duchy of Warsaw, with the choice to take the title of King of Poland or to incorporate the duchy into the Russian Empire. The emperor's secretary considered me quite like a Frenchman rather than a Pole, because he had seen me for some years close to the emperor; so, he could not guess the terrible trauma which took place in my heart at the sight of this proposition.

So as not to betray the confusion of my thoughts, I went out and I remained so absorbed in myself that I only came to myself when the colonel of Cossacks asked me for the letter for my father. I gave it to him with a note bearing the address. This letter arrived safely.

The Cossacks were always polite to us, as if they had not forgotten that they had been formerly allies of the Poles.

It was not a peace that was signed, as the emperor had wanted, but merely an armistice. We returned to Dresden. This is where I wrote my request for resignation which I sent to the Marshal Soult. He was very surprised and tried to persuade to stay in the service. I didn't want to compromise the secretary Fain, by revealing how I knew about the proposals made by the emperor to conclude peace, because they had been shown to me under the seal of secrecy.

However, I did communicate my knowledge of the contents of the proposal to Captain Jordan, to whom I was bound by a close friendship, and to General Chlopicki. This gentleman, after having sworn vehemently as usual, added: "That he would rather break stones than continue to serve such a man!" Both also gave their resignations shortly afterwards.

When I received the acceptance of the resignation that I had sent to Marshal Soult, I began *en route* to Paris. I took advantage of the hospitality of my childhood friends Caraman, and in their home in Paris. I fell there seriously ill in consequence of the two painful campaigns I had just completed and lay in bed for some months. Very few of those who took part in the Russian campaign were fortunate enough to avoid the putrid fever which attacked its victims sometimes after a year and more.

Peace was signed in Paris. The province of Posen (later Grand Duchy), returned to the Prussia, but the Russians still occupied it. I left Paris for England, with the resolution to wait there until the Russians had left Posen, because I learned that the Russian governor general forced all Poles to give the oath of allegiance to the Emperor Alexander and I preferred escape this painful formality.

I spent the winter of 1814 to 1815 in London. I was there during the English parliamentary session. They were just debating the law on wheat, which was advantageous and at this time necessary for landowners, but the inhabitants of the cities and especially the owners of factories were stubbornly opposed to it. They succeeded several times in provoking violent demonstrations among the people of London: several thousand inhabitants assembled, smashing the windows of the houses of the deputies who voted for the law, and those of the palace of ministers.

The whole city of London looked like it was in a state of revolution. Once, in wanting to see the gatherings up close, I was forced to hide on a staircase, tight against the door, so as not to be taken away by the crowd which filled the street carrying flags with the inscriptions:"Down with the law! Down with the ministers!" They carried in triumph a Mr. Bardett, favourite of the people, who voted against the law.

The cavalry of the English guard and the 10th Hussars camped in the streets, sending a squadron on to the squares where the people broke the windows and tried to penetrate the houses of deputies. Always, in front of each squadron marched a constable, carrying a white cane, and when the people massed to destroy the house of a deputy or a minister, he was reading the law on insurgencies, called the Riot Act. He was reading this act first, then a second time, in the middle screams so loud you couldn't hear them: but when he began the third reading, there was hardly anyone on the street, all had dispersed.

They knew very well that after this third reading the cavalry would surely fall upon them. In the evening in front of the Parliament, the people manhandled upon their arrival the deputies in favour of the law: they were forced to enter through the doors at the rear. This freedom of protest made an extraordinary impression on me. The people also let quietly pass everyone who was not a deputy. I had met a few deputies and often dined with them around seven o'clock, during deliberations; the restaurant for members of parliament stood in the same building as the session hall.

One day we were talking about Poland. It was known that England, France and Austria wanted the Duchy of Warsaw to retain its autonomy and did not want to allow the Russia to take over this part of Poland. I received a special invitation to attend the deliberation on the question of Poland. In the House

CHLAPOWSKI IN OLD AGE

of Commons is a stand reserved for foreigners authorised by the speaker to attend the sessions. We didn't talk much that day; we only explained the state of affairs, that is to say the state of the peace negotiations in Vienna.

I was visiting the city of Bath at the home of Caraman's sister, the Marquise de Sommery, when the news of the landing of Napoleon at Fréjus following his escape from exile on Elba reached me. Knowing the spirit of the French Army, I had no doubt that it would almost entirely rally to Napoleon. I returned to Paris, where I had left my carriage, my wardrobe and three Polish servants, but I left town on March 20th in the morning; Napoleon made his return there as emperor on the same day, at eight o'clock of the evening.

Before my departure, I saw several French officers, my old acquaintances, arriving in Paris the day before: they told me how all the French troops had gone over to the emperor.

I learned on my arrival in Metz that Marshal Oudinot had just returned there from Nancy. I went to pay him a visit, because he had always been very kind to me. I found him in his bed. He told me with sadness that he had received the order to lead the Old Guard, whose command had been entrusted to him by King Louis XVIII with Metz as its garrison, and to join Marshal Ney at Troyes. He also told me that Marshal Ney had begged Louis XVIII to entrust him with the command of the French Army to repel Napoleon.

During his march towards Troyes the Marshal Oudinot learned that his grenadiers rejoiced to join their emperor. When he was convinced that they would not be turned against Napoleon, he ordered a counter-march and wanted to bring them back to Metz: but the head of the grenadier column refused to obey, the old grenadiers surrounded the marshal in begging him to lead them to the emperor. Oudinot reminded them of their oath of fidelity to Louis XVIII.

But all efforts to persuade them remain were in vain, the explanations of the marshal on the perjury were unsuccessful; the grenadiers, seeing that Marshal Oudinot refused to lead them, set off towards their emperor, while Oudinot returned to Metz.

When Oudinot skirted the columns in returning, the grenadiers begged him again to accompany them, but the marshal resisted, and replied that he did not want to violate his oath, that the emperor had relieved him of the oath he had given him, and that now he would remain loyal to the King of France. After passing the grenadiers, Oudinot encountered the 1st Regiment of Hussars, of which his son was the colonel. He ordered him to gather all his officers to a trumpet call, explained to them their situation, represented to them that the oath is for a man of honour sacred thing, etc.

The hussar officers, many of whom belonged to the French nobility, allowed themselves to be persuaded, and also succeeded to convince their hussars, who returned to Metz. But soon afterwards he met the 2nd regiment, with which he did not have the same success; on the contrary, the officers of this regiment urged their comrades of the 1st to take common cause with them and to join the emperor.

The result of these discussions was a battle, in which a dozen officers were injured by sabre cuts on both sides and ultimately the 2nd regiment took the road to follow the grenadiers, while the 1st Hussars returned to Metz with Marshal Oudinot. I note this incident, which may explain partly the failure of the French at Waterloo. An army in which feelings are divided always has an element of weakness, no matter its bravery. Oddly enough, it was precisely the artillery, the emperor's own weapon, which was the most hostile to him during this campaign.

Anyone who abandons his post for a battle never deserves praise, no matter the reason he invokes. My friend Caraman behaved quite differently. Before the emperor's abdication at Fontainebleau in 1814, when Napoleon was already abandoned by those who owed him their happiness and their fortune, Caraman presented himself again to take service. When he saw him, the emperor, knowing that Caraman's family had always professed monarchical sentiments, addressed these words to him:

"Why aren't you gone to recommend yourself to your new master?"

"Sire," replied Caraman, "I will not go away not without the permission and authorisation of Your Majesty. I want to show Your Majesty that we are worth the nobility he has made."

This response pleased the emperor, who gave Caraman a recommendation for Louis XVIII.

When Napoleon returned from Elba, Caraman commanded the artillery of the bodyguards, and left on the 19th with this artillery, following Louis XVIII, for Ghent. Louis XVIII sent the cannons back to the frontier, but Caraman stayed with the king and returned with him to Paris.

Napoleon, as we know, only remained in France one hundred days, from his disembarkation from the island of Elba until his departure for the island of Saint Helena.

I stopped in Berlin on the way eastwards, without visiting anyone. And when the Russians had left Posen, I went home to my parents.

www.ingramcontent.com/pod-product-compliance
Lightning Source LLC
Chambersburg PA
CBHW032039080426
42733CB00006B/131